PILGRIMAGE

A Spiritual and Cultural Journey

For Fiona & Peter
with blessings
& best wishes,

Ian Bradley

For Lucy,

A Valiant Pilgrim.

PILGRIMAGE

A Spiritual and Cultural Journey

IAN BRADLEY

LION

A Lion Book
an imprint of
Lion Hudson plc
Wilkinson House, Jordan Hill Road,
Oxford OX2 8DR, England
www.lionhudson.com
ISBN 978 0 7459 5270 3 (UK)
ISBN 978 0 8254 7868 0 (US)
Distributed by:
UK: Marston Book Services Ltd, PO Box 269, Abingdon,
Oxon, OX14 4YN
USA: Trafalgar Square Publishing, 814 N. Franklin Street,
Chicago, IL 60610
USA Christian Market: Kregel Publications, PO Box
2607, Grand Rapids, Michigan 49501
First edition 2009
10 9 8 7 6 5 4 3 2 1 0

Typeset in 11.5/13.5 Arno Pro
Printed and bound in China

Text Acknowledgments

Every effort has been made to trace and acknowledge copyright holders of all the quotations included. We apologize for any errors or omissions that may remain, and would ask those concerned to contact the publishers, who will ensure that full acknowledgment is made in the future.

Scripture quotations taken from the *Holy Bible, New International Version*, copyright © 1973, 1978, 1984 International Bible Society. Used by permission of Zondervan and Hodder & Stoughton Limited. All rights reserved. The 'NIV' and 'New International Version' trademarks are registered in the United States Patent and Trademark Office by International Bible Society. Use of either trademark requires the permission of International Bible Society. UK trademark number 1448790.

p. 22 R.S. Thomas, extract from 'Somewhere' from *Collected Poems 1945-1990*, published by JM Dent, a division of The Orion Publishing Group

p. 24 Extract from 'The Succession' by Edwin Muir from *The Collected Poems*. Reproduced by permission of Faber & Faber Ltd.

p. 76 Extract taken from the song 'How Great Thou Art' by Stuart K Hine, copyright © 1953 The Stuart Hine Trust/kingswaysongs.com, published by kingswaysongs.com (excl. North and South America) tym@kingsway.co.uk Used by permission.

p. 84 Extract taken from 'The Servant Song' by Richard Gillard ©1977 Scripture in Song/Maranatha!Music. Administered by CopyCare, P.O. Box 77, Hailsham BN27 3EF UK music@copycare.com Used by permission.

p. 85 Extract from 'One More Step' by Sydney Carter (1915-2004) © 1971 Stainer & Bell Ltd, 23 Gruneisen Road, London N3 1DZ, England.

pp. 105–6 Extract from *Therapy* by David Lodge, published by Secker & Warburg. Reprinted by permission of The Random House Group Ltd.

p. 122 'Will You Come & Follow Me?' (The Summons), from *Heaven Shall Not Wait* (Wild Goose Publications, 1987). Words John L. Bell & Graham Maule, copyright © 1987 WGRG, Iona Community, Glasgow G2 3DH, Scotland.

pp. 146–7 R.S. Thomas, 'Pilgrimages' from *Collected Poems 1945-1990*, published by JM Dent, a division of The Orion Publishing Group

p. 158 Extract taken from 'The Pilgrims' Manual,' by Christopher Irvine, 1996 © Christopher Irvine, *The Pilgrims' Manual*, Wild Goose Publications, Glasgow.

To the Pilgrim

Set out!
You were born for the road.
Set out!
You have a meeting to keep.
Where? With whom?
Perhaps with yourself.

Set out!
Your steps will be your words –
The road your song,
The weariness your prayers.
And at the end
Your silence will speak to you.

Set out!
Alone, or with others –
But get out of yourself!
You have created rivals –
You will find companions.
You envisaged enemies –
You will find brothers and sisters.

Set out!
Your head does not know
Where your feet are leading your heart.

Set out!
You were born for the road –
The pilgrim's road.
Someone is coming to meet you –
Is seeking you
In the shrine at the end of the road –
In the shrine at the depths of your heart.

He is your peace.
He is your joy!

Go!
God already walks with you!

Anonymous

Contents

Preface

Pilgrimage is enjoying a huge revival across Europe. Catholics, Protestants and others uneasy with denominational labels and uncertain of their faith are walking old and new pilgrim routes across the continent and visiting ancient and modern pilgrim places.

This book celebrates and explores this phenomenon, so striking and unexpected in an age that is usually described as secular or post-Christian. Why are so many people going on pilgrimage and what do they experience on the way and at their destinations? The first part of the book seeks to define pilgrimage, and traces its history from its biblical and early church roots through its medieval heyday to its recent and contemporary manifestations. The second part describes thirteen major European pilgrim routes and destinations, giving a flavour of the distinctive experiences they offer and providing practical hints and suggestions for modern pilgrims.

Much of the book, especially in Part 2, is based on my own experiences and on extensive research carried out over the last few years. But at heart, what I have learned about pilgrimage has more to do with putting up with your own blisters and other people's snoring than some of the more high-minded spiritual thoughts or beautiful images that appear in the following pages! However, if this book encourages you to become a pilgrim – whatever form that takes – it will have done its work.

Many people have helped me along the way in my research for this book. Gunnar Siqueland supplied me with the poem that appears after the title page. It is his own translation of verses that he saw on the wall of the monastery of Sant Honorat in Mallorca when he was on a mountain bicycling training trip in 2006. Peter Millar has kindly allowed me to reproduce his poem on Iona, which appears on page 130, and Bodvar Schjelderup graciously acceded to my request to quote the poem 'Pilgrim', which he wrote in

1992 (page 35).

My pilgrimage to Santiago was made courtesy of the BBC and I am indebted to my good friend, Stephen Shipley, senior worship producer in the religious broadcasting department, for inviting me to join the Radio 4 pilgrimage there. I also benefited much from talking to Tony Crockett, who very sadly died while this book was in production, about his pilgrimage to Santiago. I owe a debt of gratitude to David Dow, the moving spirit behind attempts to revive interest in pilgrimage to St Andrews, for involving me in what has been a rewarding and stimulating project. Father Tommy Murphy first told me about the Croagh Patrick pilgrimage during a Celtic Christianity summer school at Lampeter University and subsequently led the group with which I was privileged to make the ascent of the sacred mountain on Reek Sunday in 1999. I was introduced to the pilgrim places of Wales by Donald Allchin, Bill Pritchard and Gregory Morris during a series of wonderful day trips that were part of the annual Celtic Christianity courses at St Deiniol's Library, near Hawarden. Their knowledge and enthusiasm have been contagious.

My wife, Lucy, and I greatly enjoyed a week-long walk along the pilgrim way to Nidaros in July 2007 thanks to the kind invitation of Rolf Synnes, the pilgrim priest at Trondheim, the help of his assistant Siv Smedseng and the gentle guidance of our leader, Hans Jacob Dahl. In Trondheim I gained much from conversations with Eivind Luthen and Stein Thue. My research in Assisi was hugely helped by a chance encounter with Anne Leigh, who put me in touch with Brother Thomas of the Society of Saint Francis. He, in turn, arranged for me to meet the redoubtable Angela Maria Seracchioli, who has single-handedly created the Franciscan pilgrim way. At Lourdes I benefited from conversations with Martin Moran and at Taizé I gained much from two long discussions with Brother Jean Marc. The travel arrangements for my visit to Medugorje were considerably assisted by Tricia Nugent, and I learned much about Częstochowa from Katarzyna Potocka. Vanessa Richards kindly told me about the new Huguenot path from France to Germany. I have walked St Cuthbert's Way twice – once on my own to mark my fiftieth birthday and a second time with my good friend, Jonathan Mason. On both occasions I gained much at the end of the journey from praying and chatting with another good friend and enthusiast for pilgrimage, Ray Simpson. My ministerial colleague and 'boss' at Holy Trinity Church, St Andrews, Rory Macleod, has encouraged and supported my interest in and commitment to pilgrimage.

Grants from the Carnegie Trust for the Universities of Scotland have financed my research visits to pilgrim sites and I have also benefited from a semester of research leave granted by the University of St Andrews.

Part 1

Introduction

Pilgrimage is perhaps best defined as a departure from daily life on a journey in search of spiritual well-being. It involves leaving home, making a journey, arriving at a destination that usually has some religious significance, and then returning home. It is sometimes undertaken alone, sometimes with a group. The practice of pilgrimage is a central feature of all the world's major faiths. For Muslims, the requirement to travel to Mecca once in a lifetime to visit the Ka'ba or House of God built by Abraham and his son Ishmael is one of the five pillars of Islam. Jews are commanded in the book of Exodus to appear before God three times a year. For the thousand years before the birth of Jesus, the temple

Christian Orthodox pilgrims carry a wooden cross along the *Via Dolorosa* towards the Church of the Holy Sepulchre during the Orthodox Good Friday procession in Jerusalem's Old City

in Jerusalem was the focal point for Jewish pilgrims at the festivals of Passover, Shavu'ot and Sukkot. Many Jews still visit its Western Wall, also known as the Wailing Wall and the only part left standing after its final destruction. Hindus travel especially to sites near rivers, describing pilgrimage as tirtha, a ford or bridge to the divine. Every twelve years there is a special pilgrimage known as the Kumbh Mela to Allahabad, where the Rivers Ganges and Yamuna converge with the mythical underground Saraswati River. In 2001, this attracted 25 million pilgrims in one day in what is thought to have been the largest gathering in human history. There is a network of Buddhist pilgrim sites associated with episodes in the life of the Buddha. Among the many sacred places visited by Sikhs, the most important is the Golden Temple at Amritsar in the Punjab. Jainist pilgrims go to places associated with the twenty-four great teachers known as tirthankaras or Jinas. Japanese pilgrims climb sacred mountains in accordance with Shintoist teaching and tradition.

Although not obligatory, pilgrimage has long been a significant aspect of Christian life and devotion. Jesus sent out his disciples to preach the kingdom of God and to heal, telling them to go from house to house, taking nothing on their journey (Luke 9:1–6). Some early Christians, like the Irish monks who wandered across Continental Europe as well as around the remoter shores of the British Isles, took to perpetual pilgrimage as a form of costly witness and exiled themselves from home comforts as they sought to follow the Son of Man who 'has nowhere to lay his head' (Luke 9:58). The desire to walk in

Jesus' footsteps has led many to journey to the Holy Land. As the cult of saints developed and certain places came to be seen as especially sacred, Christian pilgrimage reached its zenith in the Middle Ages with thousands travelling for many months across Europe to Rome, Santiago, St Andrews and other shrines associated with apostles and martyrs.

Christian literature is full of images and stories of pilgrimage: the epic voyage of St Brendan the Navigator; Chaucer's famous *Canterbury Tales* told by a motley group of pilgrims on their way to the Shrine of Thomas à Becket; John Bunyan's great allegorical work of Puritan devotion, *Pilgrim's Progress*; and the nineteenth-century Russian spiritual classic, *The Way of a Pilgrim,* which describes the wanderings of a seeker after spiritual enlightenment who desires to pray without ceasing. Pilgrimage is the theme of some of the best-loved prayers and hymns in the Christian tradition. It has also been the subject of several popular and influential modern devotional classics including Thomas Merton's account of his journey to the Trappist monastery at Gethsemani in *Seven Storey Mountain* and Gerry Hughes' descriptions of his walks to Jerusalem and Rome.

The revival of pilgrimage has been one of the most striking and encouraging developments in Western Christianity over the last thirty or forty years. The medieval pilgrim route or *camino* to Santiago de Compostela has undergone a new lease of life following significant European Union funding for its infrastructure, and the number of those walking at least 62 miles (100 km), or cycling at least 125 miles (200 km), to qualify for their *Compostela* has quadrupled over the last twenty years. A series of apparitions of the Virgin at Medugorje in the Balkans since 1981 have added a major new European pilgrim destination to other long-established Marian shrines (shrines to the Virgin Mary) such as Częstochowa, Fatima and Lourdes. Such sites continue to draw ever-larger crowds of the faithful seeking healing in body, mind and spirit. New long-distance pilgrim trails have been created, such as St Cuthbert's Way, opened in 1997, which passes through the Scottish and English border country from the town of Melrose to Lindisfarne. St Olav's Way, also opened in 1997, follows a well-established medieval pilgrim route from Oslo to the shrine of St Olav in Trondheim in Norway. In 2007 the Italian Government announced a £7 million project to restore the Italian stretches of the medieval pilgrim route across France and Italy to Rome, known as the *Via Francigena*, to their former glory. The 8,000 or so pilgrims using the *Via Francigena* in 2007 included a group of twenty-seven cyclists from Canterbury who covered the 1,200-mile (1,900-km) journey to Rome in seventeen days and raised £100,000 for the English cathedral's restoration appeal.

A new organization, the *Cammini d'Europa*, backed by the European Commission and the Council of Europe and with its headquarters in Rome, is seeking to promote and develop Europe's historic pilgrimage routes, especially

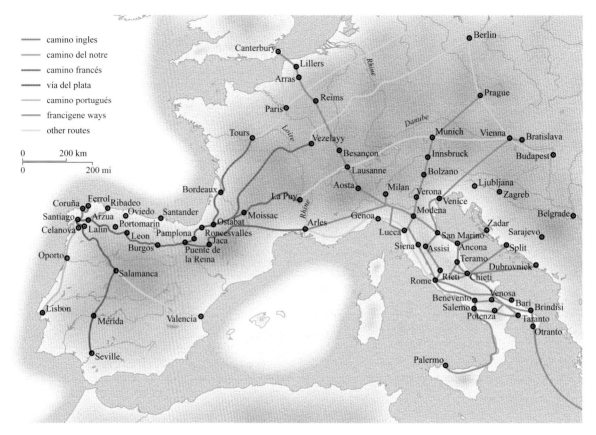

Legend:
— camino ingles
— camino del notre
— camino francés
— vía del plata
— camino portugués
— francigene ways
— other routes

0   200 km
0   200 mi

Pilgrim routes across
Europe from Cammini
de Europageie
brochure

the *camino* to Santiago, the *Via Francigena* and the various Scandinavian routes to Trondheim. Although this initiative is partly driven by a concern to encourage cultural links and tourism, it is also inspired by a realization that the contemporary revival of pilgrimage across the continent testifies to a widespread desire to recover and celebrate Europe's spiritual roots and soul. It was the German writer Goethe who observed at the end of the eighteenth century that 'the *camino* created Europe'. As a new Europe is taking shape with the incorporation of more and more countries of the old communist East into the European Union, pilgrimage offers both a metaphor for and a practical way of breaking down barriers and forging closer links. When European ministers of culture met in Santiago in 1987 to set up the Council of Europe's programme of cultural routes across the continent, they expressed this hope:

> *May the faith which has inspired pilgrims throughout history, uniting*
> *them in a common aspiration and transcending national differences and*
> *interests, inspire us today, and young people in particular, to travel along*
> *these routes in order to build a society founded on tolerance, respect for*
> *others, freedom and solidarity.*

Pilgrimage was once regarded as an exclusively Roman Catholic activity, but this is no longer the case. Protestant-inspired ecumenical communities at Taizé in Burgundy and Iona off the west coast of Scotland have become magnets, attracting thousands of young pilgrims every year. Across Scandinavia dedicated pilgrim pastors appointed by the Lutheran churches are welcoming people to shrines and helping them to explore faith through walking as well as talking. Elisabeth Lidell, the leading pilgrim pastor in the Danish Lutheran Church, has been instrumental in developing a new 175-mile (280-km) pilgrim path across Jutland between Viborg and the German border, which opened in July 2008. The project began when her architect husband, Andreas Blinkenberg, won a competition for finding new uses for redundant farm buildings. He suggested turning them into pilgrim hostels and has supervised the conversion of disused barns into ten refuges, each with thirty to forty beds, along the route of the new pilgrim path. Over twenty churches along the way have opened their doors to welcome walkers and cyclists and taken advantage of the evangelistic opportunities that the new route creates. In Germany a new 170-mile (270-km) Luther trail was opened in 2007 to link places associated with the founding father of the Reformation. The route runs from Wittenberg to Mansfeld via Bitterfeld and Eisleben. In 2008 a long-distance footpath was opened tracing the route taken by French Protestants exiled after the revocation of the Edict of Nantes in 1685. The *Sentier sur les pas des Huguenots* starts at Le Poët-Laval in the Drôme region of south-east France and ends at Marburg in south-west Germany, covering a distance of 600 miles (950 km). At a local level, numerous one-day pilgrimages to shrines and places of spiritual significance are bringing together people of different denominations, and sometimes of different faiths, to engage in physical and spiritual journeying.

A street confessional. Each year, many Christians come to Czestochowa on Assumption Day to see the Black Madonna painting, a shrine to the Virgin Mary, at the Paulite monastery of Jasna Góra.

A pilgrim prays before the statue of the Virgin Mary on Apparition Hill, Medugorje

Overall, it has been calculated that in Western Europe alone there are now well over 6,000 pilgrimage centres, generating over 100 million visits per year, 60 million of which are 'religiously motivated'. Mary Lee and Sidney Nolan, the North American academics who have come up with these figures as a result of exhaustive research, have identified 830 pilgrim shrines that all receive more than 10,000 visitors a year. This figure does not include major Protestant and ecumenical pilgrim destinations such as Taizé, nor the numerous burgeoning shrines in Eastern Europe. In 98.4 per cent of the Western European pilgrimage places that they have studied and identified, devotion is focused on a particular holy person: 66 per cent are shrines where the Virgin Mary is the primary object of devotion, in 26.7 per cent it is an apostle or saint, and in 7.5 per cent Jesus Christ. They conclude that 'European pilgrimage is a highly dynamic institution'. While some shrines are declining in popularity, new ones are constantly springing up at other places.[1]

The motives that take people on pilgrimages today are many and various, as they always have been. The quest for a deeper spirituality and for mental, physical and psychological healing is mixed with a sense of adventure, a desire to get out of the rut, to broaden horizons and enjoy a new and different experience. Pilgrimages are still undertaken, as they often were in medieval times, with a penitential purpose, as part of an attempt to re-orientate lives away from selfishness and to make a new start, face challenges and experience – if only temporarily – a simpler and less comfortable lifestyle. There is a sense of shared community about taking part in a pilgrimage that many people welcome in our increasingly atomistic culture. Victor and Edith Turner, who pioneered the anthropological study of pilgrimage, see it as an egalitarian community formed by individuals temporarily freed of the hierarchical roles and status that they bear in everyday life. For them, pilgrimages are intrinsically inclusive and universal. They strip people of their social pretensions and restore their individuality. This is certainly true in my own experience. I vividly recall the first

Some Definitions of Pilgrimage

Pilgrimage is a practical and demonstrable way of seeking. It is a sure way of putting beliefs and commitment to the crucible. It digs up the answers from deep within. Whilst physically uncomfortable, it provides spiritual reassurance and comfort. You can walk and talk, in largely uninterrupted measure, with God. Give Him an inch, and He will show you the mile. Go the mile and He will remain with you on your life's journey.
David Baldwin[2]

There is no need for souvenirs to prove that we have visited a pilgrimage site, but going there can prompt us to think of eternal things in a way that our everyday surrounding and activities cannot. The directory of pilgrimage destinations is not finite, for it is the pilgrims who make the pilgrimage and without prayer and spiritual meditation, a visit to a shrine is just a visit and the visitors, mere tourists.
Pilgrimage and Beyond[3]

Pilgrimages symbolize the experience of the homo viator *who sets out, as soon as he leaves the maternal womb, on his journey through the time and space of his existence. This is the fundamental experience of Israel which is marching towards the promised land of salvation and of full freedom; the experience of Christ who rose to heaven from the land of Jerusalem, thus opening the way towards the Father; the experience of the Church which moves on through history towards the heavenly Jerusalem; the experience of the whole humankind which tends towards hope and fullness.*

Every pilgrim should confess: 'By the grace of God, I am a human person and a Christian; by my actions, a great sinner; by my condition a pilgrim without a roof, of the lowliest species that goes wandering place to place.'
The Great Pilgrimage in the Jubilee[4]

To be a pilgrim is to opt out of one society and join another. To be a pilgrim is to tear away from the standard way of thinking. As a pilgrim you aim towards the unknown. In an age stamped by individualism and self-assertion, the pilgrim dares towards humility: there is no class distinction on the way. People will take you for what you are, not what you represent.
Eivind Luthen[5]

To become a pilgrim is to be understood as a way of looking at life itself: constantly moving and willing to break away from fixed ideas about oneself and others, breaking away from lifestyles that do not respect the earth as a community for all living creatures. The pilgrim realizes that there is a change to undergo, and afterwards to return home with extended faith and understanding of life.

The outer physical landscape people wander through with all its varying scenery is, in the pilgrim's tradition, understood as a picture of the inner landscape every person carries with them.
Arne Bakken[6]

A pilgrimage differs from a tour. It is a personal invitation from God, comprised of His offer and dependent upon the pilgrim's acceptance. God's call may vary but the purpose remains consistent: It is an individual summons to know God more fully. A pilgrimage is a spiritual journey to which the pilgrim joyfully responds 'yes' to God's invitation.

A successful pilgrimage involves a commitment to leave behind one's problems and to focus instead on seeking to learn more about God, making one's heart full of desire for special graces, praises, petitions and thanksgiving.
What is a Pilgrimage?[7]

We will come back changed. Of that I am certain. But of course that is why you go on pilgrimage in the first place, to find the holy, stumble upon God in action, and be changed for ever by the experience.
Canon Trevor Dennis introducing a pilgrimage to Russia[8]

words of our leader when my wife and I joined the group with whom we would
be spending the week walking to Trondheim. As we were about to introduce
ourselves, he said: 'It is not important where we come from or what jobs we do.
For the next week we are all simply pilgrims.'

Pilgrimage is often undertaken to mark a significant anniversary or
landmark in life. I have lost count of the number of people who have told me
that they walked the *camino* to Santiago, usually alone, either to mark their
fiftieth birthday or their impending retirement. I myself celebrated my half-
century with a more modest solitary walk along St Cuthbert's Way. Among the
predominantly North American group with whom I journeyed to Rome, Assisi
and Medugorje in September 2007 were a couple celebrating their thirtieth
wedding anniversary and another who had just got married in their late-fifties.
Both had lost their previous spouses to cancer and never expected to marry
again. They felt a pilgrimage was a more appropriate way of celebrating this
'miracle' than a conventional honeymoon. The group also included a woman
with a number of serious health problems who was seeking healing, and an
elderly couple from Australia on a lengthy pilgrimage across Europe, which had
already taken in Canterbury, Lourdes and Fatima, paid for by their two sons as a
thank you for all that they had given them.

Pilgrimages are traditionally associated with a search for the miraculous,
whether it be a vision, a cure or some particularly intense supernatural
encounter. Victor and Edith Turner define pilgrimage sites as 'places where
miracles once happened, still happen and may happen again'.[9] Yet even in
Lourdes I met no pilgrims, however sick, who were actively expecting a
miraculous cure, and there is little or no emphasis on this aspect in any of
the pilgrim shrines that I visited during the research for this book. For most
contemporary pilgrims it is miracle enough if faith is strengthened and they
return home with a sense of renewal. I myself can testify to one small, but in
its own way miraculous, spiritual benefit that being a pilgrim has given me.
It has made me less inclined to judge others. I think of the fellow pilgrim to
Trondheim whose heavy snoring kept me awake all night and whom I was
ready to dismiss as an irritating and uninspiring encumbrance. By the end
of our week together, he had shown himself to be the most considerate and
helpful of all of us in helping the oldest member of our band, who was visibly
flagging and would not have fulfilled her lifetime's dream of walking St Olav's
Way without his steadying arm and patient support. I think, too, of one of my
North American companions on the pilgrimage across Italy. At first, I thought
her brash and superficial, but over our ten days together a story of considerable
hardship and an astonishingly deep faith emerged. If I have learned one lesson
from my own experiences of pilgrimage it is to be less judgmental.

The revival of interest in pilgrimage also ties in with the recovery of a
sense of the sacredness of place and landscape in an increasingly fragile and

urbanized world, the growing emphasis on physical well-being and exercise, and the widespread desire to rediscover and connect with roots, traditions and history. Many people find it easier to walk rather than talk their faith and find encouragement in treading in the footsteps of countless pilgrims before them. Walking has clear psychological as well as physical benefits. An experienced Christian therapist shared with me how beneficial it can be for people to make confession, formal or otherwise, and get things off their chest while walking side by side with a companion/confessor rather than in a confrontational face-to-face encounter. In her book of pilgrim stories from the *camino*, Nancy Frey quotes a letter she received from Marina, a 33-year-old physical therapist from Madrid, about the benefits of walking: 'I learned to love a healthy life and how good I felt in nature, as part of it. I found myself living exclusively in the present, in the moment, living without news or daily life and even in another stage of the century or another world where the well-being, the enjoyment, the energy, the freedom, and above all the walking are all that matter.'[10]

The Cammini d'Europa's Product Line of branded pilgrimage merchandise

Not all pilgrimages involve strenuous and prolonged physical activity. There are those where the journey along the way is at least as important as the final point of arrival, but there are also pilgrimages where the destination is all-important and the means of reaching it are of little significance. Cheap air travel has made it easy and inexpensive to reach most places in Europe and has created a new category of multi-destination pilgrim holidays. Even the Vatican has followed suit, with its pilgrimage arm, *Opera Romana Pellegrinaggi*, launching a dedicated chartered airline service for pilgrims in 2007. Instead of the usual in-flight movies and bags of peanuts, those travelling to destinations including Santiago, Częstochowa, Lourdes and Rome are treated to religious videos and the inscription 'I search for your face, Lord' emblazoned on the outside of the plane and on seat backs inside. *Opera Romana Pellegrinaggi*, which shuttles over 400,000 pilgrims a year to shrines across Europe and beyond, is one of a growing number of specialist travel operators catering for this developing market in what is sometimes called 'spiritual tourism'. Its glossy brochures feature '*Itinerari dello Spirito*' and promote packages combining visits to major shrines with a few added days at nearby beach resorts. It is also responsible for marketing walking and bus tours along the *Cammini d'Europa*, advertised as 'grand tours and weekend breaks' and supported by a product line of branded merchandise including rain capes, backpacks, walking sticks, flashlights and drinking bottles.

The dividing line between pilgrims and tourists has long been blurred and is becoming increasingly more so. It has been said that while tourists return

'We will come back changed. Of that I am certain. But of course that is why you go on pilgrimage in the first place, to find the holy, stumble upon God in action, and be changed for ever by the experience.'

Canon Trevor Dennis introducing a pilgrimage to Russia

from their travels with souvenirs, pilgrims come back with blessings and with their lives somehow changed. Yet pilgrims have long returned home with souvenirs, and many camera-toting and coach-borne visitors to churches and sacred places pause to light a candle and pray. If some of what passes for pilgrimage today is really tourism, it is also the case that many modern tourists are searching for something beyond a holiday. One of the greatest opportunities for Christians and churches today is, perhaps, to help tourists become pilgrims.

Pilgrimage has much to offer an age such as ours in which there is so much anxiety, yearning and seeking. It fits the needs of a restless generation – but perhaps restlessness is, in fact, part and parcel of the human condition. Bruce Chatwin, the travel writer, has suggested in his book *Songlines* that humans are born to be nomads and that our natural inclinations turn us towards movement and journeying. A document issued by the Vatican in 1998 argues that 'pilgrimages symbolize the experience of the *homo viator* who sets out, as soon as he leaves the maternal womb, on his journey through the time and space of his existence.'[11] Over 1,600 years ago St Augustine observed that 'our hearts are restless until they find their rest in God'. The desire to be pilgrims perhaps reflects yearnings to find a deeper purpose and sense of rest. It also chimes in with the way that increasing numbers of people see their faith. Surveys suggest that far more Christians now describe their faith as an ongoing journey rather than a sudden decisive conversion experience. The road to Emmaus, along which the resurrected Jesus travelled with two of his disciples for many miles before they recognized him, seems to resonate with more believers nowadays than the road to Damascus, where Paul underwent a sudden blinding conversion.

Part of the reason why the number of people making pilgrimages is on the increase is undoubtedly because of the growing appeal of sabbaticals, gap years and taking time out from ever more stressed lives. In almost every one of the major pilgrim destinations that I have visited over the last few years I have found clergy, especially for some reason ministers from the Presbyterian Church of the United States, on sabbaticals. One of them – who had already visited the desert monasteries of Sinai, walked the *camino* to Santiago and was going on to Iona and Ireland – told me when I met him in Taizé, 'My congregation sent me away because they want me to pray more deeply and have a more fulfilling spirituality. That is why I am visiting these wellsprings of faith and communities of renewal.' Taizé in particular attracts students who are taking a gap year or who have dropped out of their studies. In Lourdes I met a Scottish couple who were taking six months out of their jobs to help care for the sick pilgrims. Especially for those taking part in walking or cycling pilgrimages, much of the appeal and the satisfaction lies in slowing down and travelling at the speed that has been the norm for humankind for nearly all of its time on this planet. Reflecting on the benefits of walking the *camino* to Santiago in 2005 in a web-post entitled 'Pilgrimage as Therapy', George Greenia, a North American academic, wrote:

> *I am now a true believer in time invested outside of our professional and familial routines. Well used as a corrective to our usual mindless trotting around, these interludes can get us to stride past our accustomed selves. The journey forces us into silence, makes us put down our books, abandon our computers, and may lead us to a disciplined re-imagining of the life and habits of another age.*[12]

Pilgrimage is often described as a liminal activity. It involves an interruption from ordinary life, deliberately casting off into the unknown and crossing the boundary between the routine and familiar and the unpredictable and strange. Pilgrims to Rome in the Middle Ages were described as journeying *ad limina apostolorum* – 'to the threshold of the apostles'. Pilgrim places are 'thin places' where it seems possible to step over the threshold from one world to another and where ultimate realities are somehow easier to access than they usually are. Modern anthropologists have followed the Turners in seeing pilgrimage as a journey towards the 'sacred centre', where heaven and earth intersect and time stands still. The Latin word *peregrinus* from which the word 'pilgrim' is derived means stranger or traveller (literally *per ager* or 'through the land'). Pilgrimage is a provisional, transitory state, often taken as a metaphor for the journey of life, hastening irrevocably from the cradle to the grave. It is a reminder that all things in this world are temporary and that everything is in motion, nothing is ever static. In several religious traditions, pilgrimages to remote places are often undertaken towards the end of life to prepare for death by stripping away the comforts and distractions of this world. For some, pilgrimage is a perpetual state of life, as it was for the wandering Irish monks of the Dark Ages and is now for the Hindu *sadhus,* who have renounced the world and perpetually travel from one shrine to another. For most of us, however, pilgrimage is an occasional rather than a perpetual state – one for which we prepare and from which we return in some small way changed, healed, refreshed and enriched with our horizons broadened. In practical terms, it gives those of us who are not monks or free spirits, who are tied to the responsibilities and obligations that come with family or employment, the chance to leave our settled routines for a while, walk in the footsteps of the saints and the faithful of countless ages and find new companions on the way.

In pilgrimage, the journey back is as important as the outward journey or the destination. We arrive only to depart again and coming home is as significant as setting out. The pilgrim comes back changed and hopefully more open as well as more faithful than before. The late-eighteenth-century French writer Chateaubriand maintained that 'there was never a pilgrim that did not come back to his own village with one less prejudice and one more idea'. The twentieth-century Welsh poet and priest, R.S. Thomas, expressed the central purpose of pilgrimage thus:

The point of travelling is not
To arrive but to return home
Laden with pollen you shall work up
Into honey the mind feeds on.

Ultimately pilgrimages, especially those involving physical exertion, are like life. There are long, dull stretches along boring and uninteresting roads, some really dreary stages of trudging through driving rain and ugly suburban streets, and moments of sheer elation – walking through woods gathering blueberries or contemplating a sunset over distant hills. On a long pilgrimage, daily life comes to revolve around a set of very simple and basic human actions. In the words of a French pilgrim on the *camino*, it can be reduced to the formula: '*manger, marcher, laver, manger, dormir, manger, marcher*.' Every pilgrimage has its own rhythms and rituals, its ebb and flow of arriving and departing, exodus and return. The outer physical journey mirrors the inner spiritual journey; the excitement of setting out on a new adventure is balanced by the joy of coming home.

The Biblical Roots of Pilgrimage

The *raison d'etre* for pilgrimage among Jews and Christians is found in the Hebrew Bible, known to Christians as the Old Testament. In its pages are found three key themes that have motivated pilgrims for over 3,000 years: the sense that God travels with his people and that they are often closer to him when they are wandering through the wilderness than when they are settled and secure and begin to forget him; the theological significance of exodus and exile; and the particular importance of Jerusalem as a pilgrim destination.

Judaism began as a nomadic religion. The foundational statement of faith and identity for the people of Israel, found in Deuteronomy 26:5, begins with

The Dome of the Rock and Wailing Wall, Jerusalem

the words: 'A wandering Aramean was my ancestor.' This is generally taken as referring to Abraham, the founding father of the three great monotheistic faiths of Judaism, Christianity and Islam, who was perhaps the first recorded pilgrim, moving from his home in Ur, a city on the Euphrates in modern Iraq, to Haran, several hundred miles to the north-west in what is now Turkey, and from then on at God's bidding to Egypt. The words that God spoke to him at Haran as recorded in Genesis 12:1–2 have inspired countless pilgrims to set off from home: 'Go from your country and your kindred and your father's house to the land that I will show you. I will make of you a great nation, and I will bless you, and make your name great, so that you will be a blessing.' In the words of the epistle to the Hebrews 11:8, 'he set out, not knowing where he was going'. As Richard Giles, dean of Philadelphia Cathedral, comments: 'There was no question here of a relocation package with full removal expenses, but of a journey into the unknown; we too in our own generation are called to this perilous but rewarding adventure.'[1]

**'We through the generations came
Here by a way we do not know
From the fields of Abraham,
And still the road is scarce began.'**

Edwin Muir, The Succession

By living as a nomad with his flocks and herds and building a temporary altar to God wherever he set up camp, Abraham established a pattern of peripatetic devotional life that was to continue among the people of Israel for a thousand years. This motif of wandering and worshipping God on the move is seen most clearly in the exodus, when the people of Israel left their slavery in Egypt and set out under the leadership of Moses into the wilderness on their journey towards the promised land. In retrospect, they felt closer to God during their forty years in the wilderness – when God travelled with them, his presence symbolized in the portable tent or tabernacle, and appeared before them in a pillar of cloud by day and a pillar of fire by night – than when they settled in the promised land

The ruins of the ancient Sumerian city of Ur of the Chaldees. Iraq

and worshipped him in a permanent temple. Certainly the prophets felt that the Israelites lost their fervour and faith when they stopped being pilgrims and wanderers. God himself preferred to be worshipped on the move rather than tied down to one place, judging by his words to Nathan the prophet when King David expressed his desire to build a permanent temple, or 'house of cedar', as his dwelling place (2 Samuel 7:5–6): 'Are you the one to build me a house to live in? I have not lived in a house since the day I brought up the people of Israel from Egypt to this day, but I have been moving about in a tent and a tabernacle.'

Despite these words from God, David's successor, Solomon, went ahead and built a magnificent temple in Jerusalem. It became the principal place of pilgrimage for Jews for the next thousand years and subsequently a mecca for Christian pilgrims. Solomon's temple stood from c. 1000 BC until 587 BC, when it was destroyed by the Babylonian ruler, Nebuchadnezzar. Ten years after its destruction, Jews were banished from Jerusalem and began their period of exile, which lasted until 538 BC and inspired a longing to return to the homeland and visit the temple. A second temple was built in 538 BC and lasted until its destruction by the Roman general Pompey in 63 BC. In many ways the period of this second temple was the heyday of Jewish pilgrimage to Jerusalem, described in Psalm 48 as 'the city of God'. Two of the major festivals that brought Jews to Jerusalem commemorated their nomadic past: Passover celebrated the beginning of the exodus; and Sukkot, or the Feast of Tabernacles, recalled the temporary dwellings in which the Israelites lived while wandering in the wilderness.

Relief sculpture of an early Pilgrim

Of all the books in the Old Testament, it is the Psalms that speak most eloquently of pilgrimage. Many of them are thought to date from the period of the second temple, although some almost certainly go back to the time of Solomon. Psalm 84 encapsulates the pilgrim experience. It begins by asserting the importance of the destination – in this case the dwelling place of God: 'How lovely is your dwelling place, O Lord of hosts!' Then there is the unmistakable note of yearning and longing implicit in all pilgrimage: 'My soul longs, indeed it faints for the courts of the Lord.' The pilgrimage to Jerusalem, or Zion, is envisaged as the result of both a direct and external call from God and the inner promptings of longing and desire of those who undertake it: 'Happy are those whose strength is in you, in whose heart are the highways to Zion.' The psalmist also suggests that pilgrims bless the land through which they travel – 'as they go through the valley of Baca, they make it a place of springs' – as well as themselves being refreshed and invigorated on the journey: 'they go from strength to strength'.

An artist's impression of the Second Temple, built in 538BC. It was the main destination of Jewish pilgrims and inspired several Psalms.

'Happy are those whose strength is in you, in whose heart are the highways to Zion … They go from strength to strength; the God of gods will be seen in Zion.'

Psalm 84:5, 7

Psalms 120 to 134, which all bear the title 'A song of Ascents', are thought to have been sung by pilgrims making their way up to the temple in Jerusalem. Their sense of eagerness and anticipation is well conveyed in the opening verse of Psalm 122:

**I was glad when they said to me,
'Let us go to the house of the Lord!'
Our feet are standing
within your gates, O Jerusalem!**

These psalms of ascent highlight several more themes that were to become central in both Jewish and, later, Christian pilgrimage. Psalm 121 emphasizes the protection that God gives to pilgrims:

**The Lord will keep you from all evil;
he will keep your life.
The Lord will keep your going out and your coming in
from this time on and for evermore.**

Present, too, is that sense of walking in the ways of the Lord which was to lead early Christians to think of themselves as the people on and of the Way: 'Happy is everyone who fears the Lord, who walks in his ways' (Psalm 128). Furthermore, there is also an emphasis on the community and togetherness that pilgrimage fosters: 'How very good and pleasant it is when kindred live together in unity' (Psalm 133).

Although there is less explicit mention of pilgrimage in the New Testament, the Gospels give us several striking images of Jesus the pilgrim: born in a stable when his parents are far away from home; going up to Jerusalem at the age of twelve as a pilgrim for Passover and desiring to stay behind in the temple; walking alone by the lakeside, through the hills and into the desert; wandering through Galilee teaching, preaching and healing; making his own fateful journey to Jerusalem on a donkey; and, following his resurrection, walking with two of his disciples on the road to Emmaus and inspiring their comment, 'Were not our hearts burning within us while he was talking to us on the road?'

Jesus depicted as a pilgrim in a mural of the Emmaus encounter in the monasterey of Santa Domingo at Silos in Spain

1. O God of Bethel, by whose hand
thy people still are fed,
who through this earthly pilgrimage
hast all our fathers led:

2. Our vows, our prayers, we now
present
before thy throne of grace:
God of our fathers, be the God
of their succeeding race.

3. Through each perplexing path of
life
our wandering footsteps guide;
give us each day our daily bread,
and raiment fit provide.

4. O spread thy covering wings
around,
till all our wanderings cease,
and at our Father's loved abode
our souls arrive in peace.

Scottish Paraphrases (1781) based on a hymn
by Philip Doddridge (1702–1751)

(Luke 24:32). A painting of the Emmaus encounter in the Benedictine monastery of Santo Domingo at Silos on the *camino* to Santiago actually depicts Jesus as a pilgrim carrying a satchel on which is carved a scallop shell.

New Testament scholars have pointed to the way in which Jesus' public life enfolds in two stages, both of which involve journeying: first, his itinerant ministry around Galilee, and then his long ascent to the holy city of Jerusalem and the hill of Calvary. While he does not specifically call people to go on pilgrimage, he does very clearly call on them to take up their own cross and follow him. He also suggests that following him will involve a life of wandering and renunciation: 'A scribe then approached and said, "Teacher, I will follow you wherever you go." And Jesus said to him, "Foxes have holes, and birds of the air have nests; but the Son of Man has nowhere to lay his head." ' (Matthew 8:19–20)

One of Jesus' most celebrated parables is essentially the story of a pilgrimage, albeit with an unusual twist. In the case of the prodigal son, the outward journey is not that of the traditional pilgrim seeking a closer relationship with God, but rather that of a young man bent on worldly pleasures and self-fulfilment. It is the return journey that is the pilgrimage in the true sense of the word, undertaken in penitence, contrition and yearning. The prodigal is welcomed home by his father as a pilgrim, to the chagrin of his elder brother, who has never left home and therefore never taken the pilgrim path. 'The King of Love', a well-known nineteenth-century hymn, beautifully expresses the longing of the pilgrim and the wanderer to come home. It also reminds us of the fact that, like the prodigal's father, God himself goes out to seek and meet us, journeying much further than we do to seek and find him:

Perverse and foolish oft I strayed,
And yet in love he sought me,
And on his shoulder gently laid
And home rejoicing brought me.
Henry W. Baker (1821–77)

One of the key messages of the New Testament is that God is to be encountered everywhere and not just in certain special holy places. Having come to earth in the person of his son, he is not a distant deity, nor one who can only be approached and encountered in the tabernacle or the temple. Rather, he is accessible to all who come to him through Jesus and who worship him in spirit and in truth. Jerusalem is relocated from earth to heaven: it is the heavenly Jerusalem that becomes the destination for Christian pilgrims, and to that extent the whole of life on earth becomes a pilgrimage towards the life to come. This is supremely expressed in a passage from the letter to the Hebrews in which the author reflects on the importance of faith in the lives of Old Testament figures such as Abel, Noah, Enoch and Abraham:

> *All of these died in faith without having received the promises, but from a distance they saw and greeted them. They confessed that they were strangers and foreigners on the earth, for people who speak in this way make it clear that they are seeking a homeland. If they had been thinking of the land that they had left behind, they would have had opportunity to return. But as it is, they desire a better country, that is, a heavenly one.*
> **Hebrews 11:13–16**

At one level, this new understanding of God's accessibility renders the kind of pilgrimages that the Jews had made regularly to the Jerusalem temple redundant. Yet the insistence in this passage that true believers are 'strangers and pilgrims on earth' (as the Authorised Version puts it) does not diminish the importance of the theme of pilgrimage, but rather changes its emphasis. In Christianity, life itself becomes a pilgrimage and faith a journey following the way and call of Jesus:

> *Therefore, since we are surrounded by so great a cloud of witnesses, let us also lay aside every weight and the sin that clings so closely, and let us run with perseverance the race that is set before us, looking to Jesus the pioneer and perfecter of our faith…*
> **Hebrews 12:1–2**

2

Pilgrimage in the Early Church

Because Christianity is above all an incarnational faith, asserting that God entered his world at a particular time and place in the person of Jesus, both history and geography have always been important in Christian faith and experience. From the earliest days of the church, some Christians felt a desire to visit and see the places associated with key episodes in Jesus' life, death, resurrection and ascension as described in the Gospels. They were motivated as much by intellectual curiosity and a concern to verify and amplify the details of the stories that they read in the Bible as by any sense of sacred places or spiritual yearning. As such, these early visitors to what was to become known as the Holy Land were perhaps explorers rather than pilgrims. Before long, however, a whole itinerary of sacred sites had developed, elaborate shrines and places of worship were erected at significant sites mentioned in both the New and Old Testaments, and considerable numbers of pilgrims were making the journey to Palestine, armed with gazetteers and guides and seeking to deepen their faith and gain spiritual benefit from direct contact with holy places.

Jerusalem acted as a particular magnet for the first Christian pilgrims, principally because it was the location of Jesus' crucifixion and resurrection. For most of the first three centuries of Christianity, there was, in fact, little to be seen at the city's principal biblical sites. Jerusalem was comprehensively destroyed by the Roman emperor Titus when he crushed the Jewish revolt in AD 70. In AD 130–32 Hadrian rebuilt and re-founded it as a pagan Roman city, *Aelia Capitolina*. Most of the sacred Jewish and Christian sites were adorned with shrines to pagan deities and the caves where Jesus had been born and where his tomb had been were filled in and covered over. Sporadic Roman persecution throughout this period made travelling to Palestine overtly as a Christian a hazardous business, but this did not deter some hardy souls from making the journey on an individual basis.

One of the earliest known Christian visitors to Palestine was Melito, bishop

of Sardis in Asia Minor, who went there around AD 170 in order to establish the number and order of the books of the Old Testament. Although he is often described as the first Christian pilgrim to the Holy Land, he went there essentially as a scholar. Around AD 200 Alexander, a bishop in Cappadocia, made the journey to Jerusalem, according to the church historian Eusebius, 'for the purpose of prayer and investigation of the sacred places'. This is the earliest reference to someone visiting biblical sites in order to pray rather than just out of interest or for scholarly motives. In fact, Alexander made such an impression on the inhabitants of Jerusalem that they asked him to stay on and become their bishop, which he did. Strictly speaking, his failure to return rules him out from being counted as a true pilgrim. Most other early visitors to Palestine were on study tours rather than pilgrimages. Around AD 230 Origen, the Egyptian theologian and one of the Greek fathers of the church, made extensive investigations of biblical sites, including Bethlehem and Bethany.

The prospects for and the nature of Christian pilgrimage to Palestine and Jerusalem were dramatically changed by the conversion to Christianity of the Roman emperor Constantine in AD 312. With Christianity henceforth the favoured and established religion of the Roman empire, Constantine enthusiastically set about restoring the biblical sites that had been obliterated or turned into pagan shrines by his predecessors, building churches to make them centres of worship and encouraging pilgrimage to them. It is from his reign, which continued until AD 337, that the widespread and systematic development of Christian pilgrimage to what had by then become known as the Holy Land really dates. Under his patronage, churches were built over what Eusebius refers to as 'three mystical caves' – the supposed sites of Jesus' birth, resurrection and ascension. Constantine also ordered places of worship to be built at Capernaum and at the oak of Mamre, near Hebron, where Abraham's visitation from God recounted in Genesis 18 had taken place. As early as AD 315 Eusebius, who had just become bishop of Caesarea, was claiming that visitors came from 'all over the world' to visit Bethlehem and view the ruins of Jerusalem from the Mount of Olives. He himself did much to promote pilgrimage to the Holy Land by producing a gazetteer entitled *Onomastikon,* which listed most of the biblical sites.

> 'She accorded suitable adoration to the footsteps of the Saviour, following the prophetic word which says "Let us adore in the place where his feet have stood". '

Eusebius, Life of Constantine

Constantine himself never visited the Holy Land, although he said at his baptism shortly before his death that he had hoped to be baptized in the River Jordan. His mother Helena, however, made a journey taking in the key biblical sites around AD 326, when she was in her seventies. Eusebius noted that 'she came, though old, with the eagerness of youth to apply her outstanding intellect to enquiring about the wondrous land … and to inspect with imperial concern the eastern provinces with their communities and peoples'. Alongside her intellectual curiosity and maternal concern for the subjects of her son's far-flung empire, Helena seems to have been motivated by what was to become one of the hallmarks of the Christian pilgrim to the Holy Land, the desire to walk in the footsteps of Christ: 'She accorded suitable adoration to the footsteps of the Saviour, following the prophetic word which says "Let us adore in the place where his feet have stood".'[1] Her much-publicized journey was influential in promoting pilgrimage to Palestine, especially among women. According to Eusebius, during her visit the empress founded the Christian shrines at the site of Jesus' nativity in Bethlehem and at the site of his ascension on the Mount of Olives. Her son ordered the building of a church at the site of Jesus' crucifixion and resurrection, being determined that 'that sacred place should be adorned with beautiful buildings'. All traces of the pagan temple there were removed and the rock tomb in which Jesus had lain was excavated and cleared of the earth and rubble with which it had been filled. The new church, known as the Church of the Holy Sepulchre, was dedicated in AD 335, and consisted of an atrium through which pilgrims entered, a large and elaborate *martyrion* or basilica and a colonaded courtyard,

which enclosed the rock of Calvary.
Later in the fourth century the rock
tomb, which originally stood outside
the complex, was covered with a
rotunda, known as the Anastasis, and
linked to the inner court.

Over subsequent decades churches
were built at other important places
mentioned in the Bible, including
Gethsemane, Mount Tabor, Nazareth,
on the shore of Lake Galilee at
Tabgha, and at the supposed sites of
Jacob's Well and the first Pentecost.
The identification in this period of
biblical sites – such as Mount Tabor
as the location of Jesus' transfiguration
and the place now known as Kefr
Kenna as Cana in Galilee – has
been regarded by many scholars as
dubious and highly speculative, but it
provided an ever-expanding pilgrim
trail through the Holy Land. An
anonymous pilgrim from Bordeaux
in AD 333 was able to write a
comprehensive travelogue describing
his circuit round a recognized
itinerary of sacred sites; and Egeria, a
Spanish nun from Galicia who came
to the Holy Land in AD 381–84,
described an extensive network of
churches attached to biblical sites and the development of liturgies for pilgrims
visiting them.

Jezreel Valley; with
Mount Tabor in the
distance, Israel

The practice of pilgrimage was greatly encouraged in the latter part of the
fourth century by the development of a conscious theology of holy places.
Eusebius had no qualms about describing certain places as 'sacred'. Cyril, bishop
of Jerusalem from c. AD 350 to 386, held that the principal sites associated with
Jesus 'all but showed Christ to the eyes of the faithful' and had the power to
shame, reprove and confute those who were tempted to disbelieve the Gospel
stories. Speaking of the privilege of being in Jerusalem he said, 'others merely
hear, but we see and touch'.[2] Jerome, the Italian biblical scholar and translator
who produced the first Latin Bible, the Vulgate, made extensive journeys
through the Holy Land in AD 385–86 in the company of an aristocratic

widow called Paula, her daughter, Eustochium, and other women who had dedicated themselves to the ascetic life. Consciously seeking solitude and detachment from the worldliness and decadence of Rome, they visited just about every conceivable place with Old and New Testament associations and found themselves deeply moved by direct physical contact with the sacred. Jerome described the ecstacy with which Paula kissed the stone removed by the angel from the mouth of Jesus' tomb and the slab on which his body was presumed to have lain. Echoing Cyril, he recorded the impression made by his first visit to Jerusalem: 'I saw a host of marvels, and with the judgment of my eyes I verified things of which I had previously learned by report.' Around AD 390 Jerome published *Liber Locorum* (Book of Places), a Latin version of Eusebius' *Onomastikon*, which became the indispensable guide and gazetteer for European pilgrims to the Holy Land. Anticipating Dr Johnson's famous remarks on Iona (see p.121), he reflected that 'Just as Greek history becomes more intelligible to those who have seen Athens, so that man will gain a clearer grasp of Holy Scripture who has gazed at Judaea with his own eyes.'[3]

It was not just Jerusalem and other places in Palestine that opened up to pilgrims in the fourth century. Rome, too, developed as a sacred place and a major pilgrimage destination. Once again, the initiative came from

Reliquary containing a supposed fragment of Jesus' crib in the church of Santa Maria Maggiore, Rome

Constantine, with the building of the Lateran Church in AD 313 and the great basilica to house the tomb of the apostle Peter around AD 320. In AD 366 Pope Damasus cleared, restored and embellished the catacombs, the underground tombs where Christians had been buried from the second century onwards. Pilgrims visited them in the mistaken belief that most of those buried there had died heroically as martyrs rather than of natural causes. The cult of martyrs that developed in the church in the fourth century helped to fuel the appeal of pilgrimage as people sought contact with holy men and women as well as holy places, and felt drawn to the resting places of those who had given their lives for the faith. As early as the late second century, Christians in Smyrna had gathered at the tomb of the martyred bishop

Polycarp on the anniversary of his death in c. AD 155.

The beginnings of another cult closely associated with the growth of pilgrimage in the Middle Ages first appeared at this time, based on the belief that relics – objects associated with particularly holy people – were themselves sacred and possessed miraculous powers. The earliest and most significant relic was the wood of the true cross, supposedly found during the clearing of debris from around the site of Calvary prior to the building of Constantine's *Martyrium*. Eusebius was sceptical about its authenticity and worried that the Jerusalem church would develop a relic trade for its own purposes. Cyril, as bishop of Jerusalem, had no such inhibitions. In a letter to Constantine's son, Constantius, in AD 351 he described how 'the saving wood of the Cross' had been found in the city in connection with the emperor's 'discovery of the hidden holy places'. He went on to detail the miracles and apparitions that had followed its discovery, with a huge cross appearing in the sky above Gologotha and 'flashing like lightning over Jerusalem'.[4] He later claimed that the relic had spread 'all over the world', although a substantial portion of it remained in Jerusalem where it was displayed on Good Friday. The empress Helena brought back a prodigious quantity of relics from her visit to the Holy Land. They are now distributed among the main basilicas of Rome. On a more modest scale, other pilgrims began to bring back souvenirs, which they referred to as *eulogiae*, or blessings. These included dried flowers from Gethsemane, dust from the streets of Jerusalem, water from the Jordan and oil from the lamps of the Holy Sepulchre. Small tokens of burnt clay taken from the soil around holy sites were ground up and dissolved in water, which was then drunk.

Not all the early church fathers were enthusiasts for pilgrimage. Indeed, several of the most prominent were uneasy about its growing popularity and the assumptions on which it was increasingly based. Augustine of Hippo preached that voyages were useless to carry a believer to Christ since faith made him immediately present. Gregory of Nyssa, who visited Jerusalem in AD 380, was not impressed by the experience, feeling that the 'holiness' of the Holy Land was greatly exaggerated and urging his fellow Christians, 'Ye who fear the Lord, praise him in the places ye are now. Change of place does not effect a drawing nearer to God.'[5] Even Jerome, despite the power

Pilgrim?
Today?
Yes, this very day.

Perhaps not so much
To Kailish, Jerusalem,
Mecca, Santiago, Nidaros...
As on the invisible path,
In the inner landscape.

That's where
Everything begins.
And where
Everything ends.

The inner landscape is
The terrain we know.
The invisible path
Leads towards the Middle,
Where life is always new.

Bodvar Schjelderup

'Access to the courts of heaven is as easy from Britain as it is from Jerusalem for the kingdom of God is within you. Nothing is lacking to your faith though you have not seen Jerusalem.'

Jerome, Letter 58

of his own experiences in the Holy Land, pointed to the absurdity of supposing that prayers offered in one place could be more acceptable than the same prayers offered in another: 'Access to the courts of heaven is as easy from Britain as it is from Jerusalem for the kingdom of God is within you. Nothing is lacking to your faith though you have not seen Jerusalem.'[6]

Despite these strictures, however, by the end of the fourth century pilgrimage to both the Holy Land and Rome had become a significant expression of Christian devotion and was being actively encouraged by the church. Meanwhile, another very different kind of pilgrimage had taken root in the deserts of Egypt and Syria. Monasticism – both in its solitary form as pioneered by hermits and anchorites such as St Antony, and in communities such as those set up by Pachomius – emphasized the inner spiritual pilgrimage as much as a physical journey of exile away from distractions and comforts. Ironically, although their aim was to retreat into isolation and solitude, the desert monks found themselves the objects of pilgrimage as visits to holy people became as attractive as visits to holy places. Many pilgrims to the Holy Land tacked on a visit to the monasteries in Egypt and Syria after completing their tour of Palestine. Jerome and his female companions did this and were so impressed by the asceticism and spirituality of the monks that they themselves returned to Jerusalem to set up monastic communities there. Meanwhile, the hermits found themselves retreating into ever more remote and inaccessible places in an effort to seek the seclusion and exile to which they felt called. Notable ascetics such as St Simeon Stylites, who spent thirty years perched on a pillar at Thelmenissus near Antioch in Western Syria, became major attractions for visitors who were perhaps closer to gawping tourists than devout pilgrims.

The strict and austere disciplines of the desert fathers moved several Western Christians to emulate and join them. One such was John Cassian, who around AD 380 entered a monastery established near the Cave of the Nativity in Bethlehem where he shared a cell for several years with his friend Germanus. The two men later moved on to Egypt where they lived as hermits. Cassian subsequently moved to Gaul, where he wrote his *Institutes* to expound the principles of desert monasticism and asceticism. His writing had a profound impact on the monks of Ireland on the western fringes of Christendom, among whom it inspired a new and radical form of perpetual pilgrimage that stood in marked contrast to the burgeoning cults of holy places and sacred relics.

Celtic Pilgrimage

3

If I ever had to make a film about early Irish Christianity I would be tempted to call it 'monks on the move', if not 'nuns on the run'. Pilgrimage, or *peregrinatio* to use the Latin word by which they knew it, was central to the lives of the Irish monks who lived in the sixth and seventh centuries and ushered in what is generally seen as the golden age of Celtic Christianity. For them, it was not about journeying to holy places such as Rome or Jerusalem and venerating or touching the relics of holy people; rather it was a costly form of witness involving perpetual exile from the comforts and distractions of home.

Not that they were uninterested in sacred places. Around AD 688 Adamnan, the ninth abbot of Iona, wrote a treatise on Jerusalem and other sites in the Holy Land. Entitled *De Locis Sanctis*, it was illustrated with drawings and based on accounts by a Frankish bishop, Arculf, who had visited the Holy Land, Constantinople and Rome. On the way back from his travels Arculf was wrecked off the west coast of Scotland and found his way to Iona, where Adamnan interviewed him about his experiences and recorded them for posterity.

Iona Abbey with St Martin's Cross in the right foreground and Mull in the distance.

Beehive cells on the
remote island of
Skellig Michael off the
coast of Ireland

The prevailing view in Irish monastic circles about the benefits to be gained
from visiting holy places was profoundly sceptical, however. It is reflected in the
verse attributed to a ninth-century Irish abbot:

> **Who to Rome goes**
> **Much labour, little profit knows;**
> **For God, on earth though long you've sought him,**
> **You'll miss in Rome unless you've brought him.**

The Irish monks' approach to pilgrimage was based on biblical teaching, and
specifically on God's call to Abraham to leave his home and journey to a strange
land. It also owed much to the example and teaching of the desert fathers in Egypt
and Syria. There is evidence that Egyptian monks journeyed to Ireland: in an
eighth-century manuscript seven are described coming to Diseart Uilaig, a site
tentatively identified as Dundesert near Crumlin in County Antrim. Irish monks
sought their own desert places, often remote and wild like Skellig Michael, a rocky
island off the coast of County Kerry where they established their beehive cells
and hermit huts. This is the reason why the words Diseart, Disserth and Dysart
are quite often found as place names in Ireland, Wales and Scotland. They indicate

early monastic settlements, some of which were made up of a solitary hermit whereas others constituted a group living a communal life. Irish monks also sought out what they called their places of resurrection where they did penance and prepared for death, rather in the manner of the Hindu *sanyasi* or ascetic. This practice was not confined to the Celts: eight Anglo-Saxon kings went as pilgrims to Rome to die within fifty years in the eighth century.

Seen in terms of ascetic exile and renunciation of the pleasures and distractions of home and family, pilgrimage was a tough calling and a costly form of witness to Christ. The oldest surviving example of continuous Irish prose, dating from around AD 700 and copied into a book commissioned by the bishop of Cambrai, describes three kinds of martyrdom (*marturos* being the Greek word for witness). The first, white martyrdom, embraced a life of exile and separation from all that one loved for the sake of God, as well as mortification of the flesh through fasting and penitential exercises. The second, green martyrdom, involved fasting and penitential toil without the radical exile. The third, red martyrdom, meant dying for the faith, something that was almost impossible to achieve since there was very little persecution of Christians in the British Isles at this time. Many monks, however, practised white martyrdom, casting themselves off from their homeland and kinfolk to embark on a life of perpetual pilgrimage and exile.

Several of the most famous Celtic saints became pilgrims in this spirit. Patrick left his British homeland following a call that came to him in a dream to walk among the Irish. Columba is described by his biographer Adamnan as sailing away from Ireland to Britain with twelve companions, 'wishing to be a pilgrim for Christ'. It is not entirely clear what prompted the voyage that eventually led him to Iona – it may have been penitential, a banishment imposed for some transgression, a voluntary exile or a response to a request from the king of the new Irish colony of Dal Riata in western Scotland. Whatever his exact motives, Columba is portrayed by hagiographers as the classic 'pilgrim for Christ'. Beccan mac Luigdech, an Irish monk who seems to have come to Iona around AD 630, writes of Columba crucifying his body 'not for crimes' on the grey waves, and crossing 'the long haired sea' with 'an army of wretches':

The path I walk, Christ walks it.
May the land in which I am be
without sorrow.
May the Trinity protect me
whenever I stray,
Father, Son and Holy Spirit.
Bright Angels walk with me –
dear presence – in every dealing.
In every dealing I pray them
that no one's poison may reach
me.
The ninefold people of heaven of
holy cloud,
The tenth force of the stout
earth.
Favourable company, they come
with me,
So that the Lord may not be
angry with me.
May I arrive at every place,
may I return home;
May the way in which I spend be
a way without loss.
May every path before me be
smooth,
Man, woman and child welcome
me.
A truly good journey!
Well does the fair Lord show us a
course, a path.

Attributed to St Columba

Columbanus

Perhaps the greatest of all the Irish pilgrim monks, and certainly the one who reflected most on the theological significance and meaning of pilgrimage, Columbanus was born in Leinster around AD 540. He became a monk as a young man and was a member of the community at Bangor, which had been founded by Comgall. When he was about forty-five, Columbanus was given permission by Comgall to go on pilgrimage across Continental Europe. He had been prompted by God's words to Abraham, and according to another more irreverent tradition by the fact that he was being pursued 'by lascivious maidens'. Taking twelve monks with him, he set off from the north-east coast of Ireland, travelled down the western seaboard of Britain, crossed Cornwall and journeyed through France, founding monasteries at Annegray, Luxeuil and Fontaine in the Vosges region. He and his companions fell out with both the ecclesiastical authorities and the local rulers and were forcibly marched under guard to Nantes to be sent back to Ireland. However, a storm blew the ship that was to return them aground at the mouth of the Loire, and the captain, taking this as a sign that God did not approve of their expulsion, allowed them to go free. They wandered across northern France, rowed up the Rhine and eventually came to Bregenz on Lake Constance in Switzerland. There one of the monks, Gall, remained to found a monastery while Columbanus and the others crossed over the Alps into Lombardy. He founded his final monastery at Bobbio between Genoa and Piacenza and died there in AD 615, thirty years after leaving Ireland.

Columbanus' monastic rule was taken up by over sixty monasteries in France, Belgium and Switzerland, which were founded by his followers. Although he became something of a cult figure and was much sought out for his counsel and spiritual wisdom, he remained a solitary ascetic and spent much of his time in caves living off wild apples and herbs. He fell foul of bishops who found it hard to come to terms with the activities of this restless individual, who insisted he was first and last a 'pilgrim for Christ'. Columbanus spoke of pilgrims as *hospes mundi*, or guests of the world, a phrase that epitomizes the ambivalence of pilgrimage – at once an austere, penitential calling and a somewhat self-indulgent and parasitic lifestyle that relies on other people's generosity and living off their hospitality.

Columbanus is unique among Irish monks from the 'golden age' of Celtic Christianity in having left sermons that survive today. They speak of human life as a pilgrimage and show how his thirty years of exile and wandering reflected his own theology.

Extract from Sermon Eight

We who are on the road should hasten on, for the whole of our life is like one day's journey. Just like pilgrims we should continuously sigh for and long for our homeland, for travellers are always filled with hope and desire for the road's end. And so, since we are travellers and pilgrims in this world, let us think upon the end of the road, that is of our life, for the end of our way is our home.[3]

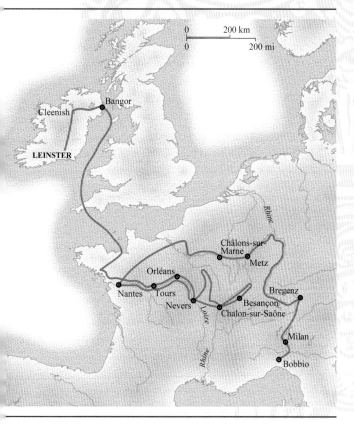

Map showing Columbanus' wanderings across Europe from his Irish home to Bobbio in Italy

**He crossed the wave-strewn wild region, foam-flecked, seal-filled,
Savage, bounding, seething, white-tipped, pleasing, doleful.[1]**

This image of the pilgrim navigating dangerous seas recurs in the lives of many Irish saints. They seem for ever on the move, criss-crossing the Irish Sea, the Minch, the Bristol Channel and even the English Channel and the North Sea, penetrating deep into Wales, the Scottish mainland, the Inner and Outer Hebrides and many parts of England, as well as journeying further afield into Continental Europe where they evangelized and set up monasteries in Belgium, France, Germany and Italy. Fursey, the Irish monk who is credited with evangelizing much of East Anglia, was described by Bede as 'a holy man from Ireland, anxious to live the life of a pilgrim for the Lord's sake'.[2] He went on to travel through France, establishing a monastery at Lagny near Paris. The eighth-century Irish *Litany of Pilgrim Saints* chronicles numerous epic journeys, some made in solitude and others in company.

To journey over water the monks used *curraghs*, stout boats 33 feet (10 metres) or so long made by stretching up to fifty oak-tanned ox hides over a central wooden rib. On land, they travelled on foot clad in a tunic covered by a cowl, carrying a staff, with a leather water bottle hanging from their belt and a gospel book in a leather case slung across their shoulder. The motives that inspired their almost perpetual pilgrimage were mixed. The desire to imitate Christ in a costly witness of ascetic exile was undoubtedly strong. Pilgrimage was also clearly seen as a penitential exercise and was prescribed as a form of punishment in many monastic rules. Several monks subjected themselves to it as a voluntary penance, like those referred to in an eleventh-century Irish poem, *The Voyage of the Ui Chorra*:

**We went on our pilgrimage
At the blast of the whistling wind
To obtain forgiveness of our sins.
There is the cause of asking.**

A commitment to mission and evangelism also took monks on pilgrimage and many preached, taught, baptized and buried as they travelled and set up monasteries along the way. Some were undoubtedly motivated too by a sense of adventure and wanderlust. Often they did not know or mind where they were going. An entry in the Anglo Saxon Chronicle for AD 891 mentions three Irish monks who stole away in a boat without oars 'because they desired for the love of God to be in a state of pilgrimage, they cared not whither'. They took enough food for seven days and eventually came ashore on the north coast of Cornwall.

Abbots and others in authority were not always very keen on their monks perpetually wandering around and sometimes tried to put a stop to the practice through which some became *gyrovagues*, itinerant hermits who could not settle

St Brendan

Of all the Irish tales of pilgrimage, the *Navigation of St Brendan* – of which there are 120 surviving manuscripts, the earliest dating from the tenth century – is the most remarkable. It recounts the wanderings of Brendan, who is regarded as the founder of the monastery of Clonfert in Galway. He was probably born in Kerry around AD 486, and died in Annaghdown in AD 575. Adamnan writes of Brendan visiting Iona and there are also accounts of him travelling to Brittany. The *Navigation* suggests a much longer and more exotic journey across the Atlantic.

In the story Brendan seeks the promised land of the saints, 'that land which God will give us and our successors on the last day', a paradise where night never falls and day never ends. Having heard about this land as a young boy from a monk called Barinthus who claimed to have been there, he is determined to find it and sets out westwards from Ireland with fourteen monks. They have many adventures as they sail the Atlantic ocean, stopping off at islands both good and bad, including Sheep Island, a Paradise of Birds and the Island of the Smiths with forges casting fire into the sea. Their visionary encounters include one with Judas Iscariot, clinging to a sea-girt rock on a day's relief from the torments of hell. When they eventually reach their destination a young man tells them: 'This is the land which you have sought for so long. You were not able to find it immediately because God wished to show you his wonders in the great ocean.

Return now to the land of your birth, taking with you fruit from this land and as many gems as your boat can carry. The day of your final journey is approaching, when you shall sleep with your father.'[4]

Some scholars have seen this story as a Christianized version of older pre-Christian *immram*, or voyages to the other world. Others maintain, however, that the Christian version pre-dates the pagan *Voyage of Braan* and that it should be read as an allegory of the monastic life. Whatever its purpose and provenance, the *Navigation of St Brendan* gives a wonderful sense of the adventure of pilgrimage and stands as one of the great classics of the literature of travel and journeying. In 1976 Tim Severin reconstructed Brendan's voyages in a traditionally made *curragh* powered by sail and oars, which is now on display at the Cragganauen Archeology Park near Limerick. He travelled from Kerry up the west coast of Ireland, through the Hebridean archipelago to the Faroes, which he suggested as the site of Brendan's islands of birds and sheep, and on to Iceland, which with its volcanoes and geysers he surmised might be the Island of the Smiths. Severin and his companions eventually reached Labrador and the Newfoundland coast. He suggested that it was quite possible that Irish monks might have reached North America nearly 1,000 years before Columbus.

'Alone in my little hut without a human being in my company, dear has been my pilgrimage before going to meet death.'

Irish hermit poem

anywhere and effectively became tramps. Samthann, a nun, icily responded to a teacher named Dairchellach who expressed the desire to cross the sea on pilgrimage: 'If God could not be found on this side of the sea we would indeed journey across. Since, however, God is nigh unto all who call upon Him, we are under no obligation to cross the sea. The kingdom of heaven can be reached from every land.' However, no vow of stability was imposed in Irish monasteries, as it was in the later foundations of St Benedict, who looked with considerable disfavour on the activities of the wandering *gyrovagues*. Despite the concerns and strictures of the authorities, there was little that they could do to restrain their monks from becoming pilgrims for Christ. Pilgrimage remained extremely popular in the monastic-dominated Christian culture of Ireland, Wales, Scotland and much of England throughout the early medieval period.

Irish monks reached as far as the Faroes by AD 700 and by the end of the eighth century they had reached Iceland. Literary epics such as the *Navigation of St Brendan* testified to the appeal of pilgrimage and it was a popular theme of poems in the Irish, Welsh and Gaelic/Hebridean spiritual traditions.

In time, the Celtic pilgrim tradition changed and became more focused on the inner pilgrimage of green martyrdom. The growing realization that the pilgrim path of renunciation and asceticism could be pursued without wandering around the world is reflected in the Irish 'hermit poems' from the ninth and tenth centuries: 'Alone in my little hut without a human being in my company, dear has been my pilgrimage before going to meet death.'

Some centuries after their deaths the pioneer Celtic saints came to inspire pilgrimages of a kind which they would almost certainly not have approved to the sites associated with them, such as Iona, Croagh Patrick, St David's and Lindisfarne. Almost as much as Rome and Jerusalem, these Celtic Christian sites became places of pilgrimage, as people sought contact with the holy men and women whose saintly lives were being written up by hagiographers in ever more fanciful and effusive ways from the ninth century onwards. Across Europe as a whole, the cult of saints was about to usher in the golden age of Christian pilgrimage and take it far away from the lonely and austere lives of exile practised by the Irish monks.

Woodcut illustrating an episode in the *Navigation of St Brendan* when the saint and his companions are said to have travelled on the back of a whale

4 The Golden Age of Pilgrimage

The five hundred years from the early eleventh to the early sixteenth century were the golden age of pilgrimage in Europe. It has been estimated that in certain years one-fifth of the population of Europe was either on pilgrimage or engaged in servicing the booming pilgrim trade. Men and women left their homes for up to a year and trekked across the continent to one or more of the growing number of holy places and saints' shrines, impelled by piety, religious enthusiasm, the search for a physical cure and/or spiritual benefit, curiosity and a sense of adventure. Others felt motivated by a desire to escape the pressures and responsibilities of everyday life. The Council of Chalons-sur-Saône in AD 813 formally condemned poor people who went on pilgrimage primarily because it offered them an easy opportunity to beg. It also condemned clergy who did so to escape their pastoral duties. However, a good number of medieval pilgrims seem to have left their homes largely to deny interfering parish priests a monopoly over their spiritual welfare.

A growing popular preoccupation with death, hell and judgment increased many people's belief in the need for the prayers of saints and contact with relics to help promote their passage into heaven. The cult of relics was boosted by a decree of the Council of Nicea in AD 787 that a church could not be validly consecrated unless it contained a relic. Holy people became as important as holy places, and by the twelfth century more and more pilgrims sought physical contact with the remains of saints and believed that they would be thereby touched or infused with holiness, healing and power. As the practice of pilgrimage increased, it became more regulated by the church and integrated into a developing system of penances and punishments. From the twelfth century onwards pilgrimage was prescribed by both ecclesiastical authorities and civil courts as a form of judicial punishment for a whole range of offences. While the sinner's guilt before God could only be dealt with through contrition and confession followed by absolution, pilgrimages were seen as highly effective

Chaucer's Canterbury Pilgrims, Tabard Inn by Edward Henry Corbou

penances whereby individuals could undergo the punishment due for sin after it had been forgiven.

Tables drawn up by Hamo de Hethe, bishop of Rochester from 1319 to 1352, illustrate how the ecclesiastical authorities prescribed pilgrimages as penances. Each offence had its own penance, generally involving one or more pilgrimages to a local shrine. The punishment for adultery was an annual pilgrimage for six years to the shrines of St Thomas at Canterbury, St Thomas at Hereford, St Edmund at Bury and St Richard at Chichester, together with the provision of a three-pound candle annually for six years at the feast of St Andrew at Rochester and almsgiving along the way. Clerical incontinence was punished with a pilgrimage to Walsingham and the distribution of 6s 8d in alms along the way. The penance due for adultery with one's godmother, the most serious offence on the list, was a pilgrimage to Santiago de Compostela. Civil authorities, too, prescribed pilgrimages as punishments for crimes. The treaty of peace that Philip IV of France imposed on the rebellious Flemish in 1305 stipulated his right to send 2,000 citizens of Bruges on pilgrimages in recompense for the massacre of the French carried out in that city in 1302.

The development of the notion of purgatory increased the importance of pilgrimage. With the sense of an intermediate state after death in which individuals had to work off penances that had not been performed in life, the concept of indulgences offered the chance to alleviate the burden of posthumous suffering. Pilgrimages were one of the most common forms

'[Jerusalem] is situated in the centre of the world, in the middle of the earth, so that all men may turn their steps towards her; she is the patrimony of the patriarchs, the nurse of the prophets, the mistress of the apostles, the cradle of our salvation, the home of our Lord, and the mother of our Faith.'

Jacques de Vitry, bishop of Acre

of indulgence prescribed by the church, providing a reduction in the time that the soul would have to spend in purgatory for the remission of sin. The pilgrimage to Assisi seems to have been the first for which an indulgence was formally granted. *Libri Indulgentiarum* (*Books of Indulgences*) laid down the precise benefits to be gained from particular pilgrimages. Pope Boniface VIII offered all who visited the basilicas of the apostles in Rome during the year 1300 a plenary indulgence, totally remitting their sentence to date in purgatory. Over 200,000 pilgrims came to the city during this first Holy Year. In 1343 Pope Clement VI declared that every fifty years there would be a jubilee with pilgrims to Rome being granted a plenary indulgence. He also defined the doctrine of the Treasury of Merit, available to the faithful to make up for their shortcomings by drawing on the inexhaustible store of merit gained through the sacrifice of Jesus and the merit of the saints. One of the best ways of tapping into this treasury was through making a pilgrimage.

The Holy Land in general, and Jerusalem in particular, remained the most sought after and prized pilgrim destination throughout the Middle Ages. Jacques de Vitry, bishop of Acre (the port city just north of Haifa now known as Akko) from 1216 to 1228, described it as 'the city of cities, the saint of saints, the queen of nations, and the princess of provinces. She is situated in the centre of the world, in the middle of the earth, so that all men may turn their steps towards her; she is the patrimony of the patriarchs, the nurse of the prophets, the mistress of the apostles, the cradle of our salvation, the home of our Lord, and the mother of our Faith.'[1]

A growing emphasis on the humanity of Jesus in the eleventh and twelfth centuries drew pilgrims to Jerusalem not just to visit the places associated with his life and death, but also to imagine and re-enact in their own lives his service and suffering. They often referred to their pilgrimage as an *imitatio Christi* (imitation of Christ). Many pilgrims baptized themselves in the Jordan at the point where John the Baptist was believed to have baptized Christ. Some spent several months following the exact path of Jesus' ministry, beginning at the Jordan and ending at Calvary where they found themselves overcome by tears and anguish. Rayner of Pisa fasted for forty days on Mount Tabor in remembrance of Jesus' forty days in the desert. On Maundy Thursday, 1027, Richard of St-Vannes knelt in the square in front of the Holy Sepulchre and washed the feet of the poor. Moreover, in the latter half of the twelfth century, it was common for pilgrims to have themselves flagellated at the pillar where Jesus was said to have been scourged on the orders of Pontius Pilate.

The penitential nature of pilgrimage to the Holy Land was exacerbated by the length, expense and hazards of the journey there from Europe and, from the mid-eleventh century, by the increasing Muslim antagonism towards Christians in the Levant. It was in part to ensure the future of Christian pilgrimage to the Holy Land and make it safer that the Crusades were fought between 1095 and 1291. When Pope Urban II launched the First Crusade, he referred to it as 'this holy pilgrimage', and the Crusaders' uniforms were modelled on the dress of pilgrims. The number of pilgrims journeying

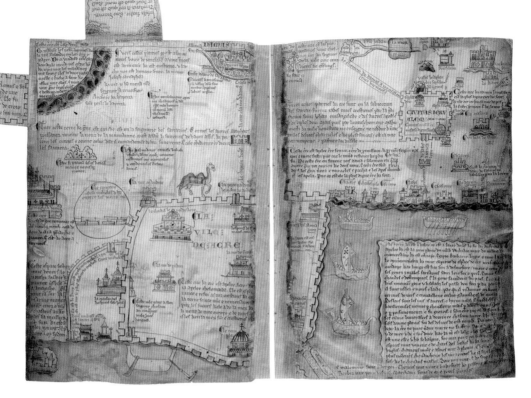

Medieval pilgrims' map of Jerusalem

to the Holy Land fluctuated depending on the strength of the Muslim presence and the impact of successive Crusades, but even after the loss of Acre, the last Christian stronghold, in 1291, intrepid individuals continued to walk in the footsteps of Jesus. Their sense that prayers offered up in places associated with him had a special significance and power is well conveyed in the writings of Felix Fabri, a preaching friar from Ulm who made two separate visits to Jerusalem in the late fifteenth century:

> *I went up to the Holy Hill of Calvary, lighted a candle, and sat down with ink in front of me close by the holy rock wherein the cross once stood him up crucified, and there I wrote down the names of all whom I had especially promised, and all for whom I was in duty bound to pray. Having written down all the names as in litanies, I went with the paper to the holy rock, and there, kneeling on my knees, I laid that paper on the holy rock, and offered a prayer for each person whose name was written thereon, and for others whose names occured to my memory.[2]*

Rome continued to be the pre-eminent place of pilgrimage within Europe, gaining significantly more visitors during those periods when access to the Middle East was more difficult or hazardous. Those who went there were known as *Romipetae* or Rome seekers. They included monarchs and other prominent figures seeking humility and pardon. Ratchis, king of the Lombards, walked to Rome with his wife and children in AD 749 and exchanged his crown for a monastic habit at the hands of the pope.

Numerous other European shrines developed in the Middle Ages as alternative or additional pilgrim destinations. One of the first, the tomb of St Martin in Tours, became a shrine shortly after his death in AD 397 and was recognized as a major place of pilgrimage by the Council of Chalons-sur-Saône in AD 813. France had a particular proliferation of medieval pilgrim shrines, including Limoges (St Martial), Vézelay (St Mary Magdalene), Poitiers (St Hilary and the head of John the Baptist), Bourges (St Stephen), Conques (St Foy), Le Puy (St Mary), Toulouse (St Saturninus) and Noblat (St Leonard). In the British Isles, the emergence in the late eighth century of a story that the bones of Andrew the apostle had been brought to a remote headland on the east coast of Scotland began the development of St Andrews as one of Britain's major places of pilgrimage. Shortly afterwards, around AD 810, a hermit living in the north-west corner of Spain was guided by a star to the tomb of another apostle, James, providing the foundation story for Santiago de Compostela, which was destined to become second only to Rome in terms of its popularity for pilgrims in medieval Europe.

Royal patronage played a key part in the development of these and other shrines. Santiago was promoted first by King Alfonso II of Asturias in the early ninth century and later by King Alfonso IV of Leon-Castile who, worried 'lest any moments of his life be lacking in good works', commanded bridges to be built across all the rivers between Logrono and Santiago. A similar boost was given to the main pilgrim route to St Andrews by Queen Margaret of Scotland when she established a ferry service across the Forth Estuary between North and South Queensferry. In the mid-twelfth century, the bequest of the supposed bodies of the Magi or three kings of the nativity story, given by Frederick Barbarossa to the archbishop of Cologne, established Cologne Cathedral as another important pilgrim destination. The tombs of the Magi were an appropriate object of pilgrimage since the Magi were perhaps the first Christian pilgrims, led by a star to worship the infant Jesus.

The rising popularity of pilgrimage across Europe was accompanied by a growing concern about the spirit in which it should be undertaken. Pilgrims were expected to ask the permission of their spouse, parish priest and feudal lord, settle their affairs and make amends to anyone they had wronged before leaving home. Those with means were encouraged to make generous donations to the poor before setting off. Sermons emphasized the penitential aspects of pilgrimage. Jacques de Vitry preached that 'nothing is more efficacious or satisfying than the labour of pilgrimage. For just as a man sins with all his limbs, so too must he make reparation with all of them.'[3] The more the pilgrim's back ached and his feet blistered, the better – the pilgrim should sweat as Christ sweated. He should also, decreed de Vitry, wear only light clothing, use money purely for charity and put his trust in Christ for his daily bread. The pilgrim accustomed to sleeping on a soft bed should lie only on a hard one, and if used to rising late, should get up early. He should never spend longer than one night anywhere and should not be distracted by anything or anyone along the way.

A similar emphasis on the austere, penitential nature of pilgrimage characterizes a sermon dating from around 1125 and printed in the *Liber Sancti Jacobi*, a manual for pilgrims journeying to Santiago attributed (wrongly) to Pope Calixtus II. It enjoins pilgrims to sell their property before leaving and give the proceeds to the poor, and to take on their journey no money for their own use but only what could be distributed to the needy along the way, warning that 'the pilgrim who dies with money in his pocket will be forever excluded from the kingdom of heaven'. The sermon, known from its opening words as *Veneranda Dies*, goes on to castigate those pilgrims who behave more as

Scenes from the Life of Saint Ursula: Arrival of the Pilgrims in Cologne from a painting by Vittore Carpaccio

Canterbury

When that Aprill with his shoures soote,
The droughte of March hath pierced to the roote…
Thanne longen folke to go on pilgrimages,
And palmers for to seken straunge strondes,
To ferne halwes, kowthe in sundry londes;
And specially from every shires ende
Of Engelond to Caunterbury they wende
The hooly blissful martir for to seke,
That hem hath holpen whan that they were seeke.

The opening lines of one of the most famous books in English literature, Geoffrey Chaucer's *Canterbury Tales*, take us to the heart of the medieval passion for pilgrimage and in particular to the importance for English pilgrims of the shrine of St Thomas à Becket at Canterbury.

Becket, who was made chancellor of England at the age of thirty-seven, became archbishop of Canterbury in 1162. He soon fell out with King Henry II over, among other issues, the respective jurisdictions of church and state. In a moment of exasperation, the king rhetorically asked who would rid him of his turbulent priest. Four knights took his remark literally and brutally killed Becket in one of the side chapels of his cathedral in 1170. He was canonized three years later. Becket's tomb became a place of pilgrimage almost immediately and his relics were eventually placed in a spectacular two-storied shrine built at the eastern end of the cathedral in 1220. Henry II himself undertook a penitential pilgrimage to Rome following Becket's murder.

For the next 350 years St Thomas' shrine at Canterbury ranked third after Rome and Santiago in terms of importance and popularity among the destinations for pilgrims within Europe. As early as 1174 a chronicler noted that Becket was being sought in pilgrimage by 'kings, princes, barons, dukes with the nobles, strangers from foreign countries speaking many languages, prelates, monks, recluses and crowds of foot travellers. They take phials home with them as a sign of their journey.' These phials, containing water supposedly mixed with Becket's blood and believed to have curative properties, have been found as far afield as Bergen in Norway and Sicily. From the fourteenth century badges showing scenes from the saint's life and miniature replicas of the sword that killed him were also sold to Canterbury pilgrims. Not all Canterbury's relics were associated with Becket: the cathedral also claimed to have a piece of the clay from which Adam had been created by God.

The *Canterbury Tales*, written in the late 1380s and early 1390s, recounts the stories told by a motley group of pilgrims (29 according to Chaucer, although his prologue actually lists 31) who gather at the Tabard Inn at Southwark and ride to Canterbury. They include a pardoner or professional seller of indulgences, tradesmen, churchmen, a nun, a prioress and the famous Wife of Bath. Chaucer's story shows the camaraderie formed during pilgrimage by a group of people who would otherwise have had little in common and whose social stations, like their outlook on life, are very different.

Chaucer's pilgrims are a jolly bunch who do not display the penitential aspects of pilgrimage lauded in so many medieval sermons. Although in his tale the parson commends those pilgrims who go naked or barefoot, he and his companions all ride to Canterbury on horseback. They do not seem to attend Mass, even on the morning of their departure, and they do not stop at any of the shrines on the way, such as the miraculous cross at Rochester or St Thomas' shoe at Broughton under Blee, which pilgrims *en route* to Canterbury customarily stopped to kiss. Chaucer, who spent much of his life as an official in the royal household, is not so much concerned with chronicling an actual pilgrimage as in using it as a convenient setting for assembling a diverse group of characters to spin their tales. He also has a clear sense of pilgrimage as a metaphor for life, with the knight reflecting in his tale that:

This world is but a thurghfare ful of woe,
And we been pilgrymes, passynge to and fro.

Such gloomy reflections about life's vicissitudes play a small part in the *Canterbury Tales*, however, and their dominant themes are of laughter, fun and the forging of a highly diverse group into a community. There is little reference to the landscape of people and places through which the pilgrims travel. The emphasis rather is on the enclosed, self-contained world that pilgrims inhabit during their time together.

Middle English glossary

straunge strondes – foreign shores
ferne halwes – distant shrines
kowthe in sundry landes – known in various lands (i.e. famous)
hem hath holpen – helped them
seeke – sick

travellers and tourists, eating and drinking their way across the roads of Europe in the hope of salvation:

> *Truly, these are not real pilgrims at all, but thieves and robbers who have abandoned the way of apostolic poverty and chosen instead the path of damnation … If the Lord chose to enter Jerusalem on a mule rather than a horse, then what are we to think of those who parade up and down before us on horseback … If St Peter entered Rome with nothing but a crucifix, why do so many pilgrims come here with bulging purses and trunks of spare clothes eating succulent food and drinking heady wine?*

For the preacher of this sermon, a pilgrimage was worthless unless it involved a total and lasting moral reformation: '… if he was previously a spoliator, he must become an almsgiver; if he was boastful, he must be forever modest; if greedy, generous; if a fornicator or adulterer, chaste; if drunk, sober. That is to say that from every sin which he committed before his pilgrimage, he must afterwards abstain completely.'[4] Walter Hilton, an English mystic writing in the late fourteenth century, similarly emphasized the harsh and demanding nature of pilgrimage in both its inner spiritual and outward physical manifestations, noting that 'a pilgrim going to Jerusalem leaves behind him house and land, wife and children. If you want to be a spiritual pilgrim you must make yourself naked of all you have … keep on your way and desire only the love of Jesus.'[5]

There is no doubt that many medieval pilgrims took these strictures to heart and undertook their long journeys in a serious and penitential spirit. Some went as far as to incise the sign of the cross on their chests so deeply as to draw blood. Others, however, took a rather different approach to their forays away from home. As early as the eighth century, St Boniface complained that several female pilgrims to Rome fell into prostitution on their way through France and northern Italy. A much quoted medieval proverb warned: 'Go a pilgrim, return a whore.' Chaucer's Wife of Bath was surely not unique in going on pilgrimage for 'dauliance' and the chance of finding a lover. William Thorpe, appearing before the archbishop of Canterbury in 1407 charged with heresy because of his attack on pilgrims, observed that most went 'more for the health of their bodies than for their souls':

> *They have with them both men and women that can sing wanton songs, and some other pilgrims will have with them bagpipes; so that every town that they come through, what with the noise of their singing, and with the sound of their piping, and with the jangling of their Canterbury bells, and with the barking of dogs after them, they make more noise than if the king came their way with all his clarions and many other minstrels.*[6]

'If you want to be a spiritual pilgrim you must make yourself naked of all you have … keep on your way and desire only the love of Jesus.'

Walter Hilton

A 15th century bas-relief sculpture depicting a group of pilgrims. They are wearing the holy dress traditional for pious travellers including a knapsack and a cap with scallop shells

There was undoubtedly a raucous element among pilgrims, who tended to travel together in large groups for their safety and security, just as there was a carnival atmosphere outside the main pilgrim churches as jugglers, souvenir sellers and pickpockets mingled with those who had finally reached their destination after walking halfway across Europe. Much like those on package holidays today, pilgrims tended to travel with those of the same nationality who spoke the same language and to have little contact with local people along the way. There was also a very serious side to medieval pilgrimage, however. It was epitomized by the dress that pilgrims universally came to espouse: a long grey gown with a red cross sewn on it; a black or grey broad-brimmed hat, also marked with a red cross, turned up at the front and often attached at the back to a long scarf that was wound round the body as far as the waist; a staff – a tough wooden stick with a metal toe; and a leather scrip or satchel either slung on the pilgrim's shoulder or strapped to the waist, which contained his meagre provisions of food, a mess-can, money for alms and 'a bottle sufficient not for luxury but barely for the necessaries of life'. Much symbolism was attached to these accoutrements. The sermon *Veneranda Dies* decreed that the pilgrim's scrip should be made of the hide of a dead animal, thereby signifying the mortification of the flesh. It should be small, to indicate the pilgrim's modesty and trust in God for all requirements, and be ever-open, containing a few coins for almsgiving. The pilgrim's staff was to be used for driving off wolves and dogs, symbols of the snares of the devil. Felix Fabri identified a fifth outward badge of the pilgrim, in addition to the gown, hat, staff and scrip, as 'a long beard growing from a face that is serious and pale on account of his labours and dangers'.

This distinctive outfit came to constitute a uniform that guaranteed protection and privileges along the way. Pilgrims were generally exempt from paying tolls and entitled to free board and lodging throughout their journey, much of which was provided by monasteries set up along the main pilgrim routes. Later the chivalric religious orders of Knights Hospitaller and Knights Templar were set up specifically to care for and protect pilgrims. The first use of the word 'hospital' dates from around AD 800 when *hospitales* were set up as pilgrim refuges, some providing specialized care for those who were sick. Subsequently the term 'hospital' came to be reserved for establishments caring for sick or infirm pilgrims, with hostels and other places that provided basic accommodation and food for the able-bodied being known as hospices.

The Knights of St John of Jerusalem, who were the first of the many orders of Hospitallers and had run a pilgrim hospital since 1023, were formally constituted as a religious order around 1113. The Hospitallers subsequently established and managed hundreds of pilgrim hospices and hospitals across Europe and the Levant. Other more basic needs were also catered for: Pope Symmachus gave instructions for the construction of a public convenience for pilgrims near St Peter's Basilica in Rome.

Long-distance pilgrimage was expensive. The costs included boat fares, fees for officials, guides and interpreters, tolls on roads and bridges, payments to churches, hire of mules, asses or camels for those going to the Middle East, food and miscellaneous expenses such as travelling clothes,

Pilgrim Badges

After visiting a shrine, pilgrims usually wore a badge or token showing where they had been. The best known and earliest of these souvenirs were pieces of palm brought back from Jerusalem, which led to pilgrims being known as 'palmers'. Initially, palm branches were gathered by pilgrims in the plain between Jericho and Jordan, but soon enterprising merchants set up stalls selling them outside the main churches and shrines in Jerusalem. Equally distinctive were the scallop or cockle shells worn by those returning from Santiago. These were originally picked up by pilgrims from the beaches to the north and west of Santiago on their way home, but from the early twelfth century they were on sale at the market held every day outside the north door of the cathedral. Later badges made of lead and tin were sold at all the major pilgrim shrines – a scallop shell for Santiago, St Andrew on his X-shaped cross of martyrdom for St Andrews and a pair of crossed keys for Rome. Most had four holes at each corner so that they could be sewn on to hats or clothing.

Much-travelled pilgrims covered the brims of their hats with badges, attached to their belts tiny bottles or *ampullae* filled with holy water or oil, and sewed on to their gowns vernicles – pieces of cloth showing a

representation of the face of Christ, based on that left imprinted on the handkerchief with which St Veronica was said to have wiped Jesus' face on the way to Calvary.

Louis XI of France, a pious monarch who visited virtually every notable French shrine of his day, wore a hat which was, according to one of his enemies, 'brim-full of images, mostly of lead and pewter, which he kissed whenever good or bad news arrived or whenever the fancy took him'. The pilgrim described in William Langland's poem *Piers Plowman* had a hundred tiny phials attached to his belt, tokens from Sinai and shells from Galicia perched on his hat, and crosses, the keys of Rome and the vernicle sewn on his gown so that 'men should know and see by his signs whom he had sought'.

Badges guaranteed those wearing them the privileges accorded to pilgrims and provided proof that they had carried out the penance or punishment required of them by ecclesiastical or civil authorities. For some, they also came to take on miraculous properties and the status and power of relics. It is not surprising that a brisk trade developed in counterfeits.

Above: 13th century pilgrim's badge depicting Madonna with Child, found in Solder, France

Margery Kempe

One of the most interesting and unusual accounts of medieval pilgrimage is provided by the *Book of Margery Kempe*, the account of the life and travels of a female mystic from King's Lynn in Norfolk who lived from around 1373 to 1438.

Margery Kempe made her first and most extensive pilgrimage in 1413, travelling in white clothes to symbolize her purity, having broken off sexual relations with her husband after conceiving fourteen children. She sailed from Great Yarmouth to Zierikzee in Zeeland and travelled on to Constance, possibly by way of the Rhine, and then on across the Alps via Milan and Bologna to Venice where she took a galley to Jaffa. She spent three weeks in the Holy Land, where she experienced dramatic visions and intense spiritual feelings at the sites associated with Jesus' suffering and death. At Calvary she first manifested the uncontrollable crying that was to be a hallmark of her devotion for much of the rest of her life. Shunned by many of her fellow pilgrims because of her unconventional and unpredictable behaviour, she returned alone from the Holy Land to Assisi and Rome, where she spent several months living as a beggar and had further powerful visions. While in the Apostles' Church she experienced a mystical 'marriage' to the Godhead. She eventually returned to England, having been abroad for at least eighteen months.

In 1417 Margery Kempe went to Santiago and in 1433, when she was around sixty, she set off from Ipswich across the North Sea. Storms blew her ship on to the Norwegian coast from where she sailed on to Danzig. She travelled on to the shrine of the Holy Blood at Wilsnack in Brandenburg, to which she had to be carried in a wagon because of her frail state, and then journeyed home via Aachen and Calais. Sometimes she travelled alone and at other times with just a solitary male companion. Nearing Calais, accompanied only by an English friar, she had to spend a night in an outhouse, lying on bracken and dreading that she might be raped or robbed.

Although she gained indulgences at several of her destinations, Margery Kempe seems to have made her pilgrimages primarily for the sake of her spiritual health and for the ecstatic mystical experiences that sustained her devotional life. She was not a typical pilgrim but her extensive travels, often carried out without money and in difficult circumstances, show the lengths to which an exceptionally spiritually inclined woman would go in the late Middle Ages to benefit from the experience of pilgrimage.

Right: Rocamadour, a hill town in South Western France which became a major place of pilgrimage in the Middle Ages because of its shrine to the Virgin Mary

tents, candles and weapons. Despite the growing network of monasteries, hospices and hospitals offering free accommodation, pilgrims sometimes had to stay at inns. They also often had to bribe local officials to prevent them from confiscating baggage or interrupting their progress with red tape. Raising enough money for the journey could involve mortgaging property, generally to a local monastery, taking out a large loan or finding a wealthy patron who might contribute to the cost. Some resorted to more original fund-raising schemes, like Ralph of Hatfield and his wife Jean, who started brewing beer in order to raise funds to go on a pilgrimage to Canterbury. Once embarked on their travels, pilgrims had to carry the entire cost of their journey with them in cash, making them a prey to robbers; and it was not uncommon for them to run out of money halfway through their pilgrimage. This happened to Gerald of Wales in Rome in 1203. He left the city with all his bills unpaid and was pursued by his creditors through northern Italy until he eventually persuaded them to accept a promissory note drawn on merchants at the Troyes fair.

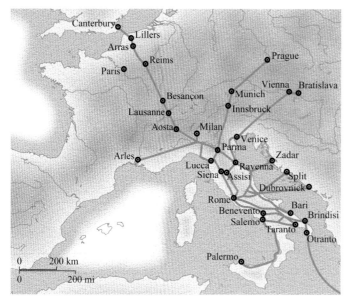

Map showing the *Via Francigena* to Rome and on to Jerusalem

As long-distance pilgrimage steadily developed, Europe became criss-crossed with well-marked and well-trodden pilgrim ways. There was significant pilgrim traffic from Scandinavia as far as Santiago and Rome – among medieval pilgrim badges found in Scandinavia, the largest number by far are from Santiago, outnumbering considerably those from local shrines such as Vadstena and Trondheim. Nikolas of Munhathvera, an Icelandic Benedictine abbot, travelled from Iceland to Rome and then on to the Holy Land in the mid-twelfth century, travelling via Norway, Denmark and Switzerland. He noted that at Vevey in Switzerland the pilgrim ways of Franks, Flemings, Southern French, English, Saxons and Scandinavians converged.

The main route from north-western Europe to Rome through France became known as the *Via Francigena*. It was first mapped in AD 990 by Sigeric, archbishop of Canterbury, on his return from a pilgrimage to Rome. The *Via Francigena* included two alternative crossings of the Alps, either via Mont Cenis or the pass of Mont Joux (Mons Iovis), and a crossing of the Apennines, usually by the pass known as Mons Bardonis. These high-level routes could often be hazardous: in AD 959 an earlier archbishop of Canterbury, Aelfsige, froze to death while crossing the Alps when on his way to Rome; and in 1077, while returning from Rome over the Mont Cenis pass, King Henry IV of England had to negotiate sheets of ice on which some of his party slipped and fell to their deaths.

Given the dangers involved in crossing the Alps, it is not surprising that some pilgrims took a considerable detour to avoid them. In 1026 Richard St-Vannes led a party of over 700 French pilgrims to Jerusalem. Subsidized by the duke of Normandy, they travelled via modern Austria, Hungary, Rumania, Bulgaria and Turkey. Overland routes such as this enabled pilgrims to visit numerous shrines on the way to their ultimate

Give me my scallop shell of quiet,
My staff of faith to walk upon,
My scrip of joy, immortal diet,
My bottle of salvation,
My gown of glory, hope's true gage,
And thus I'll take my pilgrimage.

Blood must be my body's balmer;
No other balm will there be given:
Whilst my soul, like quiet palmer,
Travelleth towards the land of heaven;
Over the silver mountains,
Where spring the nectar fountains;
There will I kiss
The bowl of bliss;
And drink mine everlasting fill
Upon every milken hill.
My soul will be a-dry before;
But, after, it will thirst no more.

Sir Walter Raleigh (1552–1618)

destination. The pilgrim ways created their own saints, notably St Bernard of Montjoux, a canon at the cathedral at Aosta in the eleventh century. He cleared the Alpine passes of robbers and built hospices for pilgrims at the top of the two passes now known after him as the Great and Little St Bernard.

Many French shrines benefited from being either on the *Via Francigena* or on one of the main overland routes from northern Europe to Santiago. Particularly well sited was Saint Gilles du Gard, 10 miles (16 km) west of Arles, and the burial place of an eighth-century hermit said to have been sought out and visited by Charlemagne. It lay on pilgrim routes to both Rome and Santiago and was also just a few miles from the departure point for boats sailing from the south of France to the Holy Land. By the end of the twelfth century around 100,000 pilgrims a week were passing through the town, staying overnight in the large abbey and associated hospices and providing employment for 109 money changers.

Many pilgrims, however, preferred sea travel to overland routes that were subject to robbers and the hazards of war, plague and pestilence. English, Irish and German pilgrims to Santiago often went by boat to Coruna, although they could be subject to long delays. Margery Kempe took seven days to sail from Bristol to Coruna in 1417, managing the return trip in just five. William Wey, a fellow of Eton College and an inveterate pilgrim, took five days when he sailed from Plymouth to Coruna in 1456, but on the return journey his ship was blown back to Coruna and he was held up there by gales for several days. He advised fellow pilgrims to carry a chamber pot 'in case you are too sick to go up on deck and use the normal facilities'. Pilgrims to Jerusalem often sailed from Bari or Venice to Jaffa or Alexandria. A favourite departure time was just after the celebration of Corpus Christi on June 7, when two or three galleys regularly set off from Venice.

Whether journeying by sea or overland, pilgrims from northern and western Europe to the Holy Land were often away from home for the best part of a year. Those going to Rome or Santiago could expect to be away for many months. Sigeric took twelve weeks to walk from the French side of the Channel to Rome in AD 990, an average of 14½ miles (23 km) a day. In 1150 Matthew Paris made the same journey in just over six weeks, averaging 25 miles (40 km) a day by travelling on horseback. Conditions in the main pilgrim destinations could be as grim as those encountered on the way, with Rome in particular often being infested with malaria in summertime; but pilgrims often stayed for several weeks before setting off for home, further prolonging the experience and delaying the return to the responsibilities and routine of family and work.

It is difficult to arrive at any precise figures for numbers travelling to the main European shrines at the height of the medieval pilgrimage boom, but estimates put the total of those going to Santiago at nearly two million a year, with around 750,000 travelling to Canterbury and 250,000 to St Andrews. Perhaps partly in reaction to the deprivations and the length of the journeys to the major pilgrim destinations, there seems to have been a trend in the later Middle Ages towards shorter pilgrimages to more local shrines, in many cases centred around devotion to the Virgin Mary. This period also saw the rise of vicarious pilgrimage and the emergence of professional pilgrims who were paid by others to go on pilgrimage on their behalf. The dead could also have their debts paid off and their time in purgatory shortened through vicarious pilgrimage. In response to these and other developments, there was increasing criticism of the system of pardons and indulgences and the crude, mechanistic theology of salvation by works that it represented. There had long been sceptical voices raised about the motivation of many pilgrims. Jacques de Vitry complained that 'some light-minded and inquisitive persons go on pilgrimages not out of devotion, but out of mere curiosity and love of novelty. All they want to do is to travel through unknown lands.' In his great epic poem *Piers Plowman*, written in the latter part of the fourteenth century, William Langland suggested that those seeking 'St James and the saints of Rome' would do better to seek 'St Truth, for he may save you all'. In the poem, a group of around a thousand pilgrims meets with Piers Plowman, who tells them that they can get much closer to St Truth by staying at home and following the example of Do Well. Anticipating John Bunyan's *Pilgrim's Progress*, he further counsels them that the way to St Truth lies via the ford of Honour-your-fathers, the pass of Swear-not-in-vain and the bridge of Pray-well rather than along the physical pilgrim routes that criss-crossed medieval Europe and provided one of its biggest businesses.

After the Reformation

Pilgrimage, as it had developed in the Middle Ages, was roundly condemned by the leading Protestant Reformers. Martin Luther felt that it reinforced an erroneous idea of God as a judge to be placated rather than a loving father. His address *To the Christian nobility* was unequivocal: 'All pilgrimages should be stopped. There is no good in them: no commandment enjoins them, no obedience attaches to them. Rather do these pilgrimages give countless occasions to commit sin and to despise God's commandments.' The doctrines that had sustained medieval pilgrimage were roundly condemned by the new Protestant churches. Article 22 of the Church of England's *Articles of Religion* describes 'the Romish doctrine concerning Purgatory, Pardons, Worshipping and Adoration of Images as well as of Reliques, and also invocation of Saints' as 'a fond thing vainly invented and repugnant to the Word of God'.

'All pilgrimages should be stopped. There is no good in them: no commandment enjoins them, no obedience attaches to them. Rather do these pilgrimages give countless occasions to commit sin and to despise God's commandments.'

Martin Luther

St David's Cathedral, St David's, Pembrokeshire, Wales

1. *Who would true valour see,*
let him come hither;
one here will constant be,
come wind, come weather;
there's no discouragement
shall make him once relent
his first avowed intent
to be a pilgrim.

2. *Whoso beset him round*
with dismal stories,
do but themselves confound;
his strength the more is,
No lion can him fright;
he'll with a giant fight,
but he will have a right
to be a pilgrim.

3. *Hobgoblin nor foul fiend*
can daunt his spirit;
he knows he at the end
shall life inherit.
Then, fancies, fly away;
he'll not fear what men say;
he'll labour night and day
to be a pilgrim.

John Bunyan (1628–88)

In those countries that became broadly Protestant after the Reformation, pilgrimage was largely suppressed by both the civil and ecclesiastical authorities. A case in point is the decisive action taken by William Barlow, who became bishop of St David's in 1536, to end pilgrimages to that remote shrine in south-west Wales. In the mid-fifteenth century a visitor had thrilled to the relics, vestments, lamps and stained glass in St David's Cathedral, declaring that 'here is the incense and smoke of another Santiago' and describing it as 'happy, beautiful Wales' Holy Sepulchre, her wonderful temple and her Rome'.[1] For Barlow, however, the cult attracted 'vagabond pilgrims' and involved 'perverse properties of execrable malignity, as ungodly image service, abominable idolatry and licentious liberty of dishonest living, popish pilgrimages, deceitful pardons and feigned indulgences'. When on St David's Day in 1538 he found that, despite his orders and the king's injunctions, 'two heads of silver plate enclosing two rotten skulls stuffed with putrified clowtes, two arm bones and a worm-eaten book covered with silver plate' were set forth as relics in the cathedral, he ordered them to be sequestered and taken away.[2] Becket's shrine in Canterbury Cathedral was destroyed in the same year.

Most of the shrines that had been the object of pilgrimages in the British Isles, Scandinavia and the Protestant Low Countries were destroyed in the sixteenth century, although some clandestine pilgrimages did continue. The 'Pilgrimage of Grace', an armed revolt in 1536 by around 50,000 men in the north of England, symbolized a new style of pilgrimage as political and social protest. The heavily armed 'pilgrims', who wore the cross of St Cuthbert on their tunics and claimed to be led by Captain Poverty, were protesting as much against rapacious landlords and interfering southerners as against what they took to be heretical Protestant innovations such as the dissolution of the monasteries, the abrogation of saints' days and the dismissal of Purgatory.

Although it effectively ended physical pilgrimages, Protestantism ushered in a new appreciation of the allegorical significance of pilgrimage as a metaphor for the journey of faith. This was expressed in a rich corpus of pilgrim hymns and supremely in John Bunyan's classic *Pilgrim's Progress*. Written in 1672 when the author – an itinerant tinker and Baptist preacher – was in prison for preaching without a licence, and published six years later, the book tells of the journey 'from this world to that which is to come, delivered under the similitude of a dream'. Bunyan's dream centres on the character of Christian, who is burdened

Christian is directed on his way by Evangelist. A copper engraving by J. Sturt from the 1728 edition of Pilgrim's Progress

down with his sins and preoccupied with the question, 'What shall I do to be saved?' He is directed in a meeting with Evangelist to set out on a journey, which will take him through a wicket-gate and along the narrow way that leads from the City of Destruction to the Celestial City. Passing through the Valley of Humiliation, the Slough of Despond, the Valley of the Shadow of Death, the town of Vanity Fair, and Doubting Castle (all based on landscapes known to Bunyan around his Bedfordshire home), Christian and his companion Hopeful eventually reach the deep and wide river that they must cross to reach the heavenly city of Jerusalem. Having been told that the depth or shallowness of the river depends on the extent to which those crossing it believe in the king of the place, Christian panics and feels himself drowning as he calls to mind his sins and his fear of death. Hopeful, however, keeps his head above water and eventually the two men find solid ground on which to stand. On the far bank of the river they are greeted by two shining men who announce themselves as ministering spirits sent to lead those who shall be heirs of salvation to the paradise of God, the heavenly city set on a hill.

> **Now, now look how the holy pilgrims ride,**
> **Clouds are their chariots, angels are their guide:**
> **Who would not here for him all hazards run,**
> **That thus provides for this when this world's done.**

In those parts of Europe that remained predominantly Roman Catholic, pilgrimage continued and, indeed, flourished in the wake of the Counter-Reformation, although the apparatus of indulgences and penances was scaled down considerably.

Recent research by Mary Lee and Sidney Nolan has shown that, following a low point in the immediate aftermath of the Reformation in the 1530s, the establishment of new European pilgrim shrines reached an all-time peak in the mid-seventeenth century with a particular concentration in Germanic regions. They suggest that this increase was in part attributable to the unsettled atmosphere caused by the Thirty Years' War and the Turkish threat to much of central Europe.[3]

The pilgrim quarter in Kevelaer, Germany

Among the many Marian shrines established at this time was Kevelaer near the Dutch-German border. It was founded by a hawker, Hendrik Busman, who regularly stopped by a particular wayside crucifix to say a short prayer while travelling through the area selling his wares. On three occasions during the winter of 1641 a mysterious voice called out to him, telling him to build a chapel on the site of the crucifix. He did so, and hung inside it a devotional portrait of the Virgin Mary. Tales of miracles performed by the Virgin travelled quickly and the Chapel of Grace at Kevelaer became a significant place of pilgrimage. The first of many pilgrimages from Bonn took place in 1699 when around 400 people walked the 65-mile (105-km) route along the Rhine to bring their prayers and petitions to *Trösterin der Betrüben* (Consoler of the Afflicted), as the Virgin of Kevelaer is known. Heinrich Heine vividly described the atmosphere of the pilgrimage in his 1822 poem *Die Wallfahrt nach Kevlaar*:

Die Mutter Gottes zu Kevlaar
Tragt heut ihr bestes Kleid;
Heut hat sie viel zu schaffen,
Es kommen viel kranke Leut.

The Mother of God in Kevelaer
Is dressed in her best clothes today;
She has much to do today,
Many sick people are on their way.

Kevelaer continues to thrive today as one of the most visited of Germany's thousand or so pilgrim sites. It attracts around 800,000 pilgrims a year, a number of whom make the eight-day walk from Bonn to honour the Virgin Mary.

The rational and sceptical atmosphere of Enlightenment Europe in the eighteenth century was not conducive to pilgrimage. The church in Paris dedicated to St James, which was the starting point of one of the main pilgrim routes to Santiago throughout the Middle Ages, was razed to the ground during the French Revolution, leaving only its tower remaining. However, the rise of the Romantic movement and the cult of medievalism in the nineteenth century gave pilgrimage a significant boost. Antiquarianism stimulated the rediscovery and reopening of old pilgrim ways and renewed interest in visiting old buildings, especially churches and cathedrals. A revival in Marian devotion contributed to the development of three major modern European pilgrim shrines: Lourdes (1858), Fatima (1917) and Medugorje (1981). Medieval shrines also received a boost in the later nineteenth century following a loosening of Protestant sensibilities and improvements in travel. In June 1876, Parson Kilvert noted in his diary: 'At noon I became a Canterbury Pilgrim and went to Canterbury on pilgrimage, nine miles, but by train.' Pilgrimage to the English Marian shrine at Walsingham was revived in the 1920s and a new Anglican shrine built there in 1931.

Easier travel, growing antiquarian and scholarly interest and missionary zeal also helped to boost pilgrimages to the Holy Land in the later nineteenth century. David Wilkie, Edward Lear and William Holman Hunt were among the many artists who went there to paint or draw biblical scenes. Thomas Cook, the staunch Methodist and pioneer travel agent who is regarded as the inventor of the package tour, led his first party of fifty-two pilgrim–tourists to Jerusalem in 1869, the year of the opening of the Suez Canal. He was particularly keen to organize clergy visits to the Holy Land, believing that 'it would be a glorious thing for all ministers and students of Divinity to visit the lands from which they draw so much of their pulpit inspirations'. A Cook's tour in May 1872 included 'half a dozen Christian ministers of the Church of England, Scottish Presbyterian, Welsh Methodist and American denominations united in the worship of God and all seemed animated by one spirit'. They were accompanied by forty saddle horses, sixty baggage mules, twenty-two donkeys and fifty servants. The pilgrims were accommodated in tents with 'iron bedsteads, carpeted floors, and an ample supply of excellent well-cooked food' including 'preserved meat, salmon, lobster, pickle and jams'.[4] In 1882 Cook organized a

Walsingham: England's Nazareth

In 1061 the Virgin Mary appeared to an East Anglian noblewoman and instructed her to build a replica of the house in Nazareth where Gabriel had announced the news of Jesus' birth. She did so, and soon afterwards pilgrims started coming to the small Norfolk village of Walsingham. A community of Augustinian canons built a priory nearby in 1153, and in 1226 King Henry III, one of many medieval monarchs who visited the shrine, declared that the statue of the Virgin in the Holy House at Walsingham performed miracles. The shrine held several relics, including one of St Peter's fingers and a phial of 'Virgin's milk' made up of chalk from the cave in which the Holy Family had supposedly stayed during their flight to Egypt.

The shrine was suppressed in 1538. In 1897 the first post-Reformation pilgrimage to Walsingham took place when a group of Roman Catholics walked to the Slipper Chapel, built in 1340 as the last stop on the journey where pilgrims would traditionally take off their shoes before walking barefoot to the shrine. A. H. Patten, who was inducted as the Vicar of Walsingham in 1921, revived pilgrimage, introducing medieval pageants with pennants, marquees and dressing up. Despite the lukewarm reception from several leading figures in the Church of England – Hensley Henson, the bishop of Durham, commented that 'the revived pilgrimages are rather "pageants" than religious acts' – the pilgrimages proved popular: a new Anglican shrine was established in 1931 and a large church was built in 1938. In 1934 the Slipper Chapel was declared the Roman Catholic National Shrine of Our Lady. There are several large-scale organized Anglican and Catholic pilgrimages to Walsingham every year with the biggest taking place on the last Monday of May. In a BBC poll of Britain's favourite spiritual places conducted in 2003, Walsingham came first equal with Iona.

The website www.walsingham.org.uk provides a history of the shrine and full details of both Anglican and Roman Catholic pilgrimages and accommodation.

The statue of the Virgin being carried through Walsingham. Note that the man on the right is walking bare-footed

The Way of A Pilgrim

Pilgrimage has long been important in the Russian Orthodox Christian tradition. As in the West, it received a considerable boost in the nineteenth century. St Seraphim of Sarov, a monk and ascetic who lived from 1759 to 1833 and was much visited by those seeking spiritual direction and inspiration, encouraged his followers to continue their pilgrimages after his death, using language that recalled the medieval understanding of contact with saints and holy men:

> When I am no longer with you, come to my tomb often, bring all your worries, all your troubles, tell me everything that is grieving you, talk to me as to a living person because for you, I shall go on living; I shall listen to you and your sorrow will disappear.

The Way of a Pilgrim is one of the great spiritual classics of Russian Orthodoxy. Written anonymously, it came into the hands of a monk on Mount Athos and was published in 1884. It tells the story of a peasant who introduces himself in the first paragraph as 'a homeless wanderer of humblest origin, roaming from place to place. My possessions consist of a knapsack with dry crusts of bread on my back and in my bosom the Holy Bible. This is all.' Fired by the apostle Paul's call to Christians to pray without ceasing, the author wanders from monastery to monastery seeking someone who can teach him how to achieve this state. After many adventures and encounters, he eventually meets a wise *startetz* or spiritual guide who instructs him in the Jesus prayer ('Lord Jesus Christ, have mercy on my soul'), which he repeats to himself again and again as an uninterrupted mantra. A sequel, *The Pilgrim Continues His Way*, shows the author persisting in his peripatetic life, instructing others whom he meets on his travels and himself receiving further guidance from faithful elders.

Pilgrimage continued to be a major theme of Russian writers in the twentieth century. Author and dramatist Maxim Gorky (1868–1936) wrote: 'All of us are pilgrims on this earth; I have even heard people say that the earth itself is a pilgrim in the heavens.'

---

visit to the Holy Land by Prince Albert Victor and Prince George (later King George V), and four years later, at the request of the Governor-General of India, he drew up plans for Muslim pilgrims to visit Jeddah and Yambo. In 1891 the first edition of *Cook's Tourist Handbook for Palestine and Syria* was published and in 1898 he arranged a visit to Jerusalem for Kaiser Wilhelm. By the end of the nineteenth century Thomas Cook had enabled over 12,000 people to visit the Holy Land.

Those visiting the Holy Land were enthusiastic about the spiritual benefits conferred, while acknowledging the limitations of physical pilgrimage. This was the theme of a sermon preached in Jerusalem by A.P. Stanley, dean of Westminster, during a tour through the Near East in 1862:

> To see that Holy City, even though the exact spots of his death and resurrection are unknown, is to give new force to the sound of the name whenever afterwards we hear it in church or read it in the Bible. I do not wish to exaggerate in this matter. It is, thank God, perfectly possible to be just, and holy, and good, without coming to Palestine. Pilgrimage is not really a Christian duty. Holy places are not really holy in the sight of God, except for the feelings they produce. The Crusaders were in error, when they fought to save their souls by fighting to regain the Holy Land. It is not the earthly, but the heavenly Jerusalem, which is 'the

mother of us all' – a mother in the widest and most enduring sense. But not the less are all these things helps to those who will use them rightly.[5]

In the latter half of the twentieth century, the development of cheap air travel encouraged long-distance pilgrimage. Specialist companies were set up to organize packaged pilgrim tours. Pilgrimage has, indeed, become a thriving branch of the booming tourism industry, taking us back in some respects to the golden era of the Middle Ages. While traditional destinations such as Rome and Santiago have undergone significant revival, new pilgrim places have emerged whose appeal is not contact with relics but rather the atmosphere of prayer and community. Two of the most popular places of pilgrimage for young people today are homes to ecumenical religious communities: the island of Iona, where a mixture of resident staff and volunteers live and welcome guests in the Benedictine Abbey buildings restored by George Macleod in the late 1930s and 1940s; and Taizé, where Brother Roger established a monastic community in 1940.

Pilgrimage Today

Pilgrimage is as buoyant and popular today as at any time since its medieval heyday. While figures for churchgoing continue to fall across Europe, the number of those making pilgrimages of many different kinds is steadily rising. Indeed, the two trends may be connected. Many people uncomfortable about sitting in pews and uneasy with institutionalized religion are happy to travel, walk and talk together with those of different denominations and other faiths. Their motives may not be the same as those that impelled medieval pilgrims to leave their homes for months at a time, but it is interesting that at least one of the less reputable practices associated with the pilgrimage boom in the Middle Ages has returned in the first decade of the twenty-first century. Carlos Gil, a Portuguese computer expert, has revived the role of the vicarious or proxy pilgrim. Describing himself as 'the payer-off of promises', he hires himself out to those too infirm, busy or lazy to make pilgrimages themselves and charges $2,500 to make the 100-mile (160-km) walk from his home near Lisbon to Fatima on their behalf.

Traditional pilgrim destinations such as the Holy Land, Rome and Santiago remain hugely popular, as do more recent shrines such as Lourdes, Fatima and Medugorje. Organized tours to these places are provided throughout the year by well-established specialist companies. 206 Tours, which began in 1985 and is now one of the largest pilgrim tour operators in the United States, provides 206 different itineraries, including such seemingly surprising combinations as the Holy Land and Krakow, or Ireland and Medugorje. Each tour has a spiritual director and daily Mass. Pax Travel, one of the largest British pilgrimage specialists, offers an exploration of early Christian mosaics in Ravenna, a week in Italy in the footsteps of St Benedict and a pilgrimage to the shrines and churches of Bavaria with a special emphasis on places associated with Pope Benedict XVI. Each of its tours is accompanied by a Roman Catholic or

Fatima

During the summer of 1917 three young cousins, Jacinta and Francisco Marto and Lucia dos Santos, professed to have experienced a series of apparitions of the Virgin Mary as they looked after their families' sheep in the mountainous region near Fatima in the centre of Portugal. The Virgin appeared to the children on the same day every month between May and October. News of the visions spread quickly and on the occasion of her last appearance 70,000 people gathered to watch. On that day, witnesses claimed to have seen the sun spin out of its usual orbit and dance in the sky. Fatima quickly became a major centre of pilgrimage with two million people visiting it in the ten years following the apparitions. Construction of a large neo-classical basilica began in 1928.

Among the Virgin's revelations to the children, two of whom died of influenza soon after the apparitions, were three secrets that were written down by the surviving girl, Lucia, in 1944, at a time when she herself thought she was dying. These secrets were sent to Rome where they were locked away in the Vatican archives. The first, a vision of Hell, was seen as referring to the two World Wars; the second prophesied that Russia would one day return to Christianity; and the third, involving the martyrdom of a man 'clothed in white' who fell to the ground apparently dead, was taken as a prediction of the assassination attempt on Pope John Paul II by a Turkish gunman – an event which occurred on 13 May 1981, the anniversary of the first apparition. This third secret was only revealed by the Vatican in 2000 after the Pope had conducted a special Mass in Fatima to beatify Jacinta and Francisco. Lucia, who became a nun, died in 2005.

Fatima's popularity was considerably boosted by the patronage of Pope John Paul II, who visited three times, and it remains one of the most popular Marian shrines in Europe with nearly six million pilgrims visiting it every year.

Worshippers with candles at evening mass during pilgrimage to Fatima, Portugal

Anglican priest and includes regular celebrations of the Eucharist. *Opera Romana Pellegrinaggi*, the Vatican's pilgrim arm, featured ninety-eight different destinations in its 2007 programme of '*Itinerari dello Spirito*' including: a voyage round the Norwegian fjords on the trail of Saint Sunniva; an exploration of the religious culture of the Baltic states; coach trips along the *Via Francigena*; walking along the *camino* to Santiago; and pilgrimages to Lourdes by air, bus or train.

Sites associated with Celtic Christian pilgrimage are becoming increasingly popular. A newly opened Saints' Way through Cornwall overlays a Bronze Age trade route and retraces the paths of Irish evangelists and later pilgrims. 206 Tours offers a week-long pilgrimage to Ireland 'in the footsteps of St Patrick', and one of Pax Travel's newest itineraries follows the travels of Columbanus across

France. Throughout the 1990s and into the early 2000s Cintra Pemberton, an Episcopalian nun from New York, regularly led four pilgrimages a year to Ireland, Scotland and Wales. In her view, what made the participants – North Americans of diverse denominations and persuasions – pilgrims rather than tourists was the *bendithion*, a sharing of experiences, impressions, prayers and blessings that took place every evening. Her book *Soulfaring* reflects on Celtic pilgrimage past and present.

Alongside these long-distance pilgrimages there has been a significant increase in one-day walks to local shrines and places of spiritual and historical significance. Such local pilgrimages have long been popular in Catholic strongholds such as Poland and Ireland. What has been striking in the last decade or so has been their emergence in Protestant countries. In Denmark the first organized pilgrimage since the Reformation took place in 2001 when Elisabeth Lidell led a 16-mile (25-km) walk through the countryside on a Spring Saturday. Part of the way was walked in silence and Holy Communion was celebrated on the seashore. New pilgrim paths are springing up across Scandinavia, like the cross-Jutland route opened in 2008 (see page 15). In England, the first Saturday in July sees approximately 1,500 pilgrims walking through fields from the village of Bradwell in Essex to the isolated Saxon chapel built by St Cedd, who came from Lindisfarne in the mid-seventh century. A 10-mile (16 km) ecumenical pilgrimage on the first Sunday in September to Dorchester Abbey in Oxfordshire commemorates St Birinus, the seventh-century evangelist of the Thames Valley. In Scotland a particularly successful annual pilgrimage, which takes place every May between Whitekirk and Haddington in East Lothian, brings together Presbyterians, Episcopalians and Roman Catholics. The ecumenical encounters and conversations achieved in walking together are undoubtedly one of the greatest benefits and attractions of these ventures.

St Cedd's chapel at Bradwell, Essex

Increasingly, pilgrimages are being undertaken by both individuals and groups to mark significant anniversaries and draw attention to particular issues. In 1995 Stan Lane, an English Baptist minister, made a 375-mile (600-km) pilgrimage along footpaths from north-east to south-west England to mark the fiftieth anniversary of the execution of Dietrich Bonhoeffer, the German priest and theologian, for involvement in the plot to assassinate Hitler and for helping Jews to escape from the Nazis. He only discovered after he had started planning his walk that Bonhoeffer himself used to walk through Germany every year so that he could meet and talk to people. Lane invited people to join him on his own walk and many did so, usually for short stretches. He also arranged evening meetings along the way to discuss issues of social justice. Several local initiatives to improve aspects of community life took place as a direct result of meetings he initiated during his pilgrimage to underline the continuing relevance of Bonhoeffer's stand against evil social and political forces.

Pilgrimages can make a powerful collective Christian witness. Considerable publicity was given to the pilgrimage from Canterbury to Iona in 1997 to celebrate the 1,400[th] anniversary of the coming of Augustine to Kent and the death of Columba, and to those that criss-crossed Europe in 2000 to mark the 2,000[th] anniversary of Jesus' birth. The experience of taking part in such a pilgrimage often leads to both an intense human bonding and a real deepening of faith. This was certainly true for those who walked from Glastonbury to Canterbury in May 1988 to mark the millennium of the death of Dunstan, who was abbot of Glastonbury at the age of eighteen and later became archbishop of Canterbury. The pilgrims who walked the 125 miles (200 km) together included thirteen from the United States, six Canadians, two Australians and a Ugandan, most of whom had a connection with a church dedicated to St Dunstan. The British pilgrims included four veterans, who had been blinded in battle, with their helpers and guide-dogs, representing St Dunstan's Charity for the war-blinded. Reflecting on the experience, two of the participants, John and Diana Hargreaves, felt that pilgrimage provided an allegory of life in several key respects:

- Trusting and needing each other
- Accepting the basic elements of God's created world, sun and rain, comfort and weariness, differences in nature and in human beings
- Travelling with a purpose, aware of the goal
- Discovering people as people rather than as 'roles' – the blisters of bishops and bartenders feel much the same
- Seeing yourselves as only the latest members in a long line of pilgrims
- Risking the unknown, whether fellow pilgrims or countryside
- Trusting God, who has led us far, and will lead us.[1]

Contemporary pilgrimages often have a specific focus or intention. The annual
Christian Aid walk along the Solway Firth to St Ninian's cave at Whithorn, in the
south-west corner of Scotland, raises money for a worthy cause as well as treading
in the footsteps of one of northern Britain's earliest saints. A number of bishops
have taken to walking around their dioceses soon after their appointment in order
to get to know the people better. In August 2006 the Roman Catholic bishop of
Middlesborough led a week-long walk through his diocese in the north-east of
England specifically to pray for and raise the profile of vocations to the priesthood
and the religious life. On each evening a different sacrament was celebrated, so that
during the pilgrimage people were baptized and confirmed, couples renewed their
marriage vows, new priests were ordained, the sick were anointed and the Eucharist
was celebrated.

Is a new kind of pilgrimage emerging through vigils and protest marches
focused on issues of peace and justice? Christians have taken a prominent part
in Make Poverty History rallies and Anti-Iraq War demonstrations. The Long

A 'Make Poverty History'
march to highlight the
problems of Third World
debt

> **'People make considerable sacrifices and travel a long way to join them, and there is a great feeling of purpose and a great sense of humanity and of coming into contact not just with fellow Christians but with those of other faiths.'**
>
> **Fiona Gordon**

Walk for Peace undertaken in the summer of 2006 from Faslane, the base for Britain's nuclear submarines, attracted the leaders of all of Scotland's major churches as well as many others wishing to protest at the existence of nuclear weapons. Fiona Gordon, a committed ecumenist and campaigner for peace and justice, says that the experience that she has had on these and other protest marches is akin to that of being on a pilgrimage: 'People make considerable sacrifices and travel a long way to join them, and there is a great feeling of purpose and a great sense of humanity and of coming into contact not just with fellow Christians but with those of other faiths.'

Inter-faith pilgrimages are, indeed, another extremely important and encouraging recent phenomenon. Sometimes they involve people of different faiths walking together over a period to a particular shrine, like the Hindu and Catholic pilgrimage to Kevelaer. More common are one-day pilgrimages in which members of different faith groups visit one another's places of worship. In Oxford there is an annual pilgrimage of this kind in which people walk from a church to a mosque via a synagogue, a Hindu temple and a Sikh temple. At a less ambitious level, but hardly less important for breaking down barriers of prejudice and suspicion, are the more modest pilgrimages that take people into the homes or places of worship of those who adhere to another faith.

The organization *Christians Aware* has a particular mission to promote inter-faith understanding and also to make Christians in the affluent West more aware of conditions in the rest of the world. Under the slogan of 'Wider Horizons' it organizes 'Pilgrim Journeys of Encounter' to the Middle East, Africa and Asia. The aim is to engage in meaningful encounters with people, cultures and faiths by travelling beyond the usual tourist sights, visiting local communities and congregations and learning about the issues that affect their lives today. *Christians Aware* also arranges week-long pilgrim walks through Britain to such places as Iona, Walsingham, Canterbury and the Welsh shrines. Its indefatigable executive secretary, Barbara Butler, has produced a book packed with 'information, instruction and inspiration for pilgrims' and entitled *To Be a Pilgrim*. It is full of stories of pilgrimages great and small and emphasizes the risk that lies at the heart of all pilgrimage:

> *Perhaps meeting the stranger is the most difficult challenge for the pilgrim because she or he is faced with the great risk that meeting may lead to humiliation, danger or even death. But pilgrimage is about facing up to the difficult bits and not missing them out or going round them. The people along the way can never be missed out or gone round. Meeting others is vital to pilgrimage,*

*and if meeting is to take place, risks have to be taken. There is little to learn and
there are few people to meet in a tourist hotel or through the thick glass of a
coach window.*[2]

As well as an increasing enthusiasm for direct physical pilgrim journeys, there is also
a growing interest in the idea and metaphor of pilgrimage as applied to Christian
faith and to the mission and witness of churches. Nowhere in
Europe is the commitment to developing both the practice
and the ethos of pilgrimage stronger than in Scandinavia. It is
perhaps significant that this is the region of Europe with the
lowest level of churchgoing. Recognizing that many people
who are apprehensive about going to church are happy to
walk and talk about their faith, the Scandinavian Lutheran
churches have developed an imaginative new kind of ministry.
Ordained pilgrim pastors welcome visitors to shrines and
lead people on physical pilgrimages that can be anything from
a day's walk to a three-week hike through mountains. Around
half of those who take part in the pilgrimages organized by
the pilgrim pastors in Sweden describe themselves not as
Christians but rather as seekers.

13th century sculpture
made of wood of the
holy Saint Birgitta from
Vadstena monastery in
Sweden

Hans-Erik Lindström, one of the founders of the pilgrim
pastor movement, set up a pilgrim centre at Vadstena on
Lake Vattern in the south of Sweden in 1997. It is sited
close to the shrine of Saint Birgitta, Sweden's patron
saint, who lived from 1303 to 1373 and was herself an
enthusiastic pilgrim who travelled to Rome, Santiago and
Nidaros. The centre now has twelve full-time staff and
welcomes over 15,000 pilgrims a year for retreats, courses
and walks. For Lindström the essence of pilgrimage is slowness, simplicity,
freedom, not worrying about things, silence, sharing and spirituality. Each of
the pilgrimages that he leads involves long periods of silence and every evening
pilgrims sit together in a circle to share something about their lives. He observes
that they are often frustrated when they come home by how much they have
in their wardrobes and their cellars: 'Pilgrimage helps us realize that what is
important is free.'

The Scandinavian churches are using pilgrimage in many creative and
enterprising ways. Helga Samset, a professional storyteller, is employed by
Norwegian churches to take groups of children on one-day walks telling them
Bible stories, the saga of Olav and local folk tales as they wander through the
forests. Norway produces the only journal that I know of dedicated to the
subject of pilgrimage. It is called *Pilegrimen* and is edited by the tireless and
boundlessly enthusiastic Eivind Luthen, who has written numerous books

'We are pilgrims; we are in constant movement, through life, through time, through the world. God has given us an eternal goal for this pilgrimage in his eternal Kingdom. He has promised to go with us to the close of the age.'

A Practical Pilgrimage Theology, Trondheim Liturgical Centre

A distinctive waymarker on St Olav's Way in Norway indicating 61 kilometres to the destination at Nidaros

about the Nidaros pilgrimage. The Church of Norway's Liturgical Centre, which is based in Trondheim, has produced some very impressive pilgrim liturgies. One service, prepared for use by worshippers on the way to the Olav vigil service, begins with the ringing affirmation: 'We are pilgrims; we are in constant movement, through life, through time, through the world. God has given us an eternal goal for this pilgrimage in his eternal Kingdom. He has promised to go with us to the close of the age.' The centre has also produced an interesting book that attempts to work out a practical theology of pilgrimage and what it means to see the church as 'God's people on pilgrimage'. There is much engagement with the post-modern condition of alienation and a sense that regarding themselves as pilgrims helps people rediscover their roots and traditions as well as their cultural and national identity. The book argues that the idea of pilgrimage can foster a sense of belonging to a broad, national folk church where levels of commitment and attendance are low. Thore Nome, advisor and diocesan chaplain in the Nidaros diocese, argues that pilgrimage provides an inclusive rather than an exclusive sense of belonging to a church, emphasizing the fact that all are on the way towards a goal, whether they have travelled a long or short distance along the way of faith.[3]

There are subtle differences in approach to pilgrimage between the inhabitants of the three main countries of Scandinavia. Norwegians are strongly focused on Olav, as national folk hero and patron saint. For the pioneer pilgrim priest, Arne Bakken, it is about that fusion of culture, history, nature and faith which underlies the re-creation and continuing development of the Nidaros pilgrim ways by church and state:

A pilgrim way is a meeting place between history, culture, nature and you. A pilgrim way is a human way, connecting you and fellow human beings in the past, present and future – with spiritual inspiration reverberating through it all.[4]

While the Swedish also have a patron saint, Birgitta, and a thriving pilgrimage centre near her shrine at Vadstena, they have less interest in destination and the focus is more on pilgrimage as a spiritual exercise and discipline. Anna Davidson-Bremborg from the University of Lund, who is researching the revival of pilgrimage, has found that the most valued part of pilgrimages for Swedes is the time of silence, even if it is just ten minutes in a two-hour afternoon walk. In Denmark the emphasis is different again. Here there is no patron saint and it is smaller, localized pilgrimages which are thriving. In Denmark, interestingly, there is most opposition from the church to pilgrimage, which is still seen in official Lutheran eyes as suspiciously Catholic, and yet there is also most radical grassroots interest in pilgrimage as a new way of expressing faith.

For the great Danish theologian Søren Kierkegaard it is more about the sheer physical business of walking. These words of his are quoted in the Pilgrim Passport, which is carried by those who walk to Nidaros and stamped at churches along the way:

Above all, do not lose your desire to walk. Every day I walk myself into a state of well-being and walk away every illness. I have walked myself into my best thoughts and I know of no thought so burdensome that one cannot walk away from it. If one just keeps on walking, everything will be all right.

However differently it may be conceived, *pilegrimsvandring* as it is very evocatively called is deeply ingrained in Scandinavian culture. It combines the Nordic love of nature and of retreating to mountains, forests and lakes with the Lutheran emphasis on the folk church as the religion of the people.

The Nordic enthusiasm for pilgrimage is encapsulated in the poem '*O store Gud*', written in 1886 by Carl Boberg one summer evening as he stood looking across the calm waters of the bay near his home at Monsteras, on the south-east coast of Sweden. A rainbow had formed, following a storm in the afternoon, and the church bell was tolling in the distance. Set to a Swedish folk tune and turned into a hymn in 1891, Boberg's verses celebrating God's greatness displayed through the wonders of his creation have been translated into many languages. The English version by Stuart Hine, 'O Lord my God, when I in awesome wonder', perhaps better known by the last words of its refrain 'How great Thou art', has for several years been the most popular hymn in the United Kingdom according to polls and surveys, testifying to the abiding message of its pilgrim theme:

When through the woods and forest glades I wander,
And hear the birds sing sweetly in the trees:
When I look down from lofty mountain grandeur,
And hear the brook, and feel the gentle beeze:

Then sings my soul, my Saviour God, to Thee,
How great Thou art! How great Thou art!
Then sings my soul, my Saviour God, to Thee,
How great Thou art! How great Thou art!

How To Be a Pilgrim

You don't have to pack your bags
and set off for some far off land to
be a pilgrim. Here are seven kinds of
pilgrimage that can be practised nearer
home.

1. The Stations of the Cross

The ancient devotional exercise of
following in Christ's footsteps along
the road to Calvary is well established
in Catholic churches and has in
recent years come to be taken up
much more widely by Protestants.
It almost certainly derives from the
practice of early pilgrims to Jerusalem, who walked from Pilate's house to the
place of the crucifixion and offered prayers at places along the route associated
with Christ's passion and death. When they returned home, they often set up a
series of pictures or carvings on the walls of their own church so that they could
re-enact the experience and give those unable to make the journey to Jerusalem
the chance to walk their own *Via Dolorosa*.

Services based around the Stations of the Cross are common during Lent
and Holy Week when people process round a church pausing to reflect and
pray at the stations, which can be either simple crosses on the wall or pictorial
representations of the event being commemorated. The number of stations at
first varied widely but finally became fixed at fourteen, eight based directly on
events recorded in the Gospels and six on inferences from the Gospel account
or pious legend.

Modern services need not include actual crosses, but may simply involve
being led around a church, pausing to reflect on the events of the Passion and

A pilgrim playing the
part of Jesus Christ,
complete with a crown
of thorns and actors'
'blood', carries his
cross on the way
along the *Via Dolorosa*
towards the Church
of the Holy Sepulchre
during the Good
Friday procession in
Jerusalem's Old City

Jesus is offered a cloth by a woman as he carries his cross along the *Via Dolorosa*. One of the stations of the cross at Lourdes

their message to us today. Yet more elaborate outdoor stations, consisting of life-size or larger figures cast out of bronze, are prominent features of several major pilgrim shrines, notably Lourdes, Częstochowa and Medugorje.

2. Pilgrimages Within Churches

You don't have to wait until Lent or Holy Week to make a meaningful walk round a church. A mini-pilgrimage around key items of furniture that symbolize important aspects of the church's mission and faith provides an opportunity to reflect on how it is performing and what could be improved. Here is a suggested itinerary involving seven stations:

i. The door, which allows reflection on the theme of entrances and exits – the expectations of those entering the church and the reasons why some leave.

ii. The areas of welcome – including the welcome desk and visitors' book, and the place where hymn books and orders of service are given out – which provides an opportunity to reflect on the ministry of hospitality and how hospitable the church and congregation are.

iii. The font or place of baptism, which is symbolic of dying and rising with Christ, new beginnings, joining the Christian community, receiving God's grace and being called to his service.

iv. The lectern, from which God's word is read and shared.

v. The pulpit, from which God's word is expounded.

vi. The altar or communion table, where the bread is broken, the Eucharist shared, communion and community celebrated and the heavenly banquet anticipated.

vii. The notice board, where the church meets the world, looks outwards, engages with the wider community and its concerns and spreads the good news. How effectively is this being done?

Such a pilgrimage can include symbolic acts such as lighting candles as well as silent and communal prayer and reflection. Participants may be encouraged to write down their own hopes for the church and for themselves on pieces of paper, which can be left at an appropriate station on the way. This kind of pilgrimage might lead on to more radical ways of worshipping. In many churches in the West the worshippers sit in pews passively watching and listening to what is going on at the front. Is there room, both literally and metaphorically, for less static worship involving more processions and moving around, maybe even dance and drama? Many church buildings are now being re-ordered to make them more appropriate for pilgrimage and pilgrim worship.

The Stations of the Cross

1. Jesus is condemned to death

2. Jesus takes up his cross

3. Jesus falls the first time

4. Jesus meets his afflicted mother

5. The cross is laid on Simon of Cyrene

6. A woman wipes the face of Jesus

7. Jesus falls a second time

8. Jesus meets the women of Jerusalem

9. Jesus falls a third time

10. Jesus is stripped of his garments

11. Jesus is nailed to the cross

12. Jesus dies on the cross

13. The body of Jesus is placed in the arms of his mother

14. Jesus is laid in the tomb

3. Labyrinths and Trust Walks

Labyrinths, which have their origins in Greek mythology, have long been used by Christians as an easy and accessible form of prayer walk. One of the earliest and best known was laid out on the floor of Chartres Cathedral in France around 1200. Its single meandering path, winding through eleven concentric circles to reach the centre, was designed to allow those unable to visit the Holy Land to experience something of the feel and flavour of a pilgrim journey. It can still be walked today, but only on Friday mornings – at other times it is covered by chairs.

Although at first sight labyrinths resemble mazes, they have no blind alleys or false trails. However twisting and winding, the path always leads to the centre and then back out again. Those walking them are encouraged to pray with their feet and bodies as well as their heads, to make a physical progress that symbolizes their inner journey of faith and their return into the world to connect with its issues and responsibilities. For those who are unable to walk or visually impaired, small labyrinths mounted on tables or walls can be traced with the fingers.

Labyrinths can be combined with trust walks in which participants divide into pairs and take turns to be blindfolded. The person who is blindfolded is led

A Modern Labyrinth

The labyrinth at Broughton St Mary's Parish Church in central Edinburgh, Scotland, was started by the new minister, Joanne Hood, in October 2005. Discovering that there was no evening worship, she decided that rather than try to start up a traditional service, she would build a labyrinth and make it available for people to walk on a Sunday evening in the hope that it would attract people who would not normally come to church.

The Broughton labyrinth measures 33 feet by 26 feet (10 by 8 metres) and fills the floor of the sanctuary area at the front of the church, where there are normally chairs that can be easily removed. The pathway is marked out in black tape on white sheets, which are stapled together. There are ten stations on the way representing the theme of journey to and from the centre, a journey towards God and then out again into the world, a journey of receiving and giving. Each has a particular feature and a printed card inviting participation in a symbolic ritual or task.

The stations on the way in focus on obstacles that might hinder the pilgrim in their relationship with God.

The first explains the purpose of the labyrinth, and the second invites those walking it to listen to a CD and consider the noises that come both from within and from outside that might distract them from their relationship with God: 'Let God still your soul, turn the noises off and give you peace.' The third station is about letting go. A pile of stones lies in front of a bowl full of water: 'Take a stone, representing a care or a worry that you have; hold it over the pool of water and in your own time let it go.' The fourth station consists of a pad of paper and a pencil beside a dustbin: those reaching it are invited to write down the hurtful things that have been done to them and that they have done to others, and then cast them into the bin, letting go of them as just as God does. This, Joanne Hood points out, is a form of confession. The final station on the way in to the centre consists of a map of the world with small magnets dotted around it and a compass in the middle. If you bring the magnets too close to the compass, it swings around wildly and loses its proper orientation. Take them away, and the compass finds true

north again. 'What are the false norths distracting you?' those walking the labyrinth are asked as they are encouraged to turn from distractions and re-focus on God.

The sixth station at the centre of the labyrinth is the Holy Space – 'God is here and you are welcome.' A wooden cross, a large candle, an open Bible, a piece of pitta bread broken in two and a cup of wine stand between two cushions: 'You are invited to break a bit of the bread off, dip it in the wine and enjoy the sustenance God provides for the journey.'

At the start of the outward journey back into the world, the seventh station encourages people to reflect on how their encounter with God might change them and affect their lifestyle. The eighth invites them to stand in front of a mirror and think about what they see and what God sees when he looks into their souls: 'Ask God to show you the real you.' The next station has a television monitor showing images of space, and a tray of earth in which those walking the labyrinth are invited to plant a seed, and in doing so connect with the world – 'You are participating in a mystery, co-creating with God, giving birth to new life.' The penultimate station, designed to foster intercession, is a table with small candles that can be lit for one or more people who are held in prayer before God. The final station, entitled 'Impression', consists of a bowl of sand with the instruction: 'Take off your socks and shoes and leave a footprint. What will be left of us when we have left? What impression have you made?'

Joanne Hood points out that the Broughton labyrinth is constructed to follow the contours of a service of worship, with an initial approach to God, involving confession and letting go, and a later time of intercession, framed by the central encounter with God through the Bible, bread and wine. Those not comfortable with receiving communion in a formal service will often take a piece of pitta bread and dip it in wine. In her words, 'The labyrinth allows people different possibilities that aren't easy to cater for in communal worship. They can do things in their own time and respond in ways that they feel are appropriate rather than everyone having to follow me when I say "Now we will stand to sing Hymn 486". It doesn't tell people what they should be thinking. It makes them think about themselves and their journey.'

Left: The labyrinth laid out in Broughton St Mary's Parish Church, Edinburgh

through the labyrinth, encouraging trust and also reliance on senses of touch, taste, hearing and smell.

4. Outdoor Prayer Walks and Worship

Outdoor prayer walks through both urban and rural areas are proving increasingly popular as a spiritual exercise as well as an effective form of Christian witness. Sometimes they can involve considerable distances, like the 'Prayer across Scotland' project in 2007, which lasted for several weeks and took a small group of people right across the country, stopping in each major town to carry a cross through the streets and pray at significant points. More often, they are shorter and involve a walk of a few hours. Several churches have revived the old tradition of beating the bounds of the parish and organise a summer walk round the parish boundaries with stops to pray and sing. For example, Church of Scotland minister Rory Macleod, has inaugurated an all-night walk round his parish on 21 June, the shortest night of the year, with prayer at various points along the way. Christine Polhill, an Anglican priest, has devised a series of inter-church 'Faith and Nature Trails' combining reflection on a gospel theme with local natural history features of interest. She got the idea when, as a country vicar, she noticed how many people would walk from one village to another at the weekend:

They refreshed themselves at the pub, but seeking a different kind of refreshment, also came into any open church. I came up with the idea of having mini-pilgrimages where people could pick up details of the trail at one church and follow it to another. At one level, the walk is just a pleasant ramble from one village church/chapel to another. However, should those walking so wish, there is also food for the spiritual journey.[1]

Another growing trend is for worship to be held out of doors. There are many good places to meet and worship beyond the church walls: a garden, a park, by a river or lake, on the seashore or in the ruins of an ancient abbey. It can involve going no further than just outside the church porch, particularly if it is adjacent to a main road and passers-by can get involved if they wish. This is particularly appropriate for carol singing at Christmas. Peripatetic carol singing around city streets and country lanes is a long-established form of popular pilgrimage. Outdoor re-enactments of the Nativity and the Passion at farms and country parks increasingly involve people walking through fields to different scenes in the unfolding drama.

5. Pastoral Pilgrimages

Visits to friends or relatives who are ill and housebound or to the graves of loved ones may be among the most meaningful and important pilgrimages that we make. A middle-aged Muslim business man remarked during an inter-faith dialogue on the theme of pilgrimage: 'The first journey for any pilgrim is to your mother. Mohammed says, "Heaven lies at the feet of your mother."' He went on to speak of the daily journey that he made to massage the tired limbs of his elderly mother after she had suffered a stroke. For him, it was a more important and meaningful pilgrimage even than the *Hajj* to Mecca. I think of my own regular visits to my elderly father in his nursing home in the same way. Visits to cemeteries to lay flowers on graves also have some of the characteristics of a pilgrimage. One of the most moving scenes in the musical *Phantom of the Opera* involves Christine visiting the tomb of her father and singing 'Wishing you were somehow here again'. Grieving is a form of pilgrimage, as is that slow process whereby we let go of a loved one, and, of course, death itself.

6. Virtual Pilgrimages

New technology allows us to become pilgrims without leaving our living rooms. Internet sites offer virtual tours through all the well-known pilgrim sites and several have live web cameras installed at key points. A number of major pilgrim shrines, including Medugorje and Częstochowa, relay live services over the Internet and via satellite. Slide shows and PowerPoint® presentations, creatively assembled by those who have themselves been on a physical pilgrimage, can

'We are pilgrims on the earth and strangers; we have come from afar and we're going far. The journey of our life goes from the loving breast of our mother on earth to the arms of Our Father in heaven. Everything on earth changes; we have no abiding city here; it is the experience of everybody.'

Vincent van Gogh (from his first sermon as a seminarian)

allow the experience to be shared by others who have not been able to make the journey. The challenge is to provide more than a lengthy show of holiday snaps. A creative virtual pilgrimage will weave together images, symbols, prayer and reflection. It will engage the audience so that it is not just a passive experience of looking at what someone else has been doing.

Pilgrims on the *Camino* to Santiago de Compostela, Galicia

Another way to experience pilgrimage while staying in one's own room is to set up a station or shrine. I have one on a shelf in my office, which takes me to Iona whenever I look at it. A small replica of St Martin's Cross, which stands outside the abbey, is surrounded by stones collected from Columba's Bay. Behind are two icons of Columba – one a painting of the saint sitting in his cell on the island and copying from his beloved psalter. This is a good way to use souvenirs brought back from a pilgrimage.

7. Becoming a pilgrim people

Pilgrimage is as much about the inner as the outer journey. What are the marks of a pilgrim people? Here are four suggestions:

Connecting with the Saints

It is no coincidence that in the Bible the injunction to run with perseverance the race that is set before us is bracketed with the reminder that we are surrounded by a great cloud of witnesses (Hebrews 12:1). Pilgrims travel in the footsteps of those who have gone before them, not just the well-known apostles, saints and martyrs whose shrines are the object of so many pilgrimages, but countless unsung and uncelebrated faithful souls through the ages. The road stretches back as well as forwards.

Being more open

Pilgrims walk in faith and hope rather than marching in dogmatic certainty. They are welcoming and accommodating to those who are seekers and explorers on the edge or the fringes of faith, remembering the promise in Psalm 34 that 'those who seek the Lord shall not want for anything that is good'. Significantly, those were the last words that the great pilgrim, Columba, copied before his death on Iona.

Providing companionship

Pilgrims share bread and walk beside others in their sorrow and in their joy, offering a helping hand along the way. This is not necessarily a constant companionship – pilgrims may be very close for a while and then their paths may diverge. Pilgrimage is not a race – there are no prizes for being first at the destination. It creates temporary communities where differences of status, wealth and background count for little. Muslim pilgrims to Mecca all wear identical simple white robes to show their equality before God. In the eloquent words of Richard Gillard's hymn 'Brother, sister let me serve you':

> **We are pilgrims on a journey,**
> **And companions on the road;**
> **We are here to help each other**
> **Walk the mile and bear the load.**

Being on the move

This is perhaps the most important characteristic of a pilgrim people: that they are not static, wedded to the past and institutionalized, but rather on a journey and looking forward. Like the people of Israel as they wandered through the wilderness on the way to the promised land, they are conscious that God is also on the move and ahead of them, and they do not attempt to box him in or tie him down. Jean Vanier, the visionary founder of the *L'Arche* communities, has observed: 'A sect has control at its heart, a community has journey at its heart.' Pilgrims sit lightly to buildings, authority and dogmas. Richard Giles, dean of Philadelphia Cathedral, who has pioneered the development of pilgrim liturgies, notes:

In a contemporary culture where individuals in pursuit of success spend so much of their time giving you the impression that they have 'arrived', it is a beautiful thing that the Church should exult in its conviction that we are a community that never arrives. At the end of our brief span on earth the Christian comes to realise that he/she has just begun. This conviction that the community of faith is always on a journey is a refreshing tonic to a jaded world … The whole Judaeo-Christian story is a travellers' tale. Moreover, it is a cautionary tale which warns that coming to a halt, settling down and building bigger barns is usually a sign that decline and fall is imminent.[2]

Sydney Carter expresses the prayer of every pilgrim in his song:

One more step along the world I go,
One more step along the world I go;
From the old things to the new
Keep me travelling along with you:
And it's from the old I travel to the new;
Keep me travelling along with you.

Part 2

Introduction

The second part of this book describes the major and most interesting pilgrim places and routes in Europe, which were developed between the early centuries of the Christian church and the late twentieth century. They are presented in roughly chronological order, beginning with the three great shrines established to house the supposed relics of key apostles: Rome, Santiago and St Andrews. Next come places and routes in Scotland, Ireland and Wales dating from the golden age of Celtic pilgrimage, and three major pilgrim destinations that emerged in the Middle Ages: Nidaros, Assisi and Częstochowa. Finally there are descriptions of three modern places of pilgrimage – Lourdes, Taizé and Medugorje – and a brand new pilgrim route, St Cuthbert's Way, opened in the late 1990s. As well as providing historical background, the pages that follow are designed to give a flavour of the experience of pilgrimage to these places today and to provide practical hints and advice to those considering visiting them.

8 Rome

Rome is the oldest and the most popular pilgrim destination in Europe. Nearly twenty million people visit the 'Eternal City' every year and in the last Jubilee Year, 2000, the number rose to almost thirty million. There are few places where one is more constantly reminded of the factors that promoted pilgrimage in the early church and the Middle Ages – the cult of martyrs and the clamour for relics, the claims of the papacy and the missionary importance of the Roman Church.

Of all the pilgrim places featured in this book, Rome is the one that is most clearly also a tourist destination. Indeed, it could be said that to some extent it turns pilgrims into tourists. The North American pilgrimage organized by 206 Tours, for example, alongside daily Mass in one of the city's great historic churches, includes a 'Rome by Night' excursion to throw coins into the Trevi Fountain and marvel at the flood-lit Colosseum, as well as an evening entertainment of songs from Italian opera. Even among the numerous priests who are drawn to the centre of Roman Catholicism, three

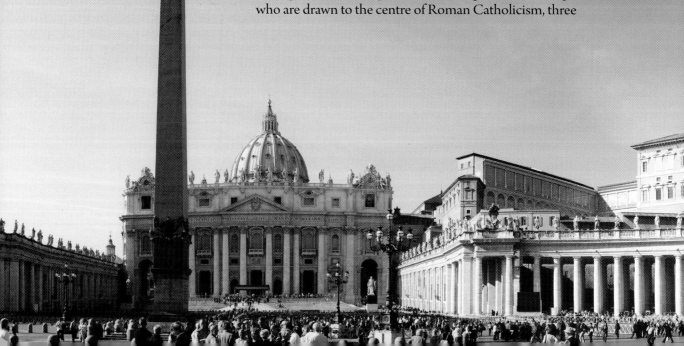

distinct types and motivations are evident from their dress: those on official church business, hurrying through the streets round the Vatican in black suits and carrying briefcases; those semi-formally dressed, conducting groups of parishioners around the city's major shrines; and a sizeable number who make no pretence of their tourist status, eating ice creams, their clerical shirts unbuttoned with the collar tucked into the side opening and their cameras

A Swiss guard on duty by St Peter's

slung round their necks. I did not see one person in Rome with a pilgrim staff or badge. The transition from pilgrim to tourist is even encouraged to some extent by the church authorities. The official Vatican bookshop next to St Peter's Church has a glossy book on Italian cooking shelved next to a learned tome on the Catacombs of Callixtus.

Notices enforcing the dress code outside St Peter's

Yet for all this, there is a genuinely reverential atmosphere in the huge basilicas that are among the prime destinations for the millions of pilgrim tourists who head to Rome each year. They are thronged all day by people wearing headsets being shepherded around by guides, who speak in hushed tones into microphones – the only mode of communication now allowed in the major churches in an effort to avoid the cacophony of raised voices as tour guides shout to make themselves heard. In even the busiest churches, side chapels are reserved for those who want to pray privately, adore the Blessed Sacrament or make confession. Notices outside prohibit skimpy tops and short skirts, and at the entrance to St Peter's there is a dress inspection checkpoint as well as airport-style security screening. Security is at a high level around the major pilgrimage sites, and especially in St Peter's Square, where *carabinieri* ride round in buggies, supplementing the work

Piazza San Pietro and St Peter's Basilica

Statue of St Peter
outside the Basilica
dedicated to him

of the ninety picturesquely attired Swiss Guards. They are a reminder not just of the troubled times in which we live but of the fact that the Vatican is an independent sovereign state with borders to be policed and patrolled.

St Peter's is where most pilgrims first head for, and it is in a real sense the place that first made Rome a pilgrimage destination. Virtually nothing now remains of the basilica erected by Constantine around AD 320 over the tomb of the apostle Peter, who is thought to have been crucified upside down on the Vatican hill during the persecutions initiated by the emperor Nero. It was the first church in the West built to house the body of a martyr and the first pilgrim place in Europe. Although Peter's tomb is not always visible to most modern visitors, and in that sense there is no actual shrine, he is an ever-present figure portrayed in massive marble statues both inside and outside the church. His most meaningful representation for pilgrims is in a thirteenth-century bronze statue situated just to the right of the high altar. It is the scene for the only piece of popular ritual in St Peter's in which visitors queue up to touch the feet of the seated apostle.

The modern St Peter's Church, which largely dates from the mid-seventeenth century and resembles a vast marble-clad railway station, is as much a mecca for art lovers – attracted by the Michelangelo *Pieta* and the swirling columns and canopies of Bernini's baroque *Baldachinno* above the high altar – as it is for pilgrims. It is always packed with tourists, but the needs of those who have come with spiritual intentions are sensitively handled. A side chapel for confessions is staffed by fourteen priests speaking twenty languages between them. Another chapel is reserved for private prayer and adoration of the Blessed Sacrament, and a third for Masses.

Many places in the vicinity of St Peter's are more for tourists and art connoisseurs than pilgrims, particularly the Vatican Museum, which receives up to 20,000 visitors a day. However, one place in this area that does speak of Rome's pilgrim past is the Church of Sancto Spirito in Sassia, which stands on the corner of the Via dei Penitenzieri and the Borgo San Spirito, a quiet backwater just a hundred yards or so from the triumphalist Via di Conciliazione that leads to St Peter's Square. It was here around AD 726 that Ina, king of Wessex, set up a church and hospice for Saxon pilgrims to the shrine of St Peter. In the twelfth century the hospice was turned into a hospital, which remains on the site to this day. The church was rebuilt in the sixteenth century. On a Saturday evening it may still be found filled with worshippers rather than tourists, with groups of nuns kneeling before its statues, those making their confession and parents bringing their children to light candles. Here it is possible to feel the continuity of faith and devotion across the centuries.

There are three other churches in Rome that are on every tourist itinerary. They have the same rather heavy and cold quality as St Peter's, but they occupy an important place in the history of pilgrimage and are worth visiting by genuine pilgrims for that reason alone. St Paul's Outside the Walls (San Paulo

An Audience with the Pope

St Peter's Square comes alive as a place of pilgrimage during the summer for the weekly papal audience on Wednesday mornings. People start gathering about two hours before the 11 a.m. start to get seats near the front. Their long wait is alleviated by spontaneous singing from different nationalities in the crowd. On the morning that I was there, a large group of Polish pilgrims from Krakow singing soulful folk hymns in four-part harmony managed to hold their own against a more raucous and rowdy Spanish party belting out more popular songs and doing Mexican waves. The atmosphere was akin to the build-up before a football match, with national banners being enthusiastically waved to the roaring of the growing crowd. Arriving in his white popemobile, the pope was driven round the square and up to the dias in front of St Peter's to the strains of Luther's defiant Reformation hymn, '*Ein feste Burg is unser Gott*', played by a band at the foot of the steps. This was followed by another Lutheran hymn tune, '*Nun danket alle Gott*' – an ecumenical gesture, if such it was, lost on the crowd who all but drowned out the music by the cheering of '*Papa*'.

Once the crowd was subdued, the pope made a lengthy speech in Italian and was then addressed in six languages (Italian, French, English, German, Spanish and Polish) by ecclesiastical dignitaries who mentioned specific pilgrim groups from their own regions, provoking more flag waving and spontaneous singing that interrupted the protocol but was enthusiastically acknowledged by the pope. The whole ceremony is filmed by the cameramen of the Vatican Television service,

immaculately dressed in black suits and ties, and relayed to their outside broadcast vehicle (which must be unique in the world in having a religious dedication – to the Knights of St Columbus). It is transmitted live across the world on Catholic satellite channels and is also shown on giant screens in the square itself. At the end of the audience, the pope greets visiting dignitaries, representatives of pilgrim groups and newly wedded couples. It makes for a spectacular piece of theatre, but also for a sense of faithful pilgrims gathering together from many different backgrounds and nations. Pope Benedict XVI has made much of the importance of pilgrimage, both literally and as a metaphor of faith, and it was a major theme in his address at the audience that I attended.

Polish pilgrims singing before the Papal audience

Fuori le Mura) was originally built at the end of the fourth century over the tomb of St Paul, who is said to have been martyred nearby in AD 67 and buried in a large pagan cemetery. By the sixth century it had become an important pilgrim site and Pope Gregory the Great rearranged the interior to place more emphasis on the saint's shrine, above which he placed the high altar. The original church was completely destroyed by fire in 1823 and rebuilt in the middle of the nineteenth century. The main draw for pilgrims is the tomb of St Paul, which can be viewed through a glass window beneath the high altar. Two marble plaques inscribed in the fourth century bear the statement: 'PAULO APOSTOLO MART.' There are holes bored through them where early pilgrims used to lower strips of cloth, known as *brandea*, which were then taken away as relics since they had come into close contact with the martyr's bones.

St John Lateran (San Giovanni in Laterano) was the first Christian church to be built in Rome, erected by Constantine soon after his conversion in AD 313 as the seat of the bishop of Rome. It remains the Cathedral of Rome and of the world. Unfortunately, like all the other important early churches in the city, it was destroyed by fire – in this case twice – and there are virtually no traces left of the original building. The present building, which dates largely from the mid-seventeenth century and is substantially the work of Borromini, with huge statues of the apostles added along the length of the nave in the eighteenth century, has little to draw the modern pilgrim – although there are claims that the high altar contains the heads of Saints Peter and Paul and that the

St Peter's Basilica – the most popular destination for pilgrims to Rome side Altar of the Holy Sacrament enshrines a cedar wood table supposedly used by Christ at the Last Supper. These claims are generally played down by the church authorities today. Their early medieval predecessors had no such inhibitions, claiming that among the sacred relics that Constantine had placed in the Lateran basilica were the original Ark of the Covenant, Aaron's rod (or staff), some of the manna that fell from heaven and John the Baptist's reed and coat. One relic that does still draw pilgrims to this area of Rome, apparently brought back from Jerusalem by Constantine's mother, Helena, is the *Scala Sancta*, supposedly the staircase of Pontius Pilate's house which Jesus descended after his condemnation. The staircase was installed in the Lateran Palace, which was built by Constantine for the bishop of Rome. Most of the palace – which remained the papal residence until the fourteenth century – is no more, but the building containing the *Scala Sancta* remains, standing across a busy road from St John's Lateran Basilica. The twenty-eight white marble steps are protected by Lebanon cedar boards, which have been replaced three times due to wear since the eighteenth century. Pilgrims can only ascend them on their knees, meditating on the Passion of Christ and repeating a short prayer at each step. The stairways on the right and left sides of the *Scala Sancta* can be ascended on foot.

Statue of St Peter in the Church of St John Lateran

The church of Santa Maria Maggiore retains rather more of its original features than the other patriarchal basilicas, most notably the impressive set of fifth-century mosaics on either side of the nave and on the triumphal arch, which were commissioned by Pope Sixtus III and illustrate Old and New Testament scenes. A reliquary below the high altar contains a supposed fragment from the crib in which Jesus was born, again brought back from her Holy Land pilgrimage by the empress Helena. It is watched over by an imposing marble statue of Pope Pius V kneeling in prayer. Overall, the atmosphere of this church is perhaps more conducive to prayer and contemplation than that of the other major Roman basilicas, although even here it is difficult to disagree with the assessment of the nineteenth-century novelist, Stendhal: 'The basilica looks like a magnificent salon and not at all like an awe-inspiring place, the dwelling of the All-Powerful.'

Perhaps the most evocative church in Rome for pilgrims is Santa Croce in Gerusalemme. Altogether simpler than the four main basilicas, it was originally built in the late fourth century on land owned by Helena. Although the church has been extensively remodelled several times, most recently in the eighteenth century, what are thought to be the remains of Helena's own private chapel can still be found at the far right-hand end, beneath the apse. The floor of the crypt-like chapel is said to be made of earth that she brought back from Calvary. Another more significant relic gives the church its name and is now on display in a specially built Chapel of the Holy Relics, reached by ascending a staircase at the far left-hand side of the nave. This is a supposed fragment of the cross on which Jesus died. Helena is said to have brought it back to be an object of veneration for pilgrims who could not make the long journey to Jerusalem. The fragment, which was discovered sealed behind a brick above the triumphal arch when repairs were being carried out to a mosaic in 1492, was long thought to be a medieval forgery. However, a diary that came to light in the nineteenth century, written by the Spanish abbess Egeria during her travels in the Holy Land in the early fifth century, includes a description of the veneration of such a relic in Jerusalem. The appearance of the word 'Nazarene' written on the piece of wood from right to left in Latin, Greek and Aramaic is generally taken as a further indication that it is not a medieval forgery.

Drawing of a fish found in the catacombs of Domitilla

If Santa Croce in Gerusalemme still points powerfully to the cult of relics that gave birth to Christian pilgrimage, an even more eloquent witness to their importance comes with a visit to the Catacombs, which are on the itinerary of just about every tourist and pilgrim to Rome. Even denuded of the bones that drew early pilgrims in their droves but were long ago stolen by grave robbers or sold and transported to more central locations, these dark and sprawling tunnels still speak powerfully of the faith and witness of early Christians. Pilgrims can visit the Catacombs of Domitilla, a network of 11 miles (18 km) of underground corridors and galleries on four levels, which are probably the largest and oldest of Rome's ancient Christian cemeteries. They contain over 150,000 tombs, all individually hewn out of the local calcareous stone known as *tufa,* which has the useful property of being soft to dig out but hardening permanently when exposed to air. Christians in Rome began to use underground burial places for their dead in the third century because their belief in an imminent general resurrection led to an insistence on burial rather than cremation, and they soon ran out of space in the already crowded city. Often they took over and enlarged existing pagan cemeteries, as in the case of the Catacombs of Domitilla, which contain a large subterranean basilica built over the tombs of Saints Nereus and Achilleus who were martyred in AD 304. It was the graves of martyrs that particularly attracted pilgrims to these vast cavernous necropolises. These can still be identified today by the fact that there are so many other tombs close by and from the murals and inscriptions on them. The rough drawings carved on the marble slabs that once sealed the tombs indicate some of the earliest use of

classic Christian symbols, such as the fish and the Good Shepherd, while the 1,600-year-old mural over one of the martyr's tombs still clearly shows Jesus and his disciples with Peter and Paul accompanied by two doves above. There is no truth in the oft-repeated stories that Christians hid in the Catacombs to escape persecution. As a silent witness to the lives and belief of the pioneers of the faith, however, the Catacombs still have the capacity to turn modern tourists into pilgrims and the celebration of Mass in one of the dark *hypogea*, or chambers, with the flickering candles illuminating ancient frescoes, remains one the most powerful memories of many a pilgrimage to Rome.

Rome, indeed, has a long history of making tourists conscious of the spiritual dimension. This is epitomized by the way in which so many of the city's great pagan classical buildings have been Christianized. The statue of the pagan emperor Trajan, which for centuries surmounted the magnificent column dating from AD 113 and still bears his name, was replaced in 1588 by one of St Peter. A large wooden cross now stands defiantly in the centre of the Colosseum, where Christians were once thrown to the lions. A plaque records that Pope Benedict XIV rededicated this architectural symbol of imperial Rome at its most proudly pagan to the passion of Jesus, and pronounced it sanctified by the blood of the martyrs and redeemed from 'impious cult and impure

The triumphal arch erected to commemorate Constantine's Victory at Milvian Bridge in AD 312. It was following this victory that Constantine converted to Christianity. The Colosseum is in the background

'Rome ... has a long history of making tourists conscious of the spiritual dimension.'

Above:
The Colosseum

Right: Detail of plaque
on the Colosseum
recording its
dedication to Jesus
by Pope Benedict XIV

Below: The Pantheon

superstition'. Even the magnificent ruins of the Roman
Baths of Caracalla were taken over by the Jesuits in the late
seventeenth century as a children's playground.
Undoubtedly the most spectacular example of the
Christianizing of a pagan temple is the Pantheon, which
should be on every pilgrim's itinerary. Originally built in
27 BC by Agrippa as a temple dedicated to the gods to
commemorate the victory of Actium over Antony and
Cleopatra, it was rebuilt in brick by Hadrian between AD
118 and 128. Abandoned
by the early Christian
emperors, it was eventually
given by the Byzantine emperor Phocas to
Pope Boniface IV, who consecrated it in AD 609
as a Christian church dedicated to Mary and
the martyrs. Legend has it that twenty-eight
wagon-loads of martyrs' bones were transferred
to it from the Catacombs. As well as being an
architectural marvel, the Pantheon still functions
as a Christian church and a shrine to Christian
monarchy. It contains the tombs of Italy's first
two kings: Victor Emmanuel, who died in 1878;

and Humbert, who was assassinated in 1900. On a lectern nearby, presided over by a man wearing a badge of the House of Savoy, there is a book of homage to the kings of Italy, which visitors are invited to sign. Monarchist-inclined pilgrims to Rome can also make their obeisances to the Stuart pretenders to the British throne. A monument to both Bonnie Prince Charlie and his father, the Old Pretender, stands behind the first pillar on the left as you enter the nave of St Peter's Church. On the wall opposite is an extraordinary monument to the Old Pretender's wife, Clementina Sobieski, which describes her in Latin – quite erroneously – as 'Queen of Great Britain, France and Ireland'!

The latest initiative to help visitors to Rome cross the boundary between tourism and pilgrimage comes from the official Vatican-run organization *Opera Romana Pellegrinaggi*. It has recently started two guided coach tours around Christian Rome, Line A being entitled 'San Pietro' and Line B 'San Paolo'. Each takes in around twenty major sites and allows unlimited stops off en route.

Rome may not be the quietest place to go as a pilgrim, but amidst the noise and the bustle of even the most crowded tourist hot spots it is possible to find oases of calm spirituality. Just across the square from the Trevi fountain, for example, stands the little church of Santi Vincenzo ed Anastasio. For most tourists, its main attraction are the steps outside which provide a superb view of the fountain and the hordes of lovers, idlers, hucksters and hangers-on gathered around it. A rather forlorn handwritten notice pinned to the railings – like many such injunctions in Rome honoured more in the breach than the observance – begs visitors not to consume their picnics there. Inside the church, nuns sit quietly saying the rosary, a young priest reads the Bible and several people light candles, kneel in prayer or sit in quiet contemplation. As is the case with almost every church in Rome, this one claims its share of relics – in this instance the hearts and lungs of almost every pope from Sixtus V (1590) to Leo XIII (1903), which are preserved in the crypt. What attracts the faithful pilgrims inside, however, is the desire to pause and be still for a few moments and to find the sacred in the midst of the secular – something that Rome is particularly good at providing.

Monument to Clementina Sobieski in St Peter's Church

'Rome may not be the quietest place to go as a pilgrim, but amidst the noise and the bustle of even the most crowded tourist hot spots it is possible to find oases of calm spirituality.'

Practicalities

The public transport system in Rome is excellent and cheap with a one-Euro ticket allowing a metro ride and unlimited travel on the buses for 75 minutes. Entrance to all churches is free. The main basilicas are open all day, while the smaller ones close for lunch. Fees are payable for entrance to church treasuries, cloisters, museums and the Catacombs. The papal audience is held every Wednesday morning at 11 a.m. when the pope is in Rome, either in St Peter's Square or in the audience chamber in the Vatican. Tickets need to be obtained in advance. The Vatican website is www.vatican.va and *Opera Romana Pellegrinaggi* has two: www.orpnet.org and www.josp.it.

Santiago

The *camino* to Santiago is the longest, most travelled and most evocative pilgrim route in Europe. It has also seen the most spectacular growth. In 1986 just under 2,500 pilgrims received their *Compostela* – the certificate awarded to those who have travelled 62 miles (100 km) on foot or 124 miles (200 km) by bicycle on consecutive days and who are prepared to testify that they made the journey for religious, spiritual or religious–cultural reasons. In 1996 the number rose to over 23,000 and in 2006 to over 100,000. Recent holy years, when the feast of St James (25 July) falls on a Sunday, have seen much higher numbers of pilgrims qualifying for the *Compostela*: just under 100,000 in 1993, 150,000 in 1999 and 180,000 in 2004.

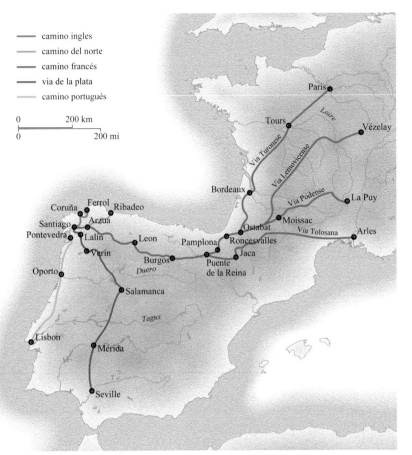

Legend:
— camino ingles
— camino del norte
— camino francés
— via de la plata
— camino portugués

0 — 200 km
0 — 200 mi

The main pilgrim routes to Santiago across France and through Spain and Portugal

There is more than one *camino*, or way, to the shrine of St James in the far north-west corner of Spain. A vast network of routes from across Europe has been used by pilgrims since the eleventh century. There are established pilgrim ways to Santiago starting from as far afield as Viborg in Denmark, Gdansk and Krakow in Poland and Budapest in Hungary. The *camino ingles* follows the route taken by many medieval pilgrims from the British Isles who sailed to La Coruna and then made the short walk south to Santiago. Others joined the *camino del norte,* a rugged route along the north Spanish coast. There are two pilgrim ways to Santiago from the south – the *camino portugués* and the *via de la plata,* which starts from Seville.

By far the most popular pilgrim route to Santiago, followed by 85 per cent of those awarded the *Compostela* in 2006, is the *camino francés.* It has four branches: the *Via Turonese,* starting from Paris, with extensions and connections from Brussels, the Low Countries and Scandinavia, and going through Tours and Bordeaux; the *Via Lemovicense* from Vézelay with connections from Germany; the *Via Podense* from Le Puy-en-Velay with connections from Switzerland; and the *Via Tolosana,* the route traditionally taken by Italians, which starts at Arles and goes through Toulouse. The first three routes converge at Ostabat, within sight of the Pyrenees, and then continue to the frontier town of St-Jean-Pied-de-Port before the long haul over the Pyrenees to the Augustinian monastery of Roncesvalles. Here pilgrims are quizzed about their motives and receive the official *credencial,* a passport that is stamped along the way and proves to the cathedral authorities in Santiago responsible for issuing the *Compostela* that the bearer has made the pilgrimage in a believable time and by a known route. The *Via Tolosana* crosses the Pyrenees further to the east at the Col de Somport and joins the other routes from France at Puenta la Reina near Pamplona. From there on, the *camino francés* – or the Camino de Santiago as it is often simply known – proceeds due westwards through northern Spain, passing the great cathedrals of Burgos and León and gradually filling up with more and more pilgrims as it approaches its destination.

The origins of Santiago as a pilgrim destination have already been described (page 48). There had long been a legend that the apostle James, the brother of John, had preached in Spain and that, denied a Christian burial by Herod Agrippa, his body had been taken by faithful disciples to the port of Jaffa. From there it underwent a miraculous journey in a stone boat, 'carried by angels and the wind beyond the Pillars of Hercules (the Straits of Gibraltar) to land near Finistere on the Atlantic coast of northern Spain'. The apparent discovery of James' bones on a hillside in a remote corner of Galicia in the early ninth century came at an opportune time. Most of the rest of Spain was then under Moorish rule and Alfonso II, whose kingdom of Asturias included Galicia and constituted a lone Christian outpost, promptly declared James (Iago in

Sign with the distinctive modern logo that marks the *camino* through Spain

Spanish) patron saint of Spain. During the long period of Moorish domination, the saint was a symbol of Christian defiance and became known as *Matamoros*, the slayer of Moors, appearing as a warrior mounted on a white horse at four critical battles. This image of the fierce opponent of Muslims co-existed with James' more benign *persona* as apostle and patron saint of pilgrims.

The first prominent pilgrim to Santiago was the bishop of Le Puy-en-Velay, who made the journey of well over 900 miles (1,450 km) from his diocese in the Haute Loire region of central France in AD 950, establishing what still remains the best-trodden of all the *caminos*. Pilgrimage to Santiago really took off when Jerusalem fell into the hands of the Turks in 1078 and it became second only to Rome as a pilgrim destination. Work began at this time on the great Romanesque cathedral, built to house James' relics, although it was not completed and consecrated until 1211, the year before the power of the Moors was finally broken. During the twelfth and thirteenth centuries, it is estimated that around half a million pilgrims a year made their way to Santiago from all over Europe to venerate the bones of one of Jesus' closest disciples. To house and feed them, a huge infrastructure of hospices was developed by the major religious orders. There was even a special religious order, the *Frères Pontiff*, set up to build and maintain bridges along the way.

As elsewhere, pilgrimage to Santiago declined considerably after the Reformation and did not significantly pick up again until the late nineteenth century when, in 1884, Pope Leo XIII declared that the remains of St James were indeed present there. More recently, Pope John Paul II did much to promote Santiago – especially among young people – through his visits there in 1982 and 1989, and that decade saw the first real revival of pilgrimage with people forsaking their cars to walk or cycle the *camino*. In 1985 UNESCO declared Santiago a World Heritage city and in 1987 the Council of Europe adopted the *camino* as the first 'European Cultural Route'. The *camino francés* was registered as a World Heritage site in 1993. With considerable European Union funding, significant improvements were made to its infrastructure and signposting.

The signs along the *camino* use various representations of the scallop shell, or *concha venera*, which has been the distinctive symbol of the Jacobean pilgrimage since at least the eleventh century. There are several stories to explain its origin: one relates how a horse bolted in terror and fled with its rider into the sea when the stone boat containing James' remains was washed up on the Galician shore. Horse and rider later emerged from the waves covered in shells. Perhaps the likeliest explanation for the scallop shell becoming the badge of pilgrims to and from Santiago is simply its ubiquity on the beaches around the Spanish coast.

The Cathedral, the Hostel de los Reyes Catolicos and other ecclesiastical buildings in the centre of Santiago

The shell came to have symbolic meaning. The sermon *Veneranda Dies* in the twelfth-century pilgrim's guide, *Liber Sancti Jacobi* (see page 49), describes it as pointing to the good works that a pilgrim must perform by reminding him of the fingers spread out on the back of his hand. The numerous statues of St James in churches and shrines along the *camino* nearly all depict him wearing the shell, often on his hat.

'**Christianity came from my head to my heart – it was an inner journey as much as an outer one.**'

Elisabeth Lidell, Scandinavian pastor

Since the early 1990s around seventy-five refuges, or *refugios*, have been built along the *camino francés* by religious groups, local authorities and private individuals. They provide basic accommodation for pilgrims, consisting of communal dormitories and bathrooms, and are unbookable with a stay of only one night allowed. A major role in the provision of these facilities, and in the general promotion of the *camino* over the last twenty or more years, has been played by the various national Confraternities of St James. The United Kingdom Confraternity has been particularly active, sponsoring a number of invaluable publications such as an English translation of the *Liber Sancti Jacobi*, which contains detailed information on the route from the Spanish border including dire warnings about the poisonous quality of the water in many of the rivers along the way.

Of the pilgrims who received the *Compostela* in 2006, 80 per cent travelled on foot and 20 per cent on bicycles. Men (60 per cent) outnumbered women (40 per cent) and by far the largest national group were the Spanish (52 per cent), with Italians (10 per cent), Germans (8 per cent) and French (6.7 per cent) coming next. Although it is now possible to walk the *camino* in some luxury, staying in comfortable hotels and having your luggage carried by van, many people still prefer to walk it alone, staying at the basic *refugios*, which in 2006 suffered a much-publicized infestation by lice. Although 76 per cent of pilgrims are 50 or under, the *camino* seems to hold a particular appeal for the middle-aged, especially those facing a significant milestone in their lives or a mid-life crisis. For many, it can be a life-changing experience. Elisabeth Lidell is one of several Scandinavian Lutheran pastors for whom the experience of walking to Santiago alone changed the direction of their ministry from parish to pilgrim priest. In her words: 'It was my desert walk. Christianity came from my head to my heart – it was an inner journey as much as an outer one.' The late Anthony Crockett,

Statue of St James as a pilgrim in one of the churches along the *camino*

bishop of Bangor in the Church in Wales until his untimely death in 2008, is one of a good number of pilgrims who walked to Santiago to mark his fiftieth birthday. He took six and a half weeks between late April and early June 1995, averaging 22 miles (35 km) a day, to cover the 1,000 miles (1,600 km) from Le Puy. Early on he established a routine of getting up around 6 a.m., 'when my collarbone and shoulder blades had not recovered from the previous day's pain', eating a meagre breakfast, saying his Morning Office and shouldering his 33-lb (15-kg) rucksack. On arrival at his *refugio* each evening, usually in the mid-to-late afternoon, he showered, washed his clothes, did some exploring and stocked up on his staple lunchtime fare of bread, tinned fish and oranges. After a substantial meal and a *demi-pichet* of red wine, he said the Evening Office, wrote up his journal and 'slept the sleep of the innocent, except on those occasions in Spanish *refugios* when one or more of my fellow pilgrims would keep me awake with their snoring'. Summing up his experience of walking the *camino* soon after his return, he wrote:

My grasp of the story of Europe is certainly much improved. I think that I now love and respect and understand my fellow human beings more than I did. I think that I love and respect and understand myself more too, and this is a good thing, for clergy often suffer from low self-esteem. I have become even more addicted to walking, probably because I am addicted to the exhilarating effects of the endorphins the body produces when exercising. As to St James and his relics, it does not matter to me at all whether it is his bones or those of anyone else in the silver coffer.

The author with fellow pilgrims on the BBC Radio 4 Pilgrimage to Santiago in 2004

What is important is that in that cathedral, the Christian good news has been and still is celebrated and preached, and millions down the ages have pilgrimaged to share in it. It was a privilege beyond price for me to be one of them.[1]

Others take to the *camino* because they want time out to reflect or meditate. The author Nicholas Luard decided to walk to Santiago when his 25-year-old daughter was diagnosed as HIV-positive in 1990. He walked the *camino* in stages both before and after his daughter's death, which took place in November 1994, and wrote of his experiences in his book *The Field of the Star*. In one of the most moving fictional accounts of the power of the *camino*, Laurence Passmore, a jaded 58-year-old writer of television sitcoms who is the central character in David Lodge's 1995 novel, *Therapy*, goes out to Spain following the break-up of his marriage to try to track down his childhood sweetheart, Maureen – a devout Catholic, who is walking from Le Puy to Santiago following the death of her son and her own recovery from breast cancer. Having discovered from the office at Roncesvalles Abbey what point along the way she is likely to have reached, he spends two weeks driving slowly up and down the roads that

Dust, mud, sun and rain
Is the Camino de Santiago.
Thousands of pilgrims
And more than a thousand years.

Pilgrim, who calls you?
What hidden force attracts you?
Not the field of the stars;
Nor the grand cathedrals.

It is not the courage of Navarra
Nor the wine of the Riochas
Nor the seafood of Galicia
Nor the plains of Castile.

Pilgrim, who calls you?
What hidden force attracts you?
It is not the people of the Camino
Nor the rural customs.

It is not the history and culture,
It is not the cock of La Calzada
Nor the palace of Gaudi
Nor the Ponferrada Castle.

I see them all as I pass
And it is a delight to see everything;
But the voice that calls to me
I feel much more deeply.

The force which pushes me,
The force which attracts me,
I cannot explain it.
Only He who is above knows it.

Verses by Eugenio Garibay painted on a wall on the outskirts of Najera, translated by Ian Bradley

Experiencing the *Camino*

In 2004 I was invited to join a BBC Radio 4 pilgrimage to Santiago as guest preacher. There was nothing penitential about this pilgrimage, I fear. We ate in fine restaurants, enjoying delicacies like the spiced octopus in wine (*pulpo*) for which Galicia is renowned. Although we only covered 45 miles (70 km) on foot – not enough to qualify for a *Compostela* – we did manage to walk to some of the most notable points of the *camino*, like the *Cruz de Ferro*, the large iron cross planted on a mass of boulders close to the highest point of the *camino* around 140 miles (225 km) from Santiago. We made the 6-mile (10-km) climb into the mountains to reach O Cerbreiro, one of the most distinctive villages along the way with its *pallozas* – round thatched buildings going back to pre-Roman Celtic times – and magnificent views over the plains of Galicia. We also walked the final stage of the *camino* from *Monte del Gozo*, the mount of joy from where pilgrims get their first sight of Santiago.

As we prepared and broadcast our services on the way to Santiago, we gained a strong sense of the importance of the churches along the *camino* as we spent so much time researching their history and worshipping in them. The first from which we broadcast was the twelfth-century church

Pallozas in O Cebreiro

of St Juan de Ortega in the *Montes de Oca*, a hilly area that divides the Rioja region from Castille and León. The church is a beautiful example of Romanesque architecture, built in a warm honey-coloured stone, wonderfully light and with a superb acoustic much appreciated by our choir as they sang traditional pilgrim hymns from the *Liber Jacobi*. The dormitories surrounding the fifteenth century cloisters next to the church have been turned into a *refugio* and are a good place from which to observe the rituals of pilgrim life.

Our second port of call was the thirteenth-century cathedral at León, a Gothic marvel with particularly impressive stained glass windows. The following day I led worship in the Church of Nuestra Senora de la Encina in Ponferada, its altar dominated by a large statue of the Virgin Mary, who is said to have appeared in the trunk of an oak tree during the time that this stretch of the *camino* was guarded by the Knights Templar. Nearby is the huge castle they built to defend the route. Our next broadcast service came from the ninth-century Church of Santa Maria La Real in O Cerbreiro, 4,000 feet (1,200 m) up in the mountains of Galicia. A fourteenth-century story tells of a peasant who trudged up from the valleys far below in a thick snowstorm to this church to take Mass. He arrived just as the priest was elevating the host. The priest, who was highly sceptical about the doctrine of transubstantiation, made fun of the simple man for making such a long and hazardous journey just for a bit of ordinary bread and wine. At this moment the bread and wine were literally transformed into flesh and blood before the eyes of the congregation. The chalice used on this occasion, known as the Holy Grail of Galicia, is kept on display in the church.

The last church from which we broadcast morning worship before reaching Santiago was St Nicolas in Portomarin, another cool and airy Romanesque building.

The Church of St Juan de Ortega

The long reputation of Portomarin as a place of healing and recuperation for weary pilgrims prompted my colleague Clair Jaquiss, who was leading this service, to reflect on what she had found most significant in the past week's pilgrimage: the bonding into a community of a group who had been total strangers when they began; the acts of acceptance and encouragement shown to each other on the way; and the gentle support when things hadn't been so good or painful memories were revived.

Finally, we arrived at Santiago Cathedral. It is difficult to capture in words the sheer size and exuberance of its massive eighteenth-century baroque façade built on to the original Romanesque frontage and the carnival atmosphere that pervades the huge square around the cathedral.

We were able to enter the cathedral by the special door that is only opened during holy years. Inside one's eye is immediately drawn to the high altar, which blazes with gold and candles and is dominated by a thirteenth-century gilded statue of St James in a jewel-bedecked cape. A constant stream of pilgrims climbs the steps behind the altar to embrace this statue. If you are sitting in the nave you have the odd sensation of seeing pairs of hands constantly appearing round his shoulders. After embracing the statue, pilgrims go down into the crypt where the saint's relics are contained in a silver

coffer. They perform other rituals, putting their hands into the five-fingered depression worn into the central pillar of the *Portico de la Gloria*, part of the original Romanesque façade, and tapping their foreheads against the little statue of Maestro Matteo, the medieval craftsman responsible for building it.

The pilgrim masses in the cathedral are dominated by the spectacle of the solid silver *botafumiero* (incense burner), which weighs a quarter of a ton and takes eight men to lift and set on its giddy course, ducking and diving over the altar as it swings on its thick hemp rope, belching out flames as the organ thunders. The original purpose of having such a large thurifier was to mask the stale and sweaty smell of the pilgrims with clouds of incense. Now it adds to the general atmosphere of theatre and excitement that pervades the cathedral.

What is striking about the pilgrims – as distinct from the tourists – both inside and outside Santiago Cathedral is the look of disappointment and sadness that often registers on their faces alongside the weariness and the exaltation. Many said that the journey had been all too short and they felt a sense of anti-climax at the end of their pilgrimage. Some go on to Cape Finisterre – the remote, rocky promontory on the Galician coast 55 miles (90 km) from Santiago often regarded in the Middle Ages as the end of the world – hoping to experience there the solitude and spiritual peace they find absent in the bustle and noise in and around the cathedral. Indeed, some pilgrims choose to by-pass Santiago altogether and avoid the main *camino francés* in favour of one of the other less-travelled pilgrim routes.

The elaborate
baroque façade of
Santiago Cathedral

run close to the *camino* looking for her:

*I met all sorts of pilgrims. The most
numerous were young Spaniards for
whom the pilgrimage was obviously
an impeccable excuse to get out of the
parental home and meet other young
Spaniards of the opposite sex. The
refugios are un-segregated. I'm not
suggesting any hanky-panky goes on
(there's not enough privacy anyway)
but I sometimes seemed to catch in them
of an evening a whiff of that puppyish
flirtatiousness I remembered from the
Immaculate Conception youth club.
Then there were the more sophisticated
young backpackers from other countries,
bronzed and muscular, attracted by the
buzz on the international grapevine
that Santiago was a really cool trip,
with great scenery, cheap wine and free
space to spread your bedroll. There
were cycling clubs from France and the
Low countries in matching T-shirts and
bollock-hugging lycra shorts and solo
cyclists pedalling pannier-festooned
mountain bikes at 78 r.p.m. There were
couples and pairs of friends with a
common interest in walking, or Spanish
history, or Romanesque architecture,
who were doing the Camino in easy
instalments, year by year. For all these
groups, it seemed to me, the pilgrimage
was primarily an alternative and
adventurous kind of holiday.*

*Then there were the pilgrims with more particular and personal motives: a
young sponsored cyclist raising money for a cancer ward; a Dutch artist aiming to
get to Santiago to mark his fortieth birthday; a sixty-year-old Belgian who was
doing a pilgrimage as the first act of his retirement; a redundant factory worker
from Nancy contemplating his future. People at turning points in their lives –
looking for peace, or enlightenment, or just an escape from the daily rat race. The
pilgrims in this category were the ones who had travelled furthest, often walking all*

the way from their homes in northern Europe, camping on the way… Their eyes had a distant look, as though focused on Santiago. A few were Catholics, but most had no particular religious beliefs. Some had begun a pilgrimage in a light-hearted experimental mood and become deeply obsessed with it. Others were probably a little mad when they started.[2]

Passmore eventually finds Maureen walking along the edge of the busy N120 road between Astorga and Orbigo, 'a plump, solitary woman in baggy cotton trousers'. Exhausted and suffering from strained ligaments, she accepts a lift from him and allows him to look after her. After a day or two of rest, they walk the rest of the way to Santiago together very slowly. It is a profoundly redemptive experience for Passmore, who is moved by Maureen's suffering and her faith. He also discovers at the end of the pilgrimage that his long-standing severe knee pain, for which he has unsuccessfully tried acupuncture, aromatherapy, physiotherapy, psychotherapy and yoga as well as conventional surgery, has been cured.

One of the statues on the Monte del Gozo from which pilgrims get their first sight of Santiago Cathedral

David Lodge captures well the mixture of motives that lead people to walk or cycle the *camino*. Pilgrims filling in the questionnaire at Roncesvalles that enables them to get their *credencial* are asked whether their reason for making the journey is religious, spiritual, recreational, cultural or sporting. A good many tick all of them. Nancy Louise Frey, a North American anthropologist who spent over a year in the mid-1990s studying and walking the *camino* for her doctoral thesis, is uncertain as to whether the word 'pilgrimage' is really appropriate to describe it:

Although the Santiago pilgrimage has a religious foundation based in Catholic doctrine regarding sin, its remission and salvation, in its contemporary permutation these religious elements endure, but they also share the same stage with transcendent spirituality, tourism, physical adventure, nostalgia, a place to grieve and esoteric initiation. The Camino can be (among many other things) a union with nature, a vocation, an escape from the drudgery of the everyday, a spiritual path to the self and humankind, a social reunion or a personal testing ground.[3]

What is pilgrimage for? Is it to reach a destination like Santiago, embrace the statue of St James and put your fingers on the stone where millions have placed them before? Undoubtedly such ritual gestures are powerful in linking today's pilgrims with centuries-long traditions and connecting them with the communion of saints who have gone before them. But for many others pilgrimage is much more about journeying than about reaching a destination. The journey back can often be the most difficult part – to face again the realities of home, family, relationships and work, but perhaps to face them in a different way, with a new resolve and intention. Nancy Frey found in her research that the weeks and months following a pilgrim's return from Santiago are often characterized by a negative sense of loss and depression as well as the positive translation of experiences. She comments:

> *Pilgrims with a religious orientation frequently repeat the same idea about the arrival in Santiago and the return home: el regreso es la salida (the return is the departure), or the real Camino begins in Santiago. As one pilgrim put it, 'You are not the same when you return as when you started out. Your very soul is on the move'... The physical journey concludes in Santiago where the real spiritual journey begins.* [1]

Practicalities

There are clearly many different possible starting points for the *camino*. For those from far afield wanting to walk the Spanish section of the *camino francés,* Bilbao Airport is probably the best point of arrival. The Confraternity of St James has an excellent website (www.csj.org.uk) and the website for Santiago is www.xacobeo.es.

10

St Andrews

St Andrews is now known principally as the home of golf and of Scotland's oldest university. Long before the Old Course attracted presidents and professionals to play on its hallowed turf, pilgrims from across Europe flocked to this small and remote coastal town to venerate the relics of the apostle Andrew. It was as a result of its status as one of the leading pilgrimage destinations in medieval Europe that St Andrews achieved supremacy in the Scottish church and acquired its university, the third oldest in Britain after Oxford and Cambridge. Although the mighty cathedral built to house the apostle's relics is now a ruin, the town centre still retains its pilgrim layout, with broad streets designed for processions running down to the site of the saint's shrine. An enterprising ecumenical project is currently underway to revive St Andrews as a place of religious pilgrimage and inter-faith understanding.

Legend has it that Andrew, the Galilean fisherman who was one of the first to follow Jesus, died as a martyr in Patras in Greece. The guardian of his relics, a monk named Regulus, or Rule, is said to have had a dream in the middle of the fourth century warning him that they were about to be moved to Constantinople on the orders of the emperor Constantius and telling him to remove at least some of them to 'the outer limits of the empire'. He duly set off with a tooth, an arm bone, a kneecap and three fingers of the apostle's right hand. His boat was apparently wrecked off the east coast of Scotland and so the relics came to rest in the place that subsequently took Andrew's name.

The Saltire

East Sands, St Andrews, showing the town and cathedral

In fact, the cult of St Andrew almost certainly came to north-east Fife from the kingdom of Northumbria during the eighth century. The Pictish kings who ruled eastern and northern Scotland were then in alliance with the Northumbrians against the Gaels. Later the Picts and the Gaels united to form the kingdom of Scotland and together resisted the Angles and Saxons. A Pictish king called Angus prayed for Andrew's help on the eve of a battle against the Saxons and subsequently saw a diagonal white cross silhouetted against the blue sky. This vision is traditionally taken as the origin of the Scottish flag, the Saltire. Gradually Andrew came to be seen as the protector of the Scots against the English, although it was not until well into the Middle Ages that he finally supplanted the Gael, Columba of Iona, as the nation's patron saint.

The first recorded pilgrimage to St Andrews was made in AD 967 by an Irish prince. In the 1120s a large church, dedicated to St Rule, was built to house the relics on the headland overlooking the town harbour and near to the site of the earliest ecclesiastical settlement in the area, which pre-dated the emergence of the story about the arrival of the apostle's bones. Its 100-foot- (30-m-) high tower survives and is a notable landmark for sailors and fishermen approaching the harbour. A community of Augustinian canons was established in the mid-twelfth century to look after the shrine and provide an appropriate religious and liturgical presence. Their expansion, together with the steadily increasing number of pilgrims, prompted the building of a much larger cathedral which was begun in 1160 but was not consecrated until 1318, four years after Robert the Bruce's victory over the English at Bannockburn, which was ascribed to Andrew's intervention and intercession.

Over 460 feet (140 m) long, St Andrew's Cathedral was by far the largest church in Scotland and only slightly smaller than the English cathedrals at York and Durham. It was also 40 feet (12 m) longer than Santiago Cathedral. Even today in its ruined state – the result of its destruction by Protestant Reformers in 1559 – it still has an imposing presence. The ultimate

St Rule's Tower and Church, the resting place of St Andrew's relics before the building of the cathedral

Right: Replica of
the *Mòr Breac* in St
Andrews Museum

destination for pilgrims was the relic chapel, which was almost certainly housed at the east end behind the high altar. The relics themselves were held in a jewelled casket known as the *Mòr Breac,* which was carried in procession round the town during major festivals, including St Andrew's Day (30 November).

Right: Replica of the *Mòr Breac* in St Andrews Museum

The heyday of pilgrimage to St Andrews was from the mid-twelfth to the early sixteenth centuries. The whole town was laid out to facilitate pilgrim processions, with the two major streets, North Street and South Street, made deliberately wide and designed to provide a circular one-way system to ease the flow of pilgrims to and from the cathedral. Between them ran Market Street where the numerous merchants catering for the pilgrims' physical needs were based. Their spiritual needs were met by the major religious orders, who established substantial houses in St Andrews. Guest houses and hospices were also provided for the pilgrims, the largest of which, dedicated to St Leonard and with special provision for lepers, was built very close to the cathedral. The chapel associated with this hospice, substantially restored in 1904 after centuries lying derelict, is now used by the university and is the setting for a candle-lit service of Compline at 10 p.m. every Thursday evening in term-time. Nearby are the impressive remains of the medieval gate into the cathedral precincts at the Pends, through which pilgrims would process on their way up from the harbour. A good number of pilgrims seem to have travelled by sea to St Andrews, which developed an international reputation even if it never came

Gateway into St Andrews Cathedral at the Pends

to rival Rome or Santiago. In 1333 a priest from Dunkirk, found guilty of manslaughter, was sentenced by a French ecclesiastical court to make a penitential pilgrimage to St Andrews. He was ordered to travel alone, reflect daily on his crime, and on his arrival arrange and pay for thirteen requiem masses for the repose of the soul of the man he had killed.

For those coming by land from other parts of the British Isles, a network of pilgrim routes was developed across Fife converging on St Andrews. To help those coming from England and southern Scotland, Queen Margaret of Scotland, who also played a major role in sustaining the monastery at Iona during the difficult years following the Viking raids, established the ferry route across the River Forth between the present rail and road bridges, giving her name to the settlements at either side of the crossing – South and North Queensferry, where she built pilgrim hospices. From North Queensferry, pilgrims walked to St Andrews via Inverkeithing, Loch Leven, Scotlandwell where a major hospice was built, Markinch, Kennoway and Ceres. Another much longer ferry passage across the Forth estuary was established by the earl of Dunbar between North Berwick and Earlsferry, near Elie, a distance of over 20 miles (32 km). Cistercian nuns set up hospices at either end of this crossing from where they supervised the manufacture and sale of pilgrim badges.

Pilgrims coming from west and central Scotland travelled via Perth and took a ferry across the River Tay where it is joined by the Earn, while those coming from the north and east crossed the Tay Estuary via Dundee and Tayport. These two routes converged to cross the River Eden by ford or ferry at the site of the modern village of Guardbridge, just 5 miles (8 km) north of St Andrews. This

The main pilgrim routes to St Andrews

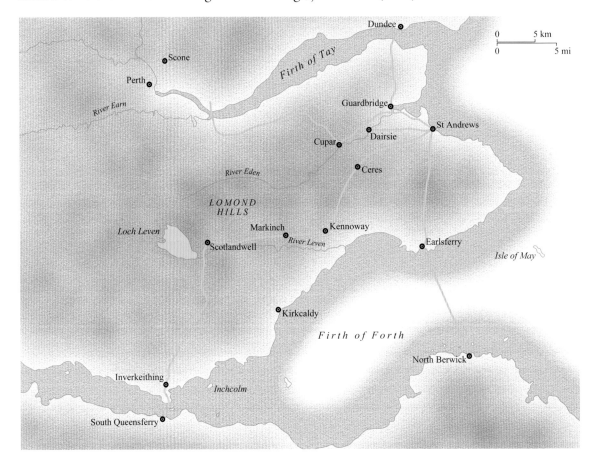

was often a hazardous crossing – on one occasion in the late fourteenth century twenty monks were drowned while attempting it – and in 1419 Henry Wardlaw, the bishop of St Andrews credited with founding the university, built a stone bridge that still survives today next to the modern bridge that carries the A91 trunk road. A large hospice was set up at Guardbridge, which functioned as an assembly station where pilgrims, many of whom had travelled alone or in small groups, would gather and spend their last night before walking together in procession to the apostle's shrine.

The atmosphere in and around St Andrews during the time when it was receiving up to 250,000 pilgrims a year has been vividly recreated by Jurek Putter in a series of meticulously researched and executed line drawings. Putter, whose Polish father came to Scotland in 1940, has been fascinated by the stories and traditions of pilgrimage to St Andrews since playing in the cathedral ruins as a boy growing up in the town in the 1950s. For each of his drawings he attempts an accurate if imaginative portrayal of what was happening at a very specific place and time. His *Statio Principalis Garebrigenses* shows the scene in and around the assembly station at Guardbridge on Maundy Thursday 1438. Within the enclosed courtyard, groups of pilgrims are resting and gossiping, while blacksmiths and stable boys attend to their horses. Near the chapel a priest is preaching to an attentive group, and in the centre of the courtyard staff from the hospice are washing the feet of incoming pilgrims. Outside, in imitation of the Good Samaritan, a pilgrim is ministering to a traveller who has been robbed and attacked on the way, while others walk past indifferent to his state. A licensed trader is doing a brisk trade in pilgrim badges and pennants and groups of pilgrims from Santiago and Venice are hoisting their banners as they prepare to leave the station for the procession into St Andrews. A 'pious picture' is being toured around in a cart for the edification of another group of pilgrims. The overall impression is of intense activity, diversity and energy but also of deep piety – almost lost in all the coming and going is the figure of Bishop Henry Wardlaw, portrayed not as a powerful ecclesiastical prince but as a humble penitent kneeling in prayer outside the walls of the *statio*.

Putter regards his works as windows into a 'world without frontiers, where pilgrims passed unmolested from country to country, even in times of war and where ideas were transmitted and dispersed for the good of all'. He is particularly struck by the internationalism of pilgrimage with its universal

*1. Courage brother! do not stumble,
though thy path be dark as night;
there's a star to guide the humble:-
'trust in God, and do the right'.*

*2. Though the road be rough and
dreary,
and its end far out of sight;
Foot it bravely; strong or weary,
trust in God, and do the right.*

*3. Some will hate thee, some will love
thee,
some will flatter, some will slight;
cease from men, and look above thee:
trust in God, and do the right.*

*4. Simple rule and safest guiding,
inward peace and inward might,
star upon our path abiding -
'trust in God and do the right'.*

Norman Macleod (1812–72)

and cosmopolitan character. His work has been one of the main catalysts in reviving interest in St Andrews' pilgrim past and reminding people that it is not just golfers for whom the city has been a mecca.

The last decade or so has seen a significant new campaign to stimulate public interest in the Christian origins and history of St Andrews as a major centre of pilgrimage and to re-interpret this traditional role in the twenty-first century by organizing and encouraging inter-denominational worship, pilgrimages of reconciliation and inter-faith dialogue. It has been spearheaded by the St Andrews Cathedral Project which was set up by David Dow, a local architect, following a suggestion by Professor Richard Demarco, an Edinburgh-based artist and impresario who has done much to foster and promote Scotland's links with Europe and who, like Putter, is much gripped

Students recreating a medieval pilgrimage to St Andrews Cathedral

by the pan-Europeanism and internationalism expressed in the great medieval pilgrim traffic. Demarco originally called for the rebuilding of the ruined cathedral as a national shrine to Scotland's patron saint following the example of the restoration of Iona Abbey and with the intention of emphasizing the country's spiritual and Christian heart at a time of growing national confidence and awareness. This rather over-ambitious project, which would have cost millions and did not find favour with Scottish Heritage, the owners of the cathedral site, was subsequently scaled down into a more realistic series of objectives including the provision of a room for prayer and meditation within the cathedral precincts and a greater emphasis in visitor displays on the spiritual reasons which drew pilgrims to the shrine of St Andrew.

Supported by Fife Council and its museums service, the Cathedral Project has put on a number of exhibitions at various locations over the last ten years that have sought to recreate the atmosphere of St Andrews as a pilgrim city and place it in the wider context of medieval and modern pilgrimage, not just in Europe but across the world. It has worked especially with young people to explore the theme of pilgrimage through artwork and stories as well as in more direct ways. On St Andrew's Day 2006 a group of primary school pupils, dressed in the costumes of medieval pilgrims, held an open-air service in the cathedral nave, and religious studies students from a local secondary school, also dressed in medieval garb, walked into St Andrews along the old pilgrim way from Guardbridge, which is now a cycle track. The cathedral ruins are being increasingly used for services of worship, including a *Songs of Praise* evening in the cloisters during the week of the Open Golf Championship in St Andrews and an ecumenical celebration of Holy Communion on the stone base of the high altar on Easter Sunday morning.

'St. Andrews is once again becoming a place of spiritual and physical pilgrimage.'

Albeit as yet on a small scale, St Andrews is once again becoming a place of spiritual and physical pilgrimage. One of the major ecumenical events in the Scottish churches' celebration of the Millennium was a four-day pilgrimage on foot from St Andrews to Edinburgh – a distance of 70 miles (110 km) – in September 2000, which followed much of the medieval pilgrims' route to North Queensferry. Described as 'a journey of discovery where past and future are reconciled', the pilgrimage was preceded by several days of performances, lectures, exhibitions and services in St Andrews, including an open-air Mass celebrated in the ruins of St Mary's on the Rock on the headland beside the cathedral, which is thought to be the site of the earliest place of Christian worship in the area. Exceptionally, a special dispensation allowed Catholics and non-Catholics to receive together at the same altar. On the Sunday when the pilgrimage proper began, the town's churches synchronized their morning services to end at the same time so that their congregations could process to the cathedral ruins for a commissioning service led by a choir from Vilnius in Lithuania. The pilgrimage then proceeded with stops at various stations in St Andrews before heading out on the old pilgrim path to Ceres. A group of Norwegians who had come especially for the occasion carried the heavy wooden cross, which was taken all the way to Holyrood Abbey in Edinburgh and subsequently erected on Inchgarvie Island in the Firth of Forth where it is clearly visible to train passengers crossing the Forth Rail Bridge.

There are other exciting dimensions to the revival of interest in pilgrimage in and around St Andrews. Fife Council is actively working on reopening and waymarking the main medieval pilgrim routes across the region so people can walk them again. Churches along the way are keen to open their doors through the week and put on interpretative displays. With a view to encouraging young people to come to St Andrews as pilgrims and seekers, thought is being given to

A Prayer Walk through St Andrews

In May 2007 I had the privilege of leading a group of pilgrims from different parts of the world, including as far away as New Zealand, on a prayer walk through St Andrews. They were making the journey as part of the 'Praying Across Scotland' initiative. I took them – as I take groups of pilgrims on or around St Andrew's Day (30 November) every year – on a route that includes many of the most significant sites in the town's important but often troubled religious history and naturally prompts reflection and prayer on issues that are still very much alive today. We begin at Holy Trinity Parish Church in the centre of town and walk to St Mary's on the Rock, overlooking the North Sea, where we reflect on the Celtic origins of Scottish Christianity and I recite Columba's prayer begging Christ to help him, 'a little man, trembling and most wretched, rowing through the infinite storm of this age'. Our next stop is at the eastern end of the cathedral where we consider the cult of St Andrew and reflect on how far the splendour of the golden jewel-encrusted shrine that once housed his supposed relics takes us from the story of the fisherman who obeyed Jesus' call. Perhaps in its ruined state, open to the sky with the gulls wheeling and crying overhead, I suggest, the cathedral speaks more eloquently than in its medieval heyday of the stark simplicity and urgency of that call.

Next we go to the castle, which was the seat of the bishops of St Andrews and the scene of two horrific killings in the name of Christianity – one of a Protestant, George Wishart, who was burned to death, and the other of a Catholic cardinal, David Beaton, who was dismembered limb from limb. Here we pray for peace and reconciliation. There are two other places associated with martyrdom that I often include in my pilgrimages around St Andrews: the memorial to Patrick Hamilton, a student who was burned to death for his Lutheran beliefs on a spot just outside the entrance to what is now the University Chapel; and a monument overlooking the West Sands erected in the nineteenth century to commemorate all the town's Protestant martyrs. St Andrews had a particularly shameful record of tit-for-tat killings of Protestants and Catholics, Presbyterians and Episcopalians, in the aftermath of the Reformation. One of my hopes in the not-too-distant future is to initiate a series of ecumenical pilgrimages in which members of different denominations will together visit the scenes of these terrible crimes perpetrated in the name of Christ by our ancestors and pray for forgiveness and reconciliation.

My pilgrim walk through St Andrews ends at the restored St Leonard's Chapel, which was originally part of the large hospice complex catering for pilgrims. The chapel lay derelict for much of the eighteenth and nineteenth centuries before being restored early in the twentieth, providing a parable for the central Christian motif of death and resurrection, which we celebrate with a closing Eucharist.

identifying places that might be turned into relatively cheap overnight hostels in a town where most of the tourist accommodation is geared to rich golfers.

One of the St Andrews Cathedral Project's most successful events so far was an inter-faith evening entitled 'Pilgrims and Pilgrimage, a Personal Experience' held in a church hall in 2004. A young Muslim student gave a presentation on his participation in the *Hajj* to Mecca and a young Christian spoke of his recent visit to Santiago. There was no attempt to convert or proselytize, but at the end of the evening we all felt that we had shared something deep and important and had grown in mutual respect. After the formal meeting was over a group of Muslim women quietly went into the sanctuary of the church next door. I had a similar experience of inter-faith pilgrimage more recently at the end of an evening service, which I took in the main parish church in St Andrews. I was conscious of a group of visitors sitting quietly at the back of the church. They turned out to be Muslims from London who had never been into a Christian church before.

Practicalities

St Andrews can be reached by road via the M90 and A91 (there are direct express buses from Edinburgh) and by rail via Leuchars station on the main Edinburgh–Aberdeen line. The Cathedral ruins are open daily free of charge from 10 a.m. to 5.30 p.m. There is an admission charge to climb St Rule's Tower and enter the excellent museum. The town's museum in Kinburn Park tells the story of pilgrimage to St Andrews well and has an excellent display of pilgrim badges with modern replicas for sale.

11 Iona

Over 250,000 people come to the tiny Scottish island of Iona each year, at the rate of 1,600 a day in the high summer, making the long journey that involves getting to Oban on the west coast of the mainland, catching the ferry to Craignure, crossing the island of Mull and then taking a second ferry that makes the short but often choppy crossing from Fionnphort.

Columba took a very different route on his fateful journey in AD 563, coming by sea from Ireland, via the islands of Jura, Colonsay and Oronsay, and possibly having stopped off on the Kintyre peninsula where some authorities suggest he first landed to meet the king of the Irish colony of Dal Riata in the west of Scotland. When he did finally arrive on Iona, it was on the remote and rocky beach at the south end of the island that is called *Port na Curaich* in Gaelic (the harbour of the curragh), often known simply as St Columba's Bay.

It is the legacy of Columba that has drawn pilgrims to Iona for nearly 1,400 years even though his relics long ago left the island, having been taken to Ireland and mainland Scotland by monks to avoid them being pillaged by

Iona Abbey seen from the jetty where modern pilgrims land

'Alone with none but thee, my God,
I journey on my way;
What need I fear when thou art near,
O King of night and day?
More safe am I within thy hand,
Than if a host did round me stand.'

Attributed to Columba

'...that man is little to be envied
whose piety would not grow
warmer among the ruins of
Iona.'

Dr Samuel Johnson

Viking raiders. There is virtually nothing left of the monastery that he founded. In accordance with the Irish tradition it was built entirely of wood and had no stone buildings. Visitors today can see the supposed site of his cell on the small rocky mound of *Torr an Aba* and the stone said to have been his pillow is on display in the small museum behind the Abbey Chapter House. The Benedictine Abbey that now dominates the island landscape was not built until the early thirteenth century, 600 years after Columba's death.

Iona has long been seen as possessing a particular spiritual aura, with the 'illustrious ruins' of its abbey having a special fascination for romantics. The English writer Dr Samuel Johnson summed up its appeal for many visitors in his often-quoted remark: 'that man is little to be envied whose piety would not grow warmer among the ruins of Iona'. In the wake of his visit in 1773, a stream of leading literary and artistic figures came to soak up its atmosphere. In 1874 the eighth duke of Argyll, who owned the island, began the process of restoring the ruined abbey and in 1899 he gave it to a trust made up of representatives of the established Church of Scotland on the condition that it be used as a place of worship open to all Christian denominations. Restoration of the Abbey Church was completed in 1910.

Lobster pots piled up on the jetty with Iona Abbey in the distance

In 1938 George Macleod, a charismatic and well-connected young Church of Scotland minister, brought out a work party made up of divinity students and unemployed shipyard workers from his inner-city Glasgow parish to begin restoring the buildings around the abbey. Over successive summers all-male groups, living in huts, taking early morning showers in the sea and generally conforming to the muscular Christian regime of Victorian public school boys,

1. Will you come and follow me
if I but call your name?
Will you go where you don't know
and never be the same?
Will you let my love be shown,
will you let my name be known,
will you let my life be grown,
in you and you in me?

2. Will you leave yourself behind
if I but call your name?
Will you care for cruel and kind
and never be the same?
Will you risk the hostile stare
should your life attract or scare?
Will you let me answer prayer
in you and you in me?

3. Will you let the blinded see
if I but call your name?
Will you set the prisoners free
and never be the same?
Will you kiss the leper clean,
and do such as this unseen,
and admit to what I mean
in you and you in me?

4. Will you love the 'you' you hide
if I but call your name?
Will you quell the fear inside
and never be the same?
Will you use the faith you've found
to reshape the world around,
through my sight and touch and sound
in you and you in me?

5. Lord, your summons echoes true
when you but call my name.
Let me turn and follow you
and never be the same.
In your company I'll go
where your love and footsteps show.
Thus I'll move and live and grow
in you and you in me.

John L. Bell (born 1949) and Graham Maule (born 1958)

gradually rebuilt the cloisters, refectory and dormitories. It is these buildings, finally completed in the mid-1960s, which now provide the main island base of the Iona Community, a dispersed ecumenical Christian community founded by Macleod which has its headquarters in Glasgow. The Community has another base on Iona, the modern Macleod Centre opened in 1988 and designed specifically for youth groups. Both centres host residential weeks every year from April to October to which people come from across the world as guests to live and work in community, worship in the restored Abbey Church and explore themes central to the Community's concerns such as racism, ecology, sexuality and non-violence.

People visiting Iona for the day sometimes express disappointment at the fact that they do not encounter cowled monks in the abbey cloisters and precincts. Those living and working in the abbey and the Macleod Centre are a mixture of resident staff – some on three-year contracts and others hired for the season – who are not necessarily members of the Iona Community, and volunteers, predominantly young people who come to Iona for periods ranging from six weeks to three months. It is the community of staff, volunteers and guests that forms and re-forms each week that constitutes the central *raison d'etre* for the Iona Community's presence on Iona. There is a huge diversity of experiences and backgrounds – a typical week can bring together middle-class Anglicans from a parish in the south of England, a group with special needs from a Glasgow housing scheme and individuals from Australia, the United States and Continental Europe.

The emphasis for those staying in the abbey or the Macleod Centre is very much on 'sharing the common life'. There are no single rooms or en suite facilities – this is a place where you have to share and put up with the snoring! A time of communal chores, including cleaning out the lavatories and shower rooms, follows breakfast each day and leads into morning worship in the abbey. The rest of the morning is given over to programme sessions and the afternoon is left free for people to explore the island or visit the neighbouring island of Staffa with its famous Fingal's Cave, which inspired Mendelssohn's *Hebrides Overture*. There are also times of singing in the Chapter House and opportunities to paint, model with clay and make mosaics in the craft room. The evening meal is followed by a talk on some aspect of the Community's work and mission and each of the 9 p.m. services in the abbey through the week has a particular theme: welcome, silence, justice and peace, healing, commitment and a Communion service.

The pilgrim theme is central to the ethos of the Iona Community. It sees itself as a movement as much as an organization, constantly searching for new ways 'to touch the hearts of all'. Its emblem, the Wild Goose, which also gives its name to the Community's publishing house and worship resource group, is (according to George Macleod) a traditional Celtic symbol of the Holy Spirit, always on the move. The songs of its leading liturgist, John Bell, have a strong pilgrim flavour, notably 'Come with me, come wander come welcome the world' and 'Will you come and follow me if I but call your name?' The Community is deeply incarnational in its focus, seeking to integrate prayer and politics, worship and work and to build

A modern replica of St John's Cross which stands in front of St Columba's shrine by the entrance to Iona Abbey

community in an increasingly individualized and divided world. Its centres on Iona are emphatically not places for escape or quiet reflection – those in search of that kind of experience would be better staying at one of the retreat houses on the island such as Bishop's House, run by the Scottish Episcopal Church, or the Roman Catholic House of Prayer. In the words of one staff member working at the abbey, 'people come to us seeking peace and quiet and we try to send them away seeking peace and justice'. As Norman Shanks, a former leader of the Iona Community, noted in a sermon preached on the occasion of the 1,400[th] anniversary of St Columba's death, 'the peace that many people find here turns out to be very different from what they expected, not the rather sanitized "God's in his heaven, all's right with the world" variety; more challenging and engaged than that'. For him, Iona is about energy, connectedness and above all an engaged spirituality.[1] It is also about vulnerability, as expressed by the statue in the middle of the cloisters entitled *The Descent of the Spirit* by the Lithuanian sculptor Jacob Lipchitz. It depicts a dove descending into the open hands of the Virgin Mary, who is portrayed womb-like, open and receptive but blind. She is supported by three angels and at her feet is a blind lamb.

Everyone who is on Iona on a Tuesday between March and October, whether a day visitor, a guest in one of the Community centres or staying

Survey of Iona Visitors

The majority of those visiting Iona are not destined for a week in the abbey or the Macleod Centre. They come to spend a night or two in one of the island's hotels or bed-and-breakfast establishments or as day visitors whose time on the island is dictated by ferry timetables. To gain an insight into the different motives that bring people to Iona, I carried out a survey over a week in September 2006 of three distinct groups: volunteers spending several months working on the island for the Iona Community; that week's crop of guests in the abbey and the Macleod Centre; and day visitors whom I interviewed outside the abbey. The results show a marked difference in geographical origin, faith commitment and motivation.

	Volunteers	Guests	Day visitors
Proportion coming from the UK	40%	44%	64%
Proportion saying they are Christian	88%	94%	58%
Main reason for coming to Iona:			
Intellectual curiosity	12%	8%	12%
Spiritual searching	52%	80%	8%
Religious feeling	16%	12%	16%
Holiday/vacation	20%	0	64%
Which of these terms best describes the reason for your visit?			
Tourist	0	0	60%
Pilgrim	32%	66%	4%
Seeker	28%	26%	4%
Adventurer/Traveller	40%	8%	32%

Of these three types of visitor, the abbey and Macleod Centre guests, who in this particular week came predominantly from Scandinavia, the United States and Australia, were the most committed in terms of Christian belief and saw themselves most clearly as pilgrims, motivated by spiritual searching. They were also clearest as to the specific reasons why they had come to Iona – several mentioned the appeal of living in community, of linking spiritual life with concern for society and the environment and of exploring Celtic spirituality and theology. Echoing George Macleod's description of Iona as a 'thin place', one guest spoke of 'the closeness of this island to heaven and earth', another spoke of experiencing 'the thin veil' and a third simply said 'this place is holy for me'. A British guest who had first come to Iona in 1977 told me: 'I have been unable to keep away. I am drawn back continually to this place which speaks in so many ways of God.'

The volunteers also predominantly identified themselves as coming to Iona for spiritual and religious reasons, although a significant minority were happy to describe themselves as motivated by intellectual curiosity or the desire for a holiday. They were the most international group, coming from twelve different countries, with Canada providing the second largest national contingent after the United Kingdom. Like the guests, they were overwhelmingly Christian although they included some who described themselves simply as spiritual or in hybrid terms. Forty per cent said they wanted to explore living in a community. Others mentioned Celtic spirituality, spiritual searching, self-development and the desire to experience Scotland and to meet different people.

The day visitors, as one might expect, gave markedly different answers, with the majority seeing themselves purely as holidaymakers. Most mentioned the island's history and wildlife or the grave of John Smith, the British Labour Party leader who was buried on the island after his sudden death in 1994.

What a survey like this does not reveal is the more personal and private motivations that bring people as pilgrims to Iona. Iona attracts those who are at a crisis point in their lives, perhaps after the break-up of a relationship, a period of illness or unemployment, when they are seeking a new direction, or as part of a much longer sabbatical or journey round Europe or even round the world. This is true also of those working for a year or two with the Community. I think of my conversations with Paul, an Australian, and Jana, a pastor and liturgist from the United States, who spent a season working in the abbey, he as one of the maintenance staff and she as the cook. They shared with me their sense that Iona offers people the spiritual equivalent of a health check, not so much a safe harbour as a mooring point where people can stay for a while before moving on, as they themselves now have to a remote part of Australia to follow their dream of setting up a way station for pilgrims – in Paul's words 'not a destination but a stopover that provides inspiration and spiritual sustenance, a kind of filling station miles from anywhere'.

elsewhere on the island, has the chance to become a pilgrim for a day. The Iona Community organizes two pilgrimages round the island: one starting at 10.15 a.m., lasting about six hours and traversing some rough and boggy ground; the other setting off at midday, taking a couple of hours or so and sticking to the roads. Both are led by a member of the resident staff group and pause for reflection, prayer and song at places of historic and religious significance around the island. They provide a chance for conversation and discussion with people from many corners of the world and widely divergent backgrounds and are a wonderful way to explore and experience both the physical beauty and the spiritual power of Iona.

Both pilgrimages set off from St Martin's Cross, the imposing 14-foot- (4.3-m-) high cross dedicated to St Martin of Tours carved during the latter part of the eighth century, which stands in front of the entrance to the abbey. Decorated on one side with biblical scenes and on the other with the distinctive Celtic intertwining knots, it provides a suitable backdrop for a meditation on Celtic Christianity and also a briefing on what lies ahead. The pilgrimages then proceed to the ruins of the Augustinian nunnery near the jetty. Built in the early thirteenth century around the same time as the Benedictine Abbey, it has been largely ignored by historians and very little is known of the life and work of the nuns who were there for over 350 years. The ruins provide an appropriate place to reflect on the neglect of women that has all-too-often blighted the Christian tradition. The next stop is at Martyrs Bay, the scene of the massacre of sixty-eight monks by Vikings in AD 806, an act of violence that prompts thoughts of the victims of torture and massacre in our contemporary world and the continuing task of reconciliation.

The on-road pilgrimage now crosses to the west side of the island to the raised beach or *Machair* that provides fertile grazing for sheep and cattle, passing on the way the Hill of Angels where Columba is said to have met with a multitude of angels who flew down and conversed with him. The off-road pilgrims climb the boggy and stony track that leads to the south-east corner of the island and, assuming that it is not pouring with rain, then descend by an even more slippery path to the quarry which supplied the marble for the communion table and

The western shore of Iona with the Atlantic ocean beyond

Pebbles on St Columba's Bay

Right: Jacob Lipchitz's sculpture *The Descent of the Spirit* in the middle of the Abbey Cloisters

St Oran's Chapel

baptismal font in the abbey. Some of the oldest rocks in the world are to be found on Iona, dating back some 2,700 million years, and the meditation here considers their stability and permanence but also their vulnerability to exploitation by humans. Another boggy track leads down to St Columba's Bay, for many the high point of the pilgrimage. Here people are invited to take up two stones from the hundreds of thousands of coloured pebbles on the shore: one representing a burden or failing they wish to be rid of which is hurled into the sea; the other representing a new commitment which is taken home. It is a powerful piece of symbolic action.

Returning from the bay, the path passes Loch Staonaig which for many centuries provided Iona's water supply. Here the reflection is on the sacred and healing nature of water and the fact that it is in desperately short supply in so many parts of the world. The off-road pilgrims then descend to the soft and springy green turf of the *Machair* to join with their on-road brothers and sisters for a cup of tea and a piece of cake. The off-road pilgrimage continues, often in silence, with a climb towards Dun I, at 300 feet (90 m) above sea level the highest point on the island, with a stop en route at the Hermit's Cell – in reality almost certainly a sheepfold but according to tradition the remains of a beehive hut where monks may have spent periods in solitude and withdrawal. The pilgrimage finishes at St Oran's Chapel, the oldest building on Iona, which may have been built at the request of Queen Margaret of Scotland in the twelfth century. It stands in the middle of the graveyard known as the *Reilig Odhráin*, which contains the graves of kings from Norway, France and Scotland as well as Columba's monks and is still used as the island's cemetery today. In Norman Shanks' words: 'It may seem strange to end the pilgrimage in a graveyard but for Christians death is not the end, and here people are encouraged to think about resurrection and new life, moving on to the next stage of their journey beyond Iona with a sense of vision and hope, open to one another and to the new possibilities to which God is calling us.' [2]

The Tuesday pilgrimage is an exhilarating experience. Physically as well as spiritually, it is a place for giving each other a helping hand – over the stile, across the bog and the slippery stones – and as on all pilgrimages it is not just a matter of the young and able-bodied helping the old and infirm but is often the other way round.

Thou shalt travel thither, thou shalt travel hither,
Thou shalt travel hill and headland,
Thou shalt travel down, thou shalt travel up,
Thou shalt travel ocean and narrow.

Christ himself is shepherd over thee,
Enfolding thee on every side;
He will not forsake thee hand or foot,
Nor let evil come anigh thee.

From the Carmina Gadelica
(collected by Alexander Carmichael from a crofter on the island of Coll)

Iona is also a good place for making individual pilgrimages – up Dun I, the summit of which is no longer on the itinerary of the Tuesday pilgrimage because of erosion, or to the silver sands on the north shore so beloved of the group of artists known as the Scottish colourists. Even though it is a small island – just 3.5 miles (5.5 km) long and 1.5 miles (2.5 km) across at its widest point – you can easily find yourself alone once you have left the main tracks.

I have a dream that there might one day be a long-distance pilgrim path to Iona on the model of the *Camino de Santiago* and the *pilegrimsleden* to Trondheim. In the manner of St Cuthbert's Way, it would follow in the footsteps of St Columba's life and trace his journey from birth to death. The starting point for this Columba Way would be Lough Gartan in Donegal in the north-west corner of Ireland, the beautiful area of lakes and mountains where Columba was born. From there it would run along the North Donegal coast, crossing into Northern Ireland and into Derry where Columba possibly founded his first monastery and where both the Roman Catholic and the Church of Ireland cathedrals are dedicated to him. The pilgrim way would continue along the Antrim coast, passing the Giant's

Campbeltown, near the tip of the Kintyre Peninsula in Argyll, where Scotland is closest to Ireland

Causeway, to the seaside town of Ballycastle. Ideally, pilgrims would then make the short sea crossing to the southern tip of the Mull of Kintyre. A ferry route from Ballycastle to Campbeltown was established in 1997 and although it has subsequently been suspended there is a concerted campaign to restore what is the shortest crossing between Ireland and Scotland.

Pilgrims arriving in Campbeltown could pick up the recently opened Kintyre Way, which meanders up the Kintyre peninsula to Tarbert. They would then walk through the forest trails of Knapdale, dropping down to visit St Columba's cave on the shores of Loch Caolisport near Ellary, where there are signs of early rock-cut crosses above a medieval altar. This atmospheric cave is already the venue for an increasing number of local pilgrimages and open-air services. Crossing the Crinan Canal and Moine Mhor, the extensive area of peat bog that is a site of special scientific interest, pilgrims would then climb the sacred hill of Dunadd, where the kings of Dal Riata were crowned in what may have been some of the earliest Christian initiation ceremonies in Europe, and enter the Kilmartin Valley with its extensive prehistoric and early Christian remains. At this point there might be a choice of routes for the Columba Way: either by boat across to Jura – perhaps the island with the greatest claim to being regarded as Hinba, described by Columba's biographer Adamnan as the saint's place of solitary retreat – and then via Colonsay to Iona; or by land continuing up the West Argyll coast to Oban and then across Mull.

There is a bid currently in for European Union funding for a Gaelic cultural trail themed around the figure of Columba and linking Ireland and Scotland, so perhaps my dream of a Columba pilgrim way may one day come true. Whether it does or not, Iona will remain a major destination for pilgrims as well as tourists. It is also one of the places where the distinction between the two is most blurred. Although only 4 per cent of the day visitors I interviewed as they went into the abbey saw themselves as pilgrims, I am sure that once inside many found themselves lighting a candle or leaving a prayer request. They would also have been brought face-to-face with the Community's current campaigns on issues of justice and peace. Even now with the abbey in the hands of Historic Scotland and presented as much as a historical monument as a living place of worship, it is impossible to visit Iona without being aware that it is the base for a religious community deeply committed to contemporary issues, many of them difficult and disturbing.

This poem by Peter Millar, Warden of the Abbey from 1994 to 1998, captures the spirit and the lure of Iona:

'A place of hope',
They say:
And in their thousands
They journey, year by year,
To this tiny island
On the margins of Europe.
Sunswept and windswept,
Yet always deeply
A place of transformation.
A sacred spot on earth:
A pilgrim's place
Of light and shadow,
Energy and challenge.

We need you, Iona,
With your alternative vision,
With your ever-present questions,
Your often uncomfortable silence.

For you are a place of prayer,
Of Christ's abiding:
Weaving a rainbow of meaning
Through the endless busyness of
our days,
Holding together the frayed
threads
Of our fleeting devotion,
Opening a path for healing
And for peace.
Not momentary healing
Nor easy faith,
But struggle, commitment,
And an ongoing conversion
Are your gifts for
Our broken yet beautiful lives.[3]

Practicalities

The Iona Community website is www.iona.org.uk. For ferries consult www.calmac.co.uk, for buses www.bowmantours.co.uk and for Bishop's House www.island-retreats.org.

St Martin's Cross, which has stood for well over 1,000 years on the same site. Behind it is the mound known as *Torr an Aba*, where Columba is said to have had his simple cell.

Ireland

The Irish have been enthusiastic pilgrims since the days of Columbanus and Columba. Today they are found in significant numbers at Lourdes and Medugorje.

Among the pilgrimages still thriving in Ireland itself today is one that is among the most strenuous and another that is undoubtedly the most penitential of any in Europe.

The most popular pilgrimage in Ireland today is the climb up Croagh Patrick, the 2,500-foot (760-m) high mountain in the north-west of County Mayo, known locally as The Reek, on which St Patrick is said to have fasted for forty

The Skelligs, Kerry, Ireland

A Reek Sunday Pilgrimage

On Reek Sunday 1999 I made the ascent up Croagh Patrick in the company of an international group assembled by Tommy Murphy, a Columban missionary priest who has spent much of his life in China. It included two Philippinoes, three Koreans, a Fijian and a French enthusiast for Celtic mythology, who had started their five-day pilgrimage at the Marian shrine of Knock and slept on the floors of village halls along the way. Equipped with stout sticks, we were set on our way by a lengthy Celtic blessing-cum-journey prayer from a Roman Catholic father. Unlike most modern pilgrims, who take the most direct way up, we followed the six-mile (10-km) *Tochar Phadraig* (Patrick's Causeway), the old pilgrim route from Ballintuber Abbey which was reopened and waymarked in 1989 by the local parish priest.

As we walked on, sharing folk songs from our various lands and conversations about our own life journeys and experiences, the great conical mass of the Reek loomed ever closer with a broad black ribbon of what looked like ants crawling slowly up its scree-laden summit. The first 2,000 feet (600 m) or so of the ascent is a reasonably gentle climb up well-defined paths over turf and heather. The last 500 feet (150 m) involve scrambling up a pile of constantly shifting loose scree and stones, which seems almost vertical in places. At this stage you are almost carried up by others, both physically by the sheer press of bodies gradually making their way up and spiritually by the constant encouragement of fellow climbers and those coming down from the top. At various points on the way up there are stations at which many of the pilgrims pause to recite a specified number of Hail Marys and Our Fathers. At the top there are other traditional penitential exercises to perform: walking seven times round *Leaba Phadraig* (Patrick's bed), a concrete slab surrounded by a tubular railing; kneeling at another shrine; and walking fifteen times in a clockwise direction round the white-washed church built on the summit in 1905. Mass is celebrated at half-hourly intervals from early morning until late afternoon by priests stationed in a little glass-covered booth at the front of the church. On one side of the booth a door marked 'Confessions' leads to a room manned by a rota of priests, with at least six on duty at any one time; and on the other a door marked 'Communion' is opened at the end of each Mass for people to file through and receive the consecrated wafer.

The experience of climbing Croagh Patrick underlines the simple pleasure of walking together. I am pretty sure that I will never again in this life see any of my companions from that ascent in 1999. I had never met any of them before. Yet in the course of that Reek Sunday we developed a close bond, all the more so because of that painful slog up the mountain and the

exhilaration of reaching the top. They were all Catholics. I am a Protestant. Most of them were non-British. Yet as we walked together we were not strangers but rather pilgrims together. Climbing Croagh Patrick also highlights the physicality and penitential aspect of pilgrimage. It is not easy and a good many pilgrims undertake it as a penitential exercise, some walking the whole way in their bare feet. One of the Poles making the climb on Reek Sunday 2007, Miroslawa Gorecka, a 17-year-old from Katowice, said: 'I'm not used to this kind of hardship but it's good to make a sacrifice.' A local pilgrim, Caroline Noone, concurred. 'It's a penance, you offer it up for family and friends, for someone who is ill. It's a sacrifice. I'm doing it for the holy souls in Purgatory. The more suffering there is on the way up, the better.' Father Martin Newell, aged 76 and making his fiftieth consecutive Reek Sunday pilgrimage in 2007, believes that as Ireland has become more secular, the more a place like Croagh Patrick attracts people for its atmosphere of prayer and devotion.

days and nights in AD 441 and from whose summit he supposedly banished snakes from Ireland. The Reek has long been regarded as a holy mountain and was almost certainly a focus in pre-Christian times for celebrations of the Celtic god Lugh. Its lower slopes are dotted with the remains of prehistoric cromlechs (monoliths), burial chambers, cup and ring markings and standing stones. It was first associated with Patrick in the life of the saint written by Tirechan in the late seventh century. By the ninth century it had become a major destination for penitential pilgrims. During the centuries of penal laws against Roman Catholicism in Ireland, the pilgrimages became a defiant focus of both Catholic and Irish sentiment. Attempts by local bishops to suppress the pilgrimages up the mountain in the latter part of the nineteenth century met fierce resistance and the Reek has continued to maintain a central position in popular Irish spirituality.

More than 100,000 pilgrims climb Croagh Patrick every year. The biggest pilgrimage takes place on the last Sunday in July, known as Reek Sunday. In 2007 around 40,000 made their way up its steep slopes, including several hundred from Eastern Europe.

> *May the road rise to meet you,*
> *May the sun shine warm upon your face,*
> *May the rain fall softly on your fields,*
> *May the wind be always at your back,*
> *May you find good companions along the way*
> *And until we meet again,*
> *God hold you in the hollow of his hand.*
>
> Adapted from an Irish blessing

Pilgrims praying in the mist at the top of Croagh Patrick in County Mayo

'Pilgrims journey together: they share each other's joy and feel each other's pain. We try to ensure that everyone's story is heard and that help is offered for the continuing journey of life.'

Lough Derg, a large lake in the south of County Donegal just over 100 miles (160 km) north-east of Croagh Patrick as the crow flies, provides an even more penitential pilgrim experience. Station Island, one of 46 small islands on the lake and known as St Patrick's Purgatory, has been a place of pilgrimage from at least the twelfth century. Legend has it that a cave on the island was revealed by God to St Patrick as a passage into the underworld. A treatise written in 1184 by a monk simply known as Brother H provides the first surviving account of a pilgrimage there. He presented the journey into the cave as a dramatization of the symbolic death experienced by the hermits who had long lived on the island and suggested that a short stay there would produce the spiritual benefits of a long period of withdrawal from the world without the need to embark on the life of a hermit. For many of those who came to Station Island in the Middle Ages, however, it is clear that the lure had more to do with the prospect of gaining a glimpse of the next world and avoiding meeting death unprepared.

St Patrick's Purgatory was vigorously promoted as a pilgrimage centre by Augustinian canons who had been introduced into Ireland in the 1140s and installed in a monastery on another of the islands on Lough Derg. By the end of the twelfth century it had become the mecca for thousands of pilgrims annually, some coming from as far away as Hungary. While the central feature of every pilgrimage remained entrance into the cave, other penitential rituals were added, with people being encouraged to plunge into the Lough and stand with the cold water up to their waists chanting psalms in imitation of a practice

associated with the early Celtic saints.

Today St Patrick's Purgatory offers a bracing and austere penitential experience for several thousand pilgrims every year. A traditional pilgrimage involves three days of fasting, starting at midnight on the evening prior to arrival and ending at midnight on the day of departure, alleviated only by a single, meagre daily meal of black tea and dry toast. Pilgrims, who must be on the island by 3 p.m. on the first day of their stay, are rowed across the Lough and taken immediately to one of the dormitories to remove their shoes and socks. They remain barefoot throughout their time on the island. They then spend the rest of the afternoon and evening of their first day walking round outdoor penitential beds dedicated to various Irish saints and made up of stones, several with sharp edges, which become extremely slippery in the rain. There are five of these beds, which may be the foundations of the cells used by early hermits, and three lengthy stations must be walked on each of them by 9.20 p.m. Pilgrims then move to the large basilica where they are required to stay up throughout the night and make four more stations before Mass is celebrated at 6 a.m. The second day of the pilgrimage includes the sacrament of reconciliation, renewal of baptismal vows and a further walk on the penitential beds as well as round the Stations of the Cross before evening Mass, night prayer and benediction. At 10 p.m. on their second night on the island pilgrims are finally allowed to go to bed in the spartan dormitories after benediction. The third day begins with Mass at 6.30 a.m., a final round of stations on the penitential beds and a return to the dormitories to put on shoes and socks before pilgrims board the boat back to the secular world and the prospect of a large post-midnight fry-up after another day of fasting.

St Patrick's Purgatory is the only purely penitential place of pilgrimage in Europe. The regime of sleep deprivation, fasting and repeated uncomfortable ritual exercises may seem very austere, but

it undoubtedly reflects the practices of the early Irish monks and, indeed, of many early Christians. Those who undertake it find that it purges both body and soul and makes them more appreciative of the creature comforts of western civilization while at the same time more aware of the circumstances of those in other parts of the world who go without food and proper shelter every day.

As one of the priests responsible for services at the basilica puts it: 'There are no outsiders here. In bare feet everyone is equal. Pilgrims journey together: they share each other's joy and feel each other's pain. We try to ensure that everyone's story is heard and that help is offered for the continuing journey of life.'

Practicalities

Croagh Patrick lies 5 miles (8 km) from the village of Westport, which can be reached by both bus and train from Dublin and Galway. There is an information centre with a car park at the base that is open daily from April to October (e-mail: info@croagh-patrick.com). There is plentiful accommodation in the area but booking ahead is necessary around Reek Sunday. There is a good website at www.croagh-patrick.com.

Lough Derg is not easily accessible by public transport and pilgrims without a car and not in an organized group would be best advised to take a taxi from Donegal or Pettigo. There is no need to book for the three-day pilgrimage and pilgrims can turn up any day between 10.30 a.m. and 3 p.m. during the pilgrimage season, which runs from June to mid-August. Less demanding one-day retreats are available on the island during May, late August and September. There is an excellent website at www.loughderg.org.

Wales

13

Wales is a pilgrim's paradise with a plethora of sacred wells, ancient shrines and pilgrims' tracks. In the Middle Ages the main road from north to south began at Holywell and ended at St David's, the shrine of the patron saint and a major centre for pilgrimage. The road to St David's was known as the *Meidr Sant* or holy way. Pope Calixtus II (d. 1124) decreed that two pilgrimages there equalled one to Rome and three were the equivalent of a pilgrimage to Jerusalem. A haunting early medieval Welsh poem describes a girl making a pilgrimage from Anglesey (*Mon* in Welsh) to St David's (*Mynyw*) down the west coast of Wales in penance for slaying a young man. It is no coincidence that one of the most striking effigies of a pilgrim in any church in the British Isles should be found in Llandyfodwg Church in Glamorganshire, nor that one of the greatest of all pilgrim hymns, 'Guide me, O Thou Great Redeemer' comes from the heart of Welsh Nonconformity, being written in 1745 by the Calvinistic Methodist poet from Carmarthenshire, William Williams, Pantycelyn.

Wales has also been at the forefront of one of the most interesting developments in the recent revival of pilgrimage. Small Pilgrim Places is a project that was set up in 2000 by Jim Cotter, an Anglican priest who is now rector of Aberdaron (see page 146), to keep open small country churches where there are not enough people to sustain regular Sunday worship. Each afternoon in the summer months a volunteer, known by the ancient medieval name of hospitaller, is on duty to welcome visitors. There are times of prayer, periods of silence and a meditation trail which takes visitors round the church and churchyard, alerting them to what they can see and inviting them to ponder and reflect. In Cotter's words:

People appreciate a church being open. Better still, if there is somebody there to welcome the visitor. In every tourist there is a pilgrim waiting to be recognized. Those who have been battered by life, the vulnerable and the wounded, the shy, the seekers: they are the ones who might like to slip into a small church, off the beaten track, hardly noticed. A place to be, a place for silence, a place for pondering, a place of unobtrusive welcome.[1]

Cotter especially remembers the very last visitors to the remote church at Llandecwyn, 600 feet (180 metres) above the estuary of the River Dwyryd, on the last afternoon that it was open in the 2003 season. They were a Muslim family from Birmingham who sat quietly in the church for ten minutes or so. At the end of their visit, the father came up to him and said, 'Thank you, I find I can pray here.'

One of the most atmospheric Welsh pilgrim places is Pennant Melangell, hidden away in the Berwyn Hills in mid-Wales. The only vehicular access is via a long and narrow track with high hedges on either side and few passing places. The story goes that in the early seventh century Melangell, the daughter of an Irish chieftain, left her homeland to escape an arranged marriage and to pursue her vocation to the religious life. She came to this remote spot and found it an ideal place to pursue the solitary life of contemplative prayer. One day, soon after arriving, she was startled by the appearance in the valley of a local prince out hunting with his dogs. The hare that they were chasing took refuge under the hem of Melangell's cloak. Amazingly, the dogs were held back by some strange power from pursuing the hare. The prince and the maiden spoke. He was impressed with her calling and devotion and promised to give her land in

the valley to set up a religious community and not to hunt again in that place.
A community of sisters gathered round Melangell and when she died her grave
became known as a place of healing and sanctuary for men and women in
distress as well as for hunted animals. During the 1150s the local landowner
rebuilt the church and replaced the simple grave of the saint with a magnificent

The restored
medieval shrine
of Melangell in
Pennant Melangell
Church

Statue of Mary at
Holywell

stone shrine in the chancel set up on pillars and decorated capitals. This was later moved to a little room attached to the east end of the church

The church at Pennant Melangell fell into considerable disrepair in the twentieth century, but it was saved thanks to the vision and dedication of one or two individuals. The medieval shrine has been reconstructed and replaced in its original place behind the altar in the chancel. It stands there now as a remarkable and rare example of a religious artefact that was almost completely destroyed during the Reformation and as an eloquent and moving reminder of the profound reverence felt by the Welsh for their Celtic Christian ancestors, great and small. The restored church was reopened for regular prayer and worship in 1992 and since then has been a mecca for pilgrims coming both alone and in groups. The adjoining buildings house a counselling and respite care centre for those suffering from cancer and other terminal illnesses, thus bringing Melangell's shrine a new role as a sanctuary of healing and hope.

The most visited Welsh pilgrim shrine is St Winefride's Well at Holywell in north-east Wales, which describes itself on road signs as 'the Lourdes of Wales'. Its foundation legend dates from the same time as the church at Pennant Melangell and also involves a pious and simple girl encountering an aggressive and manly warrior. In this case, Winefride, an innocent local girl, was accosted by Caradoc, the son of a neighbouring priest, while her parents were at Mass. Having come thirsty from hunting, he asked for a drink and then set about seducing her. Escaping from his clutches, she fled towards the church. Just before she reached the sanctuary of its porch, Caradoc caught up with her and in a moment of rage hacked her head from her body. Beuno, Winefride's uncle, came out of the church and immediately cursed the prince, who died instantly, whereupon the earth opened up and swallowed his body. Beuno then prayed that Winefride might be restored to life. Miraculously, her severed head was reattached to her body and the only sign she subsequently bore of the terrible attack was a thin white line around her neck. Winefride went on to become a nun and lived for another twenty-two years after her decapitation.

A spring gushed forth at the spot where Winefride's severed head had fallen and became a place of healing and pilgrimage. The earliest account of a healing there comes from the mid-twelfth century and concerns a man whose wrists had been bound for many years in iron chains as a penance. Hands miraculously appeared in the waters of the well and unfastened his chains. In 1119 a Cistercian monastery was founded at Basingwerk, a mile or so down the valley from Holywell, to look after the growing number of pilgrims coming to the well. Its romantic ruins can be reached today via a pleasant walk through the Greenfield Abbey industrial heritage trail, which leads down from Holywell to the Flintshire coast. Among the pilgrim routes to Holywell developed in the Middle Ages was one that started at St David's in south-west Pembrokeshire and came via *Strata Florida*, the Cistercian monastery in mid-Wales that claimed to

Holywell: A Place of Healing and Renewal

During Holywells' pilgrim season, from 1 April to 30 September, there is a brief service at 11.30 a.m. every day at the foot of St Winefride's statue. Her relic, a fingernail encased in a silver holder, is brought out of a battered suitcase to be exhibited and venerated. The pilgrim deputed to hold the relic is given a special stole to wear and a simple liturgy ends with a prayer to God to protect and bless pilgrimage. Traditionally, pilgrims plunged three times into the cold waters of the well, climbing down the steps at one side of the crypt and exiting on the other side. Nowadays, the pool under the crypt,

where the water bubbles up, is largely forsaken by bathers in favour of the large outdoor stone bath in front of the chapel. A trio of yellow and blue bathing tents more appropriate to a Moroccan beach provide somewhere to change, but the last time I was there they were ignored by a rowdy group of Liverpudlians who simply plunged fully clothed into the outdoor pool and swam several lengths. A tap by the side of the bath allows pilgrims to fill up containers with holy water, which is also on sale in plastic bottles in the adjoining shop.

Today the well is administered by the local Catholic parish on behalf of the diocese of Wrexham. An interpretative centre opened by Cardinal Cormac Murphy O'Connor in 2005 tells the history of the well and explains its contemporary significance in terms of pilgrims symbolically renewing their own baptismal vows and incorporating themselves anew into Christ by plunging into the cold waters and rising again. The many testimonies to Holywell's reputation for healing miracles include piles of crutches stacked up against the wall. A group of French nuns are renovating a building nearby as a community and retreat centre. Altogether this is a bizarre place to come across in the middle of a traditionally Nonconformist and now very secular land. On the several occasions that I have been there the atmosphere has been rather less reverential and quiet than at Lourdes, but it does have something of the same attraction for the distressed in mind and body craving healing. Perhaps with its particular history Holywell can speak especially to women who have been the victims of male violence and abuse.

Left: The source of the Holywell waters - the pool under the Crypt

Below: Crutches left by cured pilgrims and piled up against the wall of the Holywell museum

A pilgrim swimming in the stone bath at Holywell

possess the Holy Grail, the chalice used by Jesus at the Last Supper. Another route, which began at Shrewsbury where Winefride's relics were brought in 1138, was walked by King Henry V in 1416.

Early in the sixteenth century, on the initiative of Lady Margaret Beaufort, the mother of King Henry VII, a two-storey crypt and chapel was built over the well. A unique example of late perpendicular Gothic, it is now a Grade 1 Listed Building. Holywell was one of very few places of pilgrimage in the British Isles that survived the Reformation. It continued to attract pilgrims throughout the later sixteenth and the seventeenth century and became a symbol of Catholic defiance and identity. It underwent a significant revival in the later nineteenth century, especially during the 1890s when the parish priest, Father Charles Beauclerk, organized public processions through the town and commissioned banners. In 1913 a branch line was built off the main Chester-Holyhead railway specifically for pilgrims.

Holywell remains a major place of pilgrimage today, attracting more than 30,000 people every year. More than 48,000 votive candles are lit annually at the foot of the statue of Winefride that stands just inside the crypt. There is a national pilgrimage on the Sunday closest to 22 June and a special pilgrimage for the handicapped on Whit Sunday. Members of the United Kingdom's Polish community come on the last Sunday of July; there are dedicated days for Italian pilgrims in August and September; and an annual pilgrimage organized by the Knights of St Columba on the last Sunday in September closes the pilgrim season.

The most evocative pilgrim place in Wales is Bardsey Island – *Ynys Enlli* in Welsh – which lies off the remote Llŷn peninsula at the far north-western corner of the country. Known as the island of 20,000 saints, its sacred connections may well go back to pre-Christian times and belong to Celtic mythology about the isles of the blessed lying far in the west beyond the setting sun. In early Christian times, numerous monks seem to have gone there, possibly towards the end of their lives, seeking 'the place of resurrection' that was so important in Irish monastic spirituality. They included St Beuno, Winefride's uncle and a key figure in the evangelization of North Wales; St Dyfrig, a bishop and missionary in south-east Wales whose relics were later taken to Llandaff Cathedral; and St Deiniol, the first bishop of Bangor. For others Bardsey seems to have been a place of refuge from persecution by the pagan Saxons – 900 monks are said

Chapel on Bardsey Island

> '… the mariners seemed tinctured with the piety of the place; for they had not rowed far before they made a full stop, pulled off their hats, and offered up a short prayer'.

**Thomas Pennant,
Welsh traveller**

to have fled there after a particularly bloody massacre in Bangor. An early Welsh poem speaks of the ground being 'as thick with the graves of holy men as the cells in a honeycomb'.

Bardsey became a major pilgrim destination from the twelfth century at least, if not earlier. In a document dating from around 1120 it is described as 'the Rome of Britain' on account of its distance and sanctity and because of the contact it afforded with the apostles who had brought the gospel to Wales and who were, in their own way, as important as St Peter and St Paul. Throughout the Middle Ages there was a monastic community on the island. Pilgrimages came to an end at the Reformation and the monastic buildings fell into decay, but the reputation of Bardsey as a holy place continued. In 1773 the Welsh traveller, Thomas Pennant, crossing over to the island from Aberdaron on the tip of the Llŷn peninsula, noted that 'the mariners seemed tinctured with the piety of the place; for they had not rowed far before they made a full stop, pulled off their hats, and offered up a short prayer'. When in the 1870s the owner of Bardsey, Lord Newborough, offered the islanders the choice of a jetty or a chapel, they chose the latter, and a Calvinistic Methodist Chapel was built that is now used by those who come on retreat. The population dwindled through the twentieth century and by 1972 there was just one resident family left. In 1979 the island was acquired by a charitable trust committed to preserving its wildlife and religious sites.

The number of pilgrims going to Bardsey has grown greatly over recent decades. In 1950 the bishop of Bangor, J.C. Jones, led the first major pilgrimage in recent times. In the 1970s G.O. Williams, archbishop of Wales, who chaired the council of the Bardsey Island Trust, wrote:

> I see Bardsey as a place of pilgrimage into fuller, deeper life. It is a very special place that helps us to see that all places are special. I try not to be fanciful but the feeling that I have is that the air of Bardsey is impregnated with Spirit, as though the practice of prayer down the ages had soaked into the soil … It is a kind of school in which I can come to know myself better. I know this to be true of some who would not venture to make an explicitly Christian confession of faith or affirm avowedly theistic belief. They too feel that the island is holy, that it is a special place set aside from the ordinary to be a means of encounter with deeper reality.[2]

There was another major pilgrimage to Bardsey in 1992. Nowadays the island is a centre for residential retreats with increasing numbers of pilgrims making the hazardous sea crossing to stay in one of the simple, restored buildings without electricity or mains water.

Bardsey is a destination that cries out to be walked to, and thanks to the creation of the Llŷn Coastal Path by Gwynedd Council it is relatively easy to follow the ancient pilgrim route again. One possible point of departure could, in fact, be Holywell, but there is no good path from there along the North Wales coast. The Llŷn Coast Path officially starts at Caernarfon Castle, one of the most majestic castles in Wales, and indeed in the world. However, perhaps the best starting place is the great pilgrim church at Clynnog Fawr. Dedicated to St Beuno, who is said to have founded it around AD 630, this church was hugely extended in the early sixteenth century to accommodate the vast crowds of pilgrims who were flocking to Bardsey at the tail end of the Middle Ages. It is a pilgrim church without parallel in the British Isles. Its features include a triple sedilia (ceremonial seat) in the chancery dating from c. 1400 and exquisitely carved stalls in the chancel dating from around 1500. The church houses an excellent display on the history and recent revival of the pilgrimage to Bardsey. It is said that in the Middle Ages invalids were carried into St Beuno's Chapel at Clynnog at nightfall to lie on the tombstones. If they slept through the night, a cure was assured.

From Clynnog pilgrims have the choice of either skirting the steep slopes of

'A lonesome little sanctuary by the sea, whose walls are hoary with age, within whose nave the story of the centuries in silence sleeps. Pilgrim of today, canst thou pass by without kneeling here to bless and to pray?'

Thomas Michaeliones, Rector of Pistyll church

Bwlch Mawr or ascending it and passing a great granite quarry, which has long been the bedrock of the local economy. About 10 miles (16 km) on, nestling by the coast, lies the ancient hospice church of Pistyll, also dedicated to St Beuno, which was much used by pilgrims who rested at an adjacent monastery. Lepers stood outside the church to receive the blessed sacrament. Since 1969 this tiny church has been decorated by wild herbs and rushes strewn on the floor at Christmas, Easter and the Lammas festival in early August. It was well described by its last rector, Thomas Michaeliones, as: 'A lonesome little sanctuary by the sea, whose walls are hoary with age, within whose nave the story of the centuries in silence sleeps. Pilgrim of today, canst thou pass by without kneeling here to bless and to pray?'

The pilgrim way meanders down the north side of the Llŷn Peninsula eventually reaching the village of Aberdaron, the traditional departure point for pilgrims taking the boat to Bardsey, many of whom often wait for several days for a chance to cross the perilous sound. Aberdaron's huge and spacious church stands next to the sea and is dedicated to St Hywyn, himself a pilgrim who sailed to Wales from Brittany in the sixth century and is credited with founding the monastic community on Bardsey. It has recently been restored with the needs

Above: The tower of Clyynog Fawr Church and the Carved Stalls inside the church

Left: Clynnog Fawr Church
Below: The view from Pystill Church

The inside of Pistyll Church, the floor strewn with rushes

of today's pilgrims in mind and is regularly used for retreats and quiet days. There are excellent interpretative displays on the history of the area and an extensive bookshop. Visitors to the church are invited to choose a stone from the pebbled beach outside, write their name on it and place it on the cairn laid out in a side aisle, the centre of which represents Christ, 'who is at the centre of all life and so belongs to us all'. The cairn opens each year on Easter Day and closes on the last Sunday in October with a special service in the church. The stones are blessed and returned to the sea 'where they become part of the great ocean once more, washed by the tides, shaped and turned by the waves in endless, timeless movements in the great dance of life'.

The incumbent at Aberdaron between 1967 and 1978 was the poet R.S. Thomas, who wrote much about pilgrimage. Thomas was also very taken with the idea of the absent God, especially the God who has just eluded us and left the room as we entered. His poem *Pilgrimages*, inspired by the lure of Bardsey, takes us to the heart of the paradox of pilgrimage: is it an inner or an outer journey – do we find God in the landscape, the sacred places, or is he there, dark and inexplicable, within us? Do we find him on the way, at our destination, or do we take him with us? Is the pilgrim landscape more than anything else a landscape of the mind?

There is an island there is no going
To but in a small boat the way
The saints went, travelling the gallery
Of the frightened faces of
The long-drowned, munching the gravel
Of its beaches. So I have gone
Up the salt lane to the building
With the stone altar and the candles
Gone out, and kneeled and lifted
My eyes to the furious gargoyle
Of the owl that is like a god
Gone small and resentful. There
Is no body in the stained window
Of the sky now. Am I too late?
Were they too late also, those
First pilgrims? He is such a fast
God, always before us and leaving as we arrive.

A labyrinth in Aberdaron Chuch. The present rector, Jim Cotter, has replaced it with a cairn

There are those here
Not given to prayer, whose office
Is the blank sea that they say daily.
What they listen to is not
Hymns but the slow chemistry of the soil
That turns saints' bones to dust,
Dust to an irritant of the nostril.

There is no time on the island.
The swinging pendulum of the tide
Has no clock; the events
Are dateless. These people are not
Late or soon; they are just
Here with only the one question
To ask, which life answers
By being in them. It is I
Who ask. Was the pilgrimage
I made to come to my own
Self, to learn that in times
Like these and for one like me
God will never be plain and
Out there, but dark rather and
  Inexplicable, as though he were in here?[3]

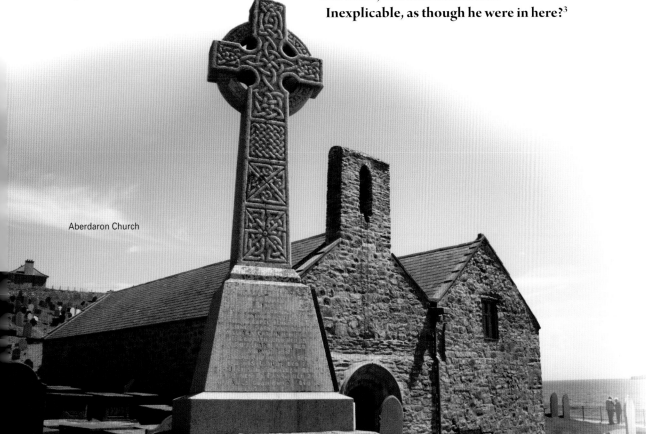

Aberdaron Church

Practicalities

More information on the Small Pilgrim Places project can be found on its website: www.smallpilgrimplaces.org.uk.

Holywell lies just off the main A55 North Wales expressway – those travelling west should exit at Junction 32 and those eastbound at Junction 31. The nearest railway station is five miles (8 km) away at Flint. The well is open every day from 10 a.m. to 4 p.m. (9 a.m. to 5.30 p.m. in the summer). Bathing is officially allowed between 9 a.m. and 10 a.m. in the summer and 10 a.m. and 11 a.m. in the winter but often seems to be permitted at other times. Further information can be found on the website: www.saintwinefrideswell.com.

The walk from Clynnog Fawr to Aberdaron is roughly 35 miles (55 km) and can be done comfortably in three days. There is an excellent booklet on the Llŷn Coastal Path produced by Gwynedd Council and up-to-date information on the route can be found on its website (www.gwynedd.gov.uk).

Residential retreats on Bardsey are available through the Carreg Trust (www.carregtruStorg.uk).

Nidaros

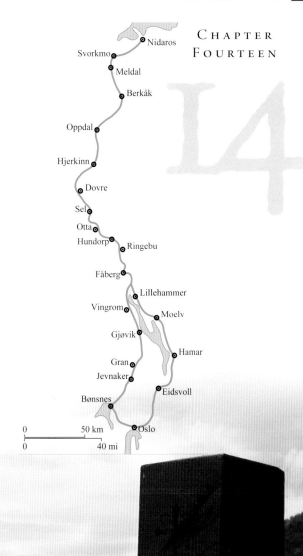

The shrine of St Olav at the cathedral at Nidaros – the old name for Trondheim, the city in the centre of Norway – is the most significant place of pilgrimage in Scandinavia. The well-trodden 402-mile (643-km) medieval pilgrim way from Oslo was reopened in 1997 by Crown Prince Haakon Magnus, reinforcing the link that Olav himself established more than a thousand years ago between church and monarchy. Many other old pilgrim routes to Nidaros have also been re-established and are being walked again; in all there are now over 3,000 miles (5,000 km) of waymarked Olav pilgrim routes in Scandinavia.

Trondheim Cathedral

'The cult of St Olav brings together Norwegian national identity, Christian devotion and sacred monarchy.'

The cult of St Olav brings together Norwegian national identity, Christian devotion and sacred monarchy. Born in AD 995, Olav Haraldson was a Viking warrior who converted to Christianity while campaigning in Europe – possibly in England while involved in an attack on London in 1009, or possibly later in France. He was baptized in Rouen in 1013 and is said to have been visited by an angel who told him to return to his native Norway as its first Christian king. He seized power from the Danes in 1015 with the help of 220 skilled warriors and four English bishops and immediately set about the dual project of unifying and Christianizing the country, which had previously been a collection of autonomous regions. This he did by force, antagonizing many local chieftains who were deprived of their authority as pagan religious leaders and unchallenged rulers in their areas.

Olav was ousted from the Norwegian throne in 1028 by the Danish king Cnut, supported by many of the disgruntled chieftains. He went into exile in Kiev in Russia and, shunning an offer to become king of Bulgaria, returned in 1030 to Norway to try to regain power. On his way back he was killed at the Battle of Stiklestad, having been wounded three times after apparently throwing away his sword and shield. Olav's body was secretly taken by supporters and buried in sand near the River Nid. Rumours soon circulated about miraculous healings taking place around his grave. In 1031 Olav was declared a saint and a martyr and his body was laid in a casket. Pilgrims started coming in large numbers to venerate his relics, not just from Norway and the rest of Scandinavia but also from the British Isles and Continental Europe. The year 1100 saw the publication of *Passio et Miraculae Olavi,* which recorded details of his life and the miracles that were said to have taken place after his death, and had soon been disseminated widely through Europe. Olav is an ambiguous figure in many ways: pilgrim badges represent him seated on his throne with a crown on his head and wielding an axe, yet he is also seen as a Christ-like martyr who healed a wound in the hand of his murderer through his own blood.

Work began on the magnificent Gothic cathedral at Trondheim that housed Olav's shrine in the late twelfth century under the direction of Archbishop Øystein Erlendsson. Construction work was not completed until around 1300. Since then, Trondheim Cathedral has had to be substantially rebuilt five times following serious fires. The present building largely dates from the late nineteenth and early twentieth centuries but it retains its Gothic splendour. The largest cathedral in Scandinavia, it dominates the Trondheim skyline and is especially suited to processions and big public occasions. It is used for the service of blessing that since 1908 has taken the place of a coronation when a new Norwegian monarch comes to the throne.

In the hundred years or so before the Black Death hit Norway in 1349, Nidaros was the fourth most important pilgrim destination after Rome, Jerusalem and Santiago. A network of hospices and overnight shelters were developed along the paths that brought pilgrims to Olav's shrine from the north, south and west of Norway and through the eastern valleys from Sweden. Every 5 or 6 miles (8 or 10 km), resting and grazing places known as Olav fields were provided for horses, and several of the springs and wells along the way became famous for their healing powers. The coming of the Reformation in the 1540s put an end to all this and the shrine containing the saint–king's relics was destroyed.

The revival of pilgrimage to Nidaros over the last twenty years has come about as a result of church and state collaborating in response to popular enthusiasm. Groups of pilgrims began coming to Trondheim in the late 1980s. In 1992 the Lutheran Church of Norway employed Arne Bakken as its first full-time pilgrim pastor to minister to them, and in the same year the Norwegian Ministry of the Environment committed itself to re-establishing the pilgrim way from Oslo, negotiating with landowners to secure rights of way and entrusting twenty-nine local authorities or *kommuner* with the task of providing signposts along their section of the route. These vary between solid granite milestones indicating the distance still to travel to Nidaros, modern blue enamel signs indicating the direction of the *Pilegrimsleden,* and stakes with red painted tops, decorated with the logo chosen to mark the pilgrim path. Combining the Christian cross of Olav with the circular sign used to designate cultural and historic monuments in Norway, the logo symbolizes the collaboration of church and state and the mingling of spiritual and cultural factors that lies behind the redevelopment of the pilgrim way, which has been deliberately

A Walk to the Shrine of St Olav

My wife and I joined a group of sixteen pilgrims, half from Norway and half from Denmark, to walk for six days along the last 63 miles (101 km) of the main Oslo–Nidaros path, a distance which qualified us to receive the official *Olavsbrevet* signed by the bishop of Nidaros. Some of our companions had already spent a week walking over the Dovre mountains. Our route took us past red-painted farmhouses, many of them now deserted, along main roads and through meadows, bogs and woods where we marvelled at the variety of wild orchids and picked blueberries and wild raspberries. We slept on school floors, in old farmhouses and even in the clubhouse of a shooting club in the middle of a forest. Our most romantic overnight stop was in the beautifully restored outbuildings of a pig farm at Sundet, which we reached by being rowed across the Gaula River, exactly as medieval pilgrims were.

Like all good pilgrimages, this one had its own routine and rhythm.

Crossing the River Gaula

Rising for an early morning service (not difficult if one has been sleeping on a mat in a school gymnasium), we then walked through the morning. A long stop for lunch and a mid-day service was followed by an hour or so of walking in silence. We usually arrived at our destination in time for a rest before the evening meal (the stores, like our sleeping bags and mattresses were transported ahead) and an evening service. These were sometimes held in one of the churches along the route, which included the unusual Y-shaped wooden Rennebu Kirke at Voll built in 1669, the highly ornate church at Meldal painstakingly rebuilt after a disastrous fire and the twelfth-century stone church in Skaun with its magnificent altar frontal dating from the height of the medieval pilgrim boom. In Skaun Church, we were addressed by Jules Bahati, who came to Norway in 2002 as an asylum seeker after being imprisoned in his native Congo. He is now the church's bell-ringer. He movingly compared modern asylum seekers to medieval pilgrims.

Our leader, Hans-Jacob Dahl, was himself the third pilgrim priest to be appointed in Norway and is now pastor of Dovre. He combines an encyclopaedic knowledge of natural history and local culture with a strong pastoral sensitivity, leading our group in discussion each evening on the biblical roots of pilgrimage and our own motivations today. For one 72-year-old lady from the island of Öland off the south-east coast of Sweden this pilgrimage was the fulfilment of a lifetime's ambition to walk to the shrine of St Olav. For a middle-aged Danish businessman it offered space in a busy life for thinking, praying and 'finding God in his creation, both big and small'.

The pilgrim liturgy that we used relied heavily on the psalms and the rich collection of Scandinavian pilgrim hymns, including the classic '*Deilig er jorden, prektig er Guds himmel, skjøer er sjelenes pilgimsgang!*' by Bernhard Ingemann. Another of his hymns was loosely translated into English by Sabine Baring-Gould as 'Through the night of doubt and sorrow, onward goes the pilgrim band'.

On our arrival in Trondheim on the eve of St Olav's Day we gradually met up with pilgrims who had come by other routes as well as with a group that had been a day ahead of us along the way from Oslo, some of whom had made the full thirty-two-day walk from the Norwegian capital. At 7 p.m. in the evening, three pilgrimages set off from different churches in outlying parts of the city. Each group walked in procession towards the city centre, stopping off at churches along the way for a hymn, prayers, a reflection and a reading from the Olav saga. At 10 p.m. the three groups joined up for a service outside a city centre church and then we walked together around the cathedral, pausing for further songs, prayers and readings by the river and in front of the magnificent west front, filled with statues of kings, apostles, prophets and saints including St James, the great apostolic pilgrim, garlanded for his own festival on July 25. We finally entered the cathedral at 11 p.m. for an hour-long vigil service, the *Olavsvaka* (Olav wake). It remained open throughout the night for personal prayer, with the choir chanting the monastic offices every hour until 6 a.m. when Lauds was sung.

The high point of the celebrations came at 11 a.m. on the morning of St Olav's Day when the cathedral was packed for the celebratory Eucharist, the *Oslokhøymesse*. I found myself robed as a Lutheran priest joining a procession of clergy from many different countries and traditions, including a delegation from the Russian Orthodox Church, and helping to dispense communion. There are special daily pilgrim masses throughout the following week and also a huge festival, the *Olavfest*, which mixes religious and secular entertainment, blending lectures on pilgrimage with jazz concerts, medieval entertainers with poetry readings and an opera café with concerts of sacred music in the cathedral.

Pilgrims are given special treatment throughout these festivities. They are given a sticker that allows free entry to the cathedral and are welcomed at the Pilgrims' House, a red wooden building prominently sited opposite the west front of the cathedral, which is the base for the current pilgrim priest, the ebullient Rolf Synnes, and offers a constant supply of waffles, coffee and sandwiches as well as housing a good library on pilgrimage. It is here that pilgrims receive their *Olavsbrevet*, having first filled in a questionnaire asking them to specify whether they have made the pilgrimage for reasons of historical interest, social contact, cultural interest, nature, religious belief or health. There is great openness in Norway about pilgrimage and no probing of people's motives or the depth of their faith. Rolf Synnes says: 'Those who now follow marked pilgrim routes have completely different reasons for

making their journey. No one has the right to criticize other people's reasons and motivations. Regardless of whether exercise, culture or faith is seen as the most important factor, we deserve the same respect.' Throughout the *Olavfest* there are events in the garden in front of the pilgrim house – we enjoyed a barbecue after which we sat under a canopy listening to Jonas Ahner, a Swedish pilgrim priest, meditating on Olav as a Christ-like figure and a symbol of vulnerability as well as aggression. As he put it, 'we have to walk to the meaning that God has given us'.

Pilgrims resting on the way to Nidaros. Hans-Jacob Dahl, the group's leader is in the foreground with a red jersey.

1. Through the night of doubt and sorrow
onward goes the pilgrim band,
singing songs of expectation,
marching to the promised land.

2. Clear before us through the darkness
gleams and burns the guiding light;
brother clasps the hand of brother,
stepping fearless through the night.

3. One the light of God's own presence
o'er his ransomed people shed,
chasing far the gloom and terror,
brightening all the path we tread;

4. One the object of our journey,
one the faith which never tires,
one the earnest looking forward,
one the hope our God inspires:

5. One the strain that lips of thousands
lift as from the heart of one:
one the conflict, one the peril,
one the march in God begun:

6. One the gladness of rejoicing
on the far eternal shore,
where the one almighty Father
reigns in love for evermore.

7. Onward, therefore, pilgrim brothers,
onward with the cross our aid;
bear its shame and fight its battle,
till we rest beneath its shade.

Sabine Baring-Gould (1834–1924) based on a Danish poem, Igjennem Nat og Traengsel, by Bernhardt Severin Ingemann (1789–1862)

routed to take in historic churches, farms and outdoor museums. There is, in fact, a choice of routes for those starting out from Oslo: the western 'cultural' path avoids going through an industrial area and skirts the west side of Lake Mjøsa before joining up north of Lillehammer with the eastern path, which follows the medieval pilgrims' route via Hamar.

Most of the organized pilgrimages to Trondheim take place in the weeks leading up to St Olav's Day on 29 July. Pilgrims making the long walk from Oslo start around 25 June while those coming from various starting points in Sweden set off in early July. An ancient and well-established route from Borgsjö takes twenty-five days, following the *Stora vägen*, which crosses central Sweden from east to west. This was, in fact, the way taken by Olav himself on his ill-fated journey to regain the Norwegian crown, which ended at Stiklestad. Today's pilgrims pause at the site of his death, where there is a national culture centre, a restored medieval church with an unusual series of wall paintings of biblical scenes dating from 1688, and an open-air stage where a drama about the martyr king is performed every July. From Stiklestad the pilgrim way to Trondheim takes another seven days' walking. Some individual pilgrims are on the road for even longer. In 2007 I met two students who had begun walking from Göteborg in the south of Sweden on 15 June and who were averaging 18 miles (30 km) a day in their determination to be in Trondheim for St Olav's Day. More leisurely pilgrims can pause on the way for special events and retreats: in 2007 a special pilgrim weekend at Dovre, high up in the mountains on the main Oslo-Trondheim route, brought people together to reflect on the spirituality of Hildegaard of Bingen. Increasingly, shorter, more localized pilgrimages are also being organized in the early weeks of July.

Finn Wagle, bishop of Nidaros since 1991, has been a strong supporter of the pilgrimage to Nidaros. To mark the tenth anniversary of its re-establishment, he spoke at a reception in the splendidly restored Archbishop's Palace – which also houses the Liturgical Centre for the Church of Norway – about the impact that it has made on many people's lives. Among those who have walked the entire way from Oslo are a group of prisoners, at least one of whom was directly inspired by the experience

to turn his life around. In 1997 a
76-year-old Finnish general walked the
whole *Pilegrimsleden* barefoot to atone
for the number of people whom he
had killed during his long career in the
army. Bishop Wagle described this act
of penance as 'a bridge to the Middle
Ages'. In 2007 a group of asylum seekers
from Afghanistan, most of whom were
Muslim, made the pilgrimage, singing
Norwegian hymns as they went. 'I have never met so many young, sad and
heavily lined faces' said the bishop.

One of the blue
enamel signs used to
mark St Olav's Way.
This sign uses the
Nynorsk language
(Pilegrimsleia rather than
Pilegrimsleden)

As yet pilgrimage to Nidaros is still on a relatively small scale and much
of the infrastructure along the way needs to be developed if it is to fulfil its
ambition of becoming the northern equivalent of the *camino* to Santiago. But
it has great potential and significant strides are being made. In 2008 a new
pilgrim hostel and centre was opened near the cathedral in a building given
by the government and previously used by the armed forces. The Norwegian
minister of culture has recently expressed his enthusiasm for developing the
infrastructure. The church also has a part to play. Nearly all the churches along
the route are currently locked. This is principally for insurance reasons and
is understandable in the case of the wooden churches, which are particularly
susceptible to fire. Their magnificent painted baroque altar screens, pulpits and
organ lofts deserve to be seen and enjoyed by pilgrims, however, and it is to be
hoped that further constructive collaboration between church and state will
enable them to become more accessible to those who walk the *Pilegrimsleden*.

Practicalities

Those wishing to walk part of the St Olav's Way to Nidaros can join it at various
points by train as the main Oslo–Trondheim railway line runs relatively close
to much of the route. Useful stations include Hamar, Lillehammer, Dovre
and Berkak. Waymarking is rather sparse in places and there is a dearth of
accommodation en route. Highly recommended are the organized group
pilgrimages led by pilgrim pastors in the weeks leading up to St Olav's Day on
which food, accommodation and transport of baggage are all arranged. Details
of these can be found on the excellent website www.pilgrim.info, which is
lovingly maintained by Eiler Prytz. Organized tours are also provided by the
Norwegian company Pilgrimtours (www.pilgrimtours.no). Information on the
Olavfest can be found on www.olavfestdagene.no.

The Danish pilgrim website is www.pilgrimsvandring.dk and the one for the
Swedish pilgrim centre at Vadstena is www.pilgrimscentrum.se.

Assisi

Pilgrimages to Assisi are focused on one particular individual, St Francis, whose witness and message of a radically simple lifestyle, a care for all creation and the imperative of peace is, if anything, more relevant now that during his lifetime in the thirteenth century. As a result, in addition to attracting thousands of tourists, this attractive walled town in Umbria draws religious and political leaders from around the world for meetings on the themes of world peace, ecology and conservation. In January 2002 the pope gathered leaders of the major world faiths there in the aftermath of the 9/11 terrorist attacks. At the other end of the scale, Third Order Franciscans and others seeking to emulate the simple lifestyle of Francis make their way to Assisi on foot along one of several newly waymarked pilgrim paths that follow in the footsteps of the saint's own wanderings in the region.

Tourism and pilgrimage overlap in Assisi as much as anywhere. In a shop on one of the steep streets of this hill town, a white plastic dove of peace whizzes giddily round and round on a wire suspended from the ceiling. In another I saw for the first and only time on my travels the term 'Pilgrim' used as a designer label for a range of women's fashions. There are any number of statuettes of Francis, usually posing with birds or animals at his feet or in his hands, and crosses for sale in the shape of the Tau symbol, based on the letter T in the Hebrew and Greek alphabets, that he used for his signature and made his distinctive logo.

As elsewhere in Italy, however, the churches manage to strike a balance between the needs of tourists and pilgrims. The audio guide for the huge basilica where Francis is buried, which provides a spoken commentary for most locations, has a special spiritual section with plainchant to encourage a few moments of contemplation and does not provide a commentary for the two most sacred places in the church: the Chapel of Relics, which includes the saint's

The cloisters at the Basilica of St Francis in Assisi

tunic, shoes and the original rule of his order; and the crypt containing his tomb. This is the ultimate destination for most pilgrims to Assisi and is a quiet sanctuary always full of people praying. The grill protecting the actual tomb is stuffed with photographs of those who are ill or have recently died. In the two-storey basilica above, packed with tourists and art lovers marvelling at the frescoes by Giotto, Lorenzetti, Cimabue and others that miraculously survived the severe earthquake of 1997, guards dressed in military-style uniforms and wearing peaked caps try to maintain a reverential atmosphere by barking out 'Silencio' at regular intervals.

The other main place of pilgrimage within the town of Assisi is the shrine of Francis' friend and follower, Clare, who like him forsook the comforts of a well-to-do upbringing for the austere and ascetic disciplines of the dedicated religious life. Her remains lie in a glass case in the crypt of the basilica built to house her tomb in the latter part of the thirteenth century. A notice nearby says: 'Her blessed remains are kept here where they can be venerated by pilgrims.' Hanging in a side chapel of this basilica is the simple twelfth-century crucifix before which Francis prayed at

God, our saviour and guide,
Who by your calling, summon us
To live as pilgrims for Christ.
Help us to travel light,
To trust your promises,
And to follow in the footsteps of the saints.

God, the source of our joy,
You gladden our hearts
As we journey towards the heavenly city.
Deepen within us a desire for peace,
A longing to see your justice done;
That sharing a common purpose,
Your people may prosper and come
To praise you with the songs of Zion.

Christopher Irvine, The Pilgrims' Manual

the age of twenty-four when, following a period in the army, he was seeking inspiration as to what he should do next. Gazing at the crucifix, he felt that he heard the voice of God saying, 'Do you not see that my house is falling

The Spirituality of St Francis

Not surprisingly, it is the places off the tourist track to the main basilicas that speak most eloquently to pilgrims of the character of Franciscan spirituality. One such for me is the little Pilgrim Oratory built in 1457 by the Confraternity of St Anthony Abbot and St James of Compostela to welcome and refresh poor pilgrims coming to the tomb of Assisi. Today it is used as a chapel by the Franciscan Missionary Sisters of Assisi, founded in 1702 and committed to the Franciscan values of conversion, penance, fraternity, poverty, prayer and practical works of mercy. A building on one of the main streets leading to St Francis' Basilica houses an interesting exhibition of the work of the Sisters, who since 1902 have been engaged in missionary and charitable work in many of the poorest parts of the world. It is just one of the many houses belonging to religious orders around Assisi, several of which provide accommodation for pilgrims.

Another atmospheric place for pilgrims is the small crypt in the Via Antonio Cristofani, which is used for Anglican services. It has a fine fourteenth-century mural of St Francis and St Leonard. I was one of just four worshippers there at a Eucharist celebrated by Brother Thomas of the Society of Saint Francis on the festival of the stigmata, which commemorates Francis receiving Christ-like wounds in his hands from a four-winged angel. He is said to be the first Christian saint to have received the stigmata. The most recent recipient was the Italian Franciscan priest Padre Pio, reported to have received the wounds in 1918. His grave in San Giovanni Rotondo has become a very popular shrine and is now the fastest growing pilgrim destination in Italy. It is quite often combined with Assisi in pilgrimage tours.

into ruins? Go then and repair it for me.' At first he took the command literally and set about physically repairing the crumbling churches in the town, but later he realized that it was a call to revive the church as a whole and set about establishing his itinerant order of mendicant friars to live out the gospel in a simple and direct way.

It is beyond the walls and away from the rather over-crowded streets of Assisi, however, that one gains a real sense of the lingering presence of St Francis and the nature of his continuing call to Christians. About 3 miles (5 km) outside the town, up a steep track which the hardy can tackle on foot and the less fit by taxi, is the hermitage known as Carceri, an ancient refuge for Christian anchorites that Francis appropriated as one of his many remote retreats. The buildings, which cling perilously to the side of Mount Subasio, enclose the rock chamber that Francis used as his cell. Behind a wooden balustrade is the rough

Above: Mural in the crypt in *Via Antonio Cristofani* used for Anglican services

Left: St Francis' cell at Carceri

Opposite page: The Basilica of St Clare, Assisi

The refectory at San Damiano

rocky floor that served as his bed. It is a good place from which to gain a sense of his extreme asceticism. Francis eschewed large communal monasteries for remote huts and caves and was himself a perpetual pilgrim, always wandering to ever more desolate places to be alone and nearer to God. A tree beside the path leading from the Hermitage to an open-air worship area is said to have been one on which birds perched while he preached to them.

Even more evocative is San Damiano, a small complex of buildings surrounded by fields just outside the walled city and dating originally from the eleventh century, where St Clare founded her community of poor sisters. It was in the church here that Francis contemplated the crucifix that was to change his direction in life – it was moved to the Basilica of St Clare when the Poor Clares left San Damiano after the death of their foundress in 1253. It was here also in 1225 that Francis wrote his famous 'Canticle of the Creatures' after, it is said, living for fifty days in a little straw hut in the garden. A modern statue of him stands in the place where he composed it. San Damiano still has a very prayerful atmosphere. A panel above the choir stalls in the little church bears the Latin inscription: '*Non vox sed votum, non clamor sed amor, non cordula sed cor psallat in aure Dei*' (Not voice but desire, not noise but love, not instruments but the heart singing in the ear of God).

As with many of the Franciscan sites, San Damiano is now the home of a small community of Friars Minor. The Marquess of Lothian, whose family owned the monastic buildings for many years, restored it to the friars in 1983 on condition that it remained primarily 'a place of prayer for pilgrims seeking inspiration from the life and teaching of St Francis'. They are helped in this work by three nuns from the Franciscan Missionaries of the Immaculate Heart of Mary, founded in Egypt. Through a little grille by the entrance to the cloisters, one of them, Sister Clothilde who comes from Malta, told me that they see their job as being to maintain an atmosphere of silence that

The garden where Francis wrote the Canticle of the Creatures

allows pilgrims to contemplate and pray quietly in the church and the adjoining convent buildings, which are still much as they were in Clare's time, with the original refectory and dormitory preserved. They do a good job: notices enjoining 'silence, respect and decorum' seem to be obeyed here more than at other churches around Assisi. The sisters also provide a counselling and listening ministry to the many people who come to San Damiano with burdens of guilt or anxiety to unload.

Doves in the cloisters of St Maria degli Angeli

There is another much more urban site in the valley below Assisi that attracts many pilgrims. The large nineteenth-century basilica of Santa Maria degli Angeli, which stands in a square in the suburban area near the railway station, encloses the tiny stone Portinuncula chapel where Francis founded his order of Friars Minor and which he always regarded as his true home. It was here that Clare received from him the religious habit and began her own order of Poor Clares. When Francis knew that he was dying, he asked to be brought back to this community and it was in its infirmary, on the site of which now stands the Chapel of the Transitus, that he died in 1226, just as the friars were singing the verse of his Canticle which welcomes 'Our Sister Bodily Death'.

The community buildings that Francis knew here consisted of a collection of wooden huts in a wooded area. It is almost impossible to imagine what it was like now as one stands in the heavy neo-Baroque splendour of the modern church. However, a pair of white doves still make their home in the adjoining

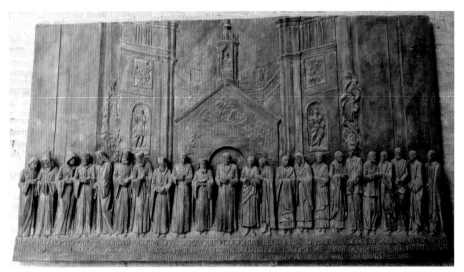

Left: Panel on the wall of St Maria degli Angeli commemorating a gathering of religious leaders from around the world in October 1986

Below: Pilgrim hostel behind St Maria degli Angeli.
Right: Cloisters at San Damiano

cloisters, a living reminder of the incident when Francis saved a basketful of doves that were being taken off to market and gave them nests around the friary. In the garden next to the cloisters there is a bed of roses without thorns, recalling another story of how, desiring to be scourged and chastened, he threw himself into a clump of thorny briars. On coming into contact with his body, the thorns miraculously disappeared and a bed of roses in bloom took the place of the briars.

Tucked away behind the church of Santa Maria degli Angeli is a small pilgrim hostel presided over by Angela Maria Seracchioli, a remarkable woman who has single-handedly created a 220-mile (350-km) pilgrim way along footpaths running from La Verna, the Tuscan mountain where Francis received the stigmata, southwards through Assisi and on to the Rieti Valley where he did much missionary work. Among the places it takes in is Greccio, where he famously set up the first-ever Christmas crib and nativity scene, using local people and a live ox and ass, to tell the story of Jesus' birth in a graphic way. Angela Seracchioli was fired to take up this project after making a pilgrimage in Tibet and then walking to Santiago de Compostela in the winter of 2002:

I felt an orphan after Compostela. Something changed in my life. All the way along the Camino, I felt the presence of my dead mother. I felt Francis walking with me too so when I got back to Italy, where I was working in mountain huts, I decided to make a long-distance walk for pilgrims to walk with him. The route is based on the places where he was and on accounts in his biographies.

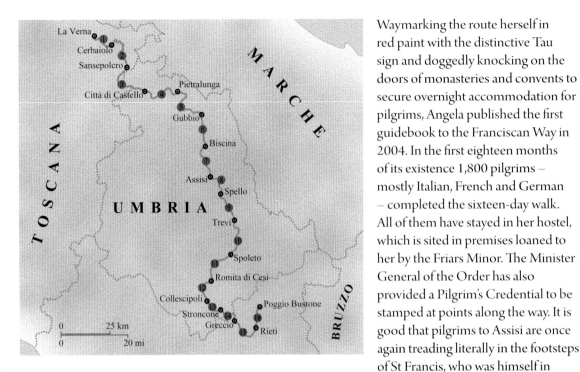

Map of the Franciscan Way from La Verna to the Riete Valley

Waymarking the route herself in red paint with the distinctive Tau sign and doggedly knocking on the doors of monasteries and convents to secure overnight accommodation for pilgrims, Angela published the first guidebook to the Franciscan Way in 2004. In the first eighteen months of its existence 1,800 pilgrims – mostly Italian, French and German – completed the sixteen-day walk. All of them have stayed in her hostel, which is sited in premises loaned to her by the Friars Minor. The Minister General of the Order has also provided a Pilgrim's Credential to be stamped at points along the way. It is good that pilgrims to Assisi are once again treading literally in the footsteps of St Francis, who was himself in many ways the pilgrim par excellence, forever on the move and, like the Son of Man to whom he devoted his life, having nowhere permanent to lay his head.

Martin Shaw, bishop of Argyll and the Isles in the Scottish Episcopal Church, who has led many pilgrimages to Assisi, has written that 'a Franciscan pilgrimage is about freedom from possession and allowing God to direct the details of life'. He recommends all pilgrims to repeat constantly the simple acclamation that Francis used to enter into a contemplative adoration of God: 'My God! My All!':

'Jesus replied, "Foxes have holes and birds of the air have nests, but the Son of Man has no place to lay his head."'

Matthew 8:20

Any pilgrimage to a holy shrine is pointless unless it is an awakening to that dynamic. If a pilgrimage to Assisi and its associated sanctuaries is to reach beyond nostalgia, history and art, then the prayer 'My God! My All!' prayed simply and constantly with St Francis will mean that there will be an immediacy, a presence which will bear with it its own awakening for the pilgrim.[1]

Practicalities

For those not coming on foot, Assisi can easily and cheaply be reached by train from Rome. The journey takes a couple of hours but make sure that you validate your ticket by stamping it in one of the (not very obvious) yellow machines at Roma Termini station. It is probably easier to book into one of the convents or

friaries if you are on an organized pilgrimage group. There are also numerous hotels and guest houses. Although the guidebooks advise getting a taxi to the Hermitage and asking it to wait for 45 minutes for the return trip, I would recommend anyone of reasonable fitness to walk back down through the oak and olive trees.

Mural of Francis and Clare contemplating the Virgin Mary and Jesus, the monastery of St Damiano

16 Częstochowa

Częstochowa is unique among the European pilgrim destinations featured in this book in that what draws people to it is a picture. Over four million people a year come to view a painting of the Virgin and Child known as the Black Madonna, which hangs behind the altar of a large chapel just off the main church in the monastery at Jasna Góra (or Shining Hill).Legend has it that the Black Madonna was painted in Nazareth by St Luke on the top of a table used by the Holy Family shortly after the assumption, and was later taken to Constantinople by the emperor Constantine. According to the excellent audio

'What continues to make Jasna Góra such an important place of pilgrimage today is undoubtedly its long association with Poland's national identity and survival, so often threatened by foreign invaders and occupiers.'

The main tower of the church at Jasna Góra

guide that leads visitors around Jasna Góra, it is rather a Byzantine icon dating from between the sixth and ninth century. In fact, the most recent and detailed analysis by art historians suggests that it is more recent and of Western rather than Eastern provenance, possibly a thirteenth-century Italian painting, repainted in the fourteenth century and reframed in the fifteenth.

Whatever its origins, the Black Madonna seems to have been in the possession of the monks of St Paul the First Hermit, an order that began in Hungary, since very shortly after the foundation of their monastery at Jasna Góra in 1382. It was given to them by Prince Ladislaus of Opole who had apparently found the painting in a Russian castle, which he had attacked while fighting the Tartars. In 1430 Bohemian followers of the early reformer, Jan Hus, looted the monastery at Jasna Góra and slashed the icon with their swords. This is said to be the reason for the prominent scars on the Virgin's right cheek.

Exactly when pilgrims started coming to venerate the painting of Our Lady of Częstochowa is not clear, but there were certainly substantial numbers by the end of the fifteenth century. What continues to make Jasna Góra such an important place of pilgrimage today is undoubtedly its long association with Poland's national identity and survival, so often threatened by foreign invaders and occupiers. A huge boost to the cult of Our Lady of Częstochowa occurred in 1655 when the heavily fortified monastery of Jasna Góra held out against Swedish attack. Its resistance proved a turning point in the bitter war between Sweden and Poland and in the following year King Jan Casimir proclaimed the Virgin Mary to be the queen of Poland and the shrine of Jasna Góra to be the Mount of Victory and the country's spiritual capital.

The peak pilgrim season to Częstochowa is in July and August, especially in the run-up to the Feast of the Assumption on 15 August when hundreds of thousands converge on the shrine from all over Poland. Many come on foot – the walk from Gdansk takes at least three weeks and from Warsaw nine days. They travel in organized parish and diocesan groups, often several hundred strong, stopping each evening at a church along the way for a service and a meal cooked by parishioners and staying overnight at people's homes or in

Jasna Góra: A National Shrine

Jasna Góra still has the feel of a castle as much as a monastery with canons standing in one corner of its heavily fortified battlements. Both its militaristic and patriotic associations were emphasized on the Sunday afternoon that I was there by the presence of a large number of Polish Air Force officers in full uniform among the pilgrims walking round the battlements following the Stations of the Cross. The stations are represented by fourteen massive bronze statues erected in 1913 on high stone pedestals around the perimeter of the monastery walls. At the head of the group, an Air Force colour party marched in tight formation between each of the stations with their flags held high. Other pilgrims carried red and white Polish flags, reinforcing the impression that Częstochowa is very much a national shrine. Over 90 per cent of those visiting it come from Poland and there are relatively few pilgrims from other countries.

local barns and schools. Katarzyna Potocka, who has made the walk several times, told me, 'For the first few days when you are still a long way off people are very friendly but the nearer you get to Częstochowa, the more pilgrims there are and you get less hospitality.' For the last few nights, pilgrims usually have to sleep in tents. Another regular pilgrim remembers the time when temperatures reached 99°F (37°C) and the asphalt on the roads was melting: 'the firemen in every village came out and hosed down the pilgrims with water as we passed'.

Many young people also go to Jasna Góra in April and May to pray for success in their exams. At other times of the year, it is common for groups of workers, like miners and shipbuilders, to hire coaches and travel together in large numbers to the shrine. Older people who can no longer make the pilgrimage cook food and offer pilgrims bottles of water.

Pilgrimages to Częstochowa reached a peak during the great Solidarity protests against Communism in the 1980s. Although there has been a slight fall-off in numbers since the collapse of Communism, it is still a hugely popular destination for Polish pilgrims. It is often impossible to get anywhere near the picture of the Black Madonna, barely visible behind a grille in the chapel where Masses are celebrated almost continually and the walls are covered by votive offerings and crutches left by pilgrims. The adjoining basilica is also often full of worshippers. The overall atmosphere of the shrine is a mixture of a family day out and a place of intense devotion. You will find couples trailing children clutching blow-up animals and balloons like a theme park or fun fair, whilst others enjoy the autumn sun at the hamburger and ice cream stalls in the area adjoining the vast car and coach parks at the back of the shrine, which also houses a large pilgrim hostel. On the ramparts high school bands can be found playing at the foot of the massive

'The overall atmosphere of the shrine was a mixture of a family day out and a place of intense devotion.'

statue of Pope John Paul II, which looks down over the sprawling industrial city below. Yet there is also a strong atmosphere of prayer and devotion both inside the basilica and in the courtyard outside where people wait on their knees as the host is consecrated. The votive offerings on display in the Treasury include numerous coral and amber rosaries and crucifixes brought by devout pilgrims over the last two centuries. Especially poignant are the artefacts made by the inmates of the nearby concentration camps during the Second World War.

Unlike most major pilgrim shrines, Częstochowa has little infrastructure. The monastic complex of Jasna Góra dominates the town and is reached by a long and impressive processional pedestrian way that climbs up the mound through parkland. It is remarkably self-contained, however, and seems to make almost no impact on the main town below. There is a complete absence of the usual shops selling rosaries and statues of the Virgin, which are confined to the area immediately around the monastery. All that the town has to offer is a rather eccentric museum of pilgrimage, opened in 2006 and tucked away half way along the main street, which mainly consists of old postcards of various pilgrim places and a rather thin display linking Częstochowa with other pilgrim places such as Lourdes, Loreto, Patmos, Fatima and Santiago. One senses that it is an attempt to integrate this very Polish shrine into the European mainstream. Interestingly, no mention is made of another major Marian pilgrimage shrine in Poland at Licheń, some 125 miles (200 km) north of Częstochowa, where a painting of the Madonna that is said to work miracles was brought to the church in 1852. A huge new basilica was built there in the late 1990s and according to some estimates Licheń now attracts more pilgrims than Częstochowa.

Statue of Pope John Paul II on the ramparts of the monastery at Jasna Góra

Stations of the Cross

A striking set of modern Stations of the Cross painted in 2000–2001 by the Polish artist Jerzy Duda Gracz decorate the walls of an unusual upper cloister built above the chapel that houses the Black Madonna. The eighteen murals depict Jesus against a background of contemporary figures and scenes: mitred bishops look on as he stumbles for the first time; the woman who offers him a handkerchief is portrayed as Mother Teresa; and Pope John Paul II stands at the foot of the cross as Jesus is dying. There is an extraordinary scene of the ascension where a semi-transparent Jesus rises above a mass of pilgrims gathered in the fields in front of Jasna Góra. The overall theme of these haunting murals is the loneliness of Christ and the incomprehension with which he was greeted by those around him.

For most visitors from other countries coming to Poland on pilgrimage, it is Krakow rather than Częstochowa or Licheń that is likely to be their destination. This is not just because of its beauty and history, which is also luring more and more tourists, but because of its central importance in the life of Pope John Paul II, who as Karol Wojtyla was a seminarian, priest and bishop there. A newly developed pilgrim trail round Krakow takes in the places where he lived and studied, including the soda factory where he was forced to work by the Nazis. The courtyard of the archdiocesan offices opposite the Franciscan church at 3 Franciszkansa Street houses an excellent display of photographs tracing his life story. In 2007 Polish Railways brought into service a special papal train,

Pociągem Papieskim, which runs three times a day in each direction between Krakow and Wadowice, Karol Wojtyla's birthplace. Intermediate stations allow pilgrims to explore churches associated with his long period as a priest in Poland. The carriages are fitted with screens showing videos on his life and there are special rates for pilgrim groups. A John Paul II Centre, which is currently being built on the edge of Krakow and which takes as its motto the words he spoke at the beginning of his Pontificate, 'Be not afraid', will house a retreat centre, a meeting place for young people and a centre for inter-faith dialogue.

More traditional pilgrims are also catered for in Krakow. Wawel Cathedral houses the magnificent silver shrine of Saint Stanislav, a bishop who, like Thomas à Beckett, was murdered on the orders of a king whom he had offended – in his case in 1079 – and became Poland's patron saint. Its crypt is filled with royal tombs. Like Częstochowa it is a place of national pilgrimage and the square outside is often filled with visiting primary school children dressed in national costume.

Perhaps the most evocative place of pilgrimage in Krakow is St Mary's Church in Rynek Główny, the great medieval square in the centre of the city. Its massive Gothic altarpiece, created by the German sculptor Veit Stoss between 1477 and 1489 and the largest of its kind in Europe, is a fulsome tribute to Mary and is bursting with gold and colour. At 11.50 a.m. every morning a nun appears before the altar, presses a remote control button to turn on some appropriately religious music and pushes back the central doors of the altarpiece with a long pole to reveal a stunning larger-than-life depiction of Mary falling asleep among the apostles with her assumption into heaven above it. The church, which also contains an unusual stone crucifix by Stoss, has a deeply

Below: Wavel Royal Cathedral, Wavel Hill, Krakow, Poland

St Mary's Church in
Rynek Glowny, the
square in the centre of
Krakow

prayerful atmosphere. A concert of sacred music put on there to celebrate the
twenty-ninth anniversary of Karol Wojtyla's election as pope and to support the
campaign for his canonization movingly brought together the proud patriotism,
staunch Catholicism and strong Marian devotion of a people whose faith has
been shaped by so much suffering.

Practicalities

Częstochowa can be reached by train from Krakow in about two and a half
hours. It is best to get a taxi from the station to Jasna Góra. The monastery is
open free of charge every day. The rear part of St Mary's Church in Krakow can
be entered free of charge by those wishing to pray. A small payment secures
entrance to the front part, recommended for gaining a good view of the
altarpiece.

Lourdes

17

The best way to come to Lourdes is undoubtedly
by train. The railway station has its own chapel, the
Oratoire Ste Bernadette, next to the main arrival and
departure platform and adjoining the Pavilion des
Malades, a special waiting room stocked high with
wheelchairs and triple-decker stretchers. There is
even a dedicated departure board for pilgrim trains.

Those arriving by rail from the direction of Paris and Bordeaux catch an early
glimpse of the grotto by the banks of the River Garve where the 14-year-old
Bernadette Soubirous apparently saw and spoke to the Virgin Mary in a series of
apparitions in 1858.

Plastic madonnas on sale in the Boulevard de la Grotte

It is because of these apparitions that this small Pyrenean town of around 15,000 inhabitants is one of the biggest pilgrim shrines in Europe with more than six million visitors a year, a considerable proportion of whom are sick or disabled.

Visitors are warned that they may find the atmosphere very commercial. Much of the literature on Lourdes, including such classics as Emile Zola's *Lourdes* (c. 1893) and J. K. Huysmans' *Les Foules de Lourdes* (1906) paints a picture of a resort town rather than a religious sanctuary. In fact it proves to be a moving blend of the sacred and the secular, combining faith, suffering and hope. Lourdes displays the mixture of piety, carnival, vulgarity, commerce and devotion that I imagine existed in the major medieval pilgrim cities. They were brought together in the sights that I took in as I sat one evening in one of the many pavement cafés in the Boulevard de la Grotte, which leads down to the sanctuary. At the adjoining table four nuns in immaculately starched white habits were sitting drinking beers. A folded wheelchair and a pair of crutches were parked next to the Pizzeria sign of the next door café where an elderly Dutch lady and her two daughters were eating. In the shops across the street rows and rows of gaudily-coloured plaster Madonnas, popes, saints and angels were stacked on shelves under a neon sign flashing the message: '*Tourisme et Religion*'. Hundreds of pilgrims clutching candles in paper holders were making their way down the crowded street past the Annunciation Bar and the Angelus Pub. They included Indians in saris, Japanese in baseball caps and nuns in every conceivable variety of habit, all en route to the torchlight procession through Rosary Square which takes place every evening in the summer and regularly attracts over 40,000 people.

For all the busy and brash vulgarity surrounding it, the sanctuary area in the centre of Lourdes is pervaded by an atmosphere of quiet respect and devotion. There is a palpable silence around the grotto where the Virgin appeared to Bernadette and where day and night a steady procession of pilgrims queues up to touch the cave walls, drop a prayer in the petition box and light a candle. Wherever you go you cannot fail to see pilgrims on their knees praying quietly, whether in front of the grotto, at the foot of one of the many crosses and statues or in one of the twenty-two different places of worship situated in the 130-acre (52-hectare) sanctuary or *domaine*, the vast sacred space shut off from the bustle of the surrounding town.

Although its shrine is relatively recent, Lourdes has long known both pilgrims and miraculous apparitions. It lay on medieval pilgrimage routes to Santiago, Rocamadour and Montserrat. The inhabitants of the Pyrenean region in which it is sited clung for much longer than those in most other parts of France to a magical pre-Christian outlook in defiance of the church's teaching and were renowned for their frequent apparitions and visions. They also have a long tradition of Marian devotion. At Garaison, 46 miles (75 km) away, the Blessed Virgin is said to have appeared three times to a twelve-year-old shepherdess in 1515. Another Marian shrine was established nearby at Betharram following her appearance to a group of shepherds around 1620. Over the next twenty years eighty-two further apparitions of the Virgin were recorded there.

So Bernadette Soubirous, who came from an impoverished family and was virtually illiterate, stood in a well-established local tradition in receiving a visitation from Mary. Her first encounter occurred on 11 February 1858 when she and her sister were out collecting firewood around a cave at the foot of a large rocky outcrop known as Mosabielle. She heard a noise like a gust of wind and looked up to see 'a young lady dressed in white' standing in a small crevice in the rock above the cave. Altogether, there were eighteen apparitions spread over the next six months, many of them witnessed by thousands of people, although only Bernadette could see or hear the woman. On her sixteenth appearance she announced

Pilgrims emerging from the grotto beneath the statue of Mary in the crevice where she appeared to Bernadette

her identity with the words, 'I am the immaculate conception', a revelation that helped to convince the initially highly sceptical ecclesiastical and civil authorities that the apparitions were authentic. The doctrine of the Immaculate Conception had only been defined by the pope four years earlier and Bernadette would have had no knowledge of such a complex theological term.

In one of her earliest appearances, the mysterious woman in white had instructed Bernadette to 'tell the priests to bring people here in procession and have a chapel built'. This command was to be taken up with alacrity. The first church, now known as the crypt, was built between 1863 and 1866 on the rocky hill directly above the grotto. Subsequently two more huge churches were built: the Basilica of the Immaculate Conception, or Upper Basilica, in 1871; and the neo-Byzantine Rosary Basilica in 1889. The River Garve was rerouted to make space for thousands of pilgrims in front of the grotto and the swampy ground over which Bernadette had walked was cleared to make the vast Rosary Square, which can accommodate over 45,000 pilgrims for open-air processions and services. The number of pilgrims coming to Lourdes has climbed steadily – by 1908 it reached one million, by 1958 five million and it is now well over six million.

The triple basilicas at Lourdes seen from the Garve River

Lourdes owed its development as a major international shrine to a combination of support from the local church, imperial patronage, and its role as a focus for Catholic identity and devotion at a time of growing anti-clericalism and rationalism in France. The Paris-based Augustinian Fathers of the Assumption organized a national pilgrimage in 1873 during the early years of the Third Republic as part of a wider Catholic movement to restore the Bourbon monarchy and reverse France's growing secularist republicanism. The story of how Lourdes came to symbolize faith in an increasingly sceptical age has been told in a sympathetic and scholarly way by Ruth Harris in her book *Lourdes: Body and Spirit in the Secular Age*. Another scholar, Suzanne Kaufman, in her *Consuming Visions: Mass Culture and the Lourdes Shrine*, has shown how the Catholic Church brilliantly exploited techniques associated

with mass tourism and mass consumption so that the
millions of women who came to Lourdes could combine
the pleasures of sightseeing, shopping and people-watching
in an environment that was sanctioned by the religious
authorities. From early on there was a brisk trade in
souvenirs around the sanctuary, with statues of the Virgin,
models of the grotto and *pastilles de Lourdes* (lozenges made
from sugar and water from the grotto) being particularly
popular. In Kaufman's view, the devotional cult established
at Lourdes modernized the act of pilgrimage and enabled
religious faith and the Catholic Church to remain relevant.

Although the sanctuary at Lourdes is in some senses
a shrine to Bernadette, there is very little emphasis on
her relics, as there would have been in a medieval pilgrim
shrine. One of her ribs is kept under the altar of an outdoor
side chapel built into the great colonnade that extends
out from either side of the main basilica, representing
the embracing arms of Christ, but it receives very little
attention from visitors. Bernadette's presence in the
sanctuary is expressed through statues of her tending sheep
and kneeling by the grotto, but it is the cult of the Virgin Mary that dominates
the architecture of the shrine. A statue of the crowned Virgin opposite the main
entrance to the basilicas is a focal point for private devotion and the railings
around it are festooned with flowers and other votive offerings. An enormous
gold crown on the dome of the Rosary Basilica commemorates the coronation
of Our Lady of Lourdes. Inside, a huge mosaic of the Virgin on the vaulted
ceiling of the choir has the words 'To Jesus through Mary' inscribed in gold
beneath it.

Crown on the dome of
the Rosary Basilica

One of the first decisions taken by the church authorities, as early as 1874,
was to transport groups of suffering and disabled pilgrims to Lourdes and make
'service to the sick' a central feature of the religious devotion there. Although
the Virgin made no mention of healing the sick to Bernadette, miraculous cures
appeared to take place in the waters of the grotto shortly after the apparitions.
The procession of the Blessed Sacrament was introduced in 1888 with sick
pilgrims being lined up on either side of the basilica and urged, if they were able,
to rise up and follow the consecrated host after it had been paraded before them
in a monstrance (a vessel used to display the consecrated bread).

The enormous respect and care afforded to the *malades*, who are given pride
of place in every service and procession, remains one of the most striking and
moving features of Lourdes. An army of volunteers known as *hospitaliers*, or
sometimes by the traditional name of *brancardiers* if they are male and *dames
hospitalières* if they are female, spends much of the day pushing wheelchairs,

carrying stretchers or pulling the distinctive blue rickshaw-like sedan chairs known as *voitures* that transport the sick around the sanctuary. Every year over 100,000 *hospitaliers* volunteer their services on an individual basis, quite apart from those who come out with pilgrim groups. During my visit I met a retired French general who comes to Lourdes as a *brancardier* for eight days every summer. He was on duty from 5 a.m. until late in the evening quietly shepherding pilgrims round the grotto, making sure those in wheelchairs were always brought to the front of the queue and firmly but with great courtesy enforcing the rule of silence. A married couple from Scotland were spending six months prior to their retirement working as *hospitaliers*, the wife as a nurse and the husband meeting disabled pilgrims at the airport or the station. *Hospitaliers* operate like a religious or chivalric order – they are formally commissioned at a church service, live together in a designated building near the gates to the sanctuary and proudly wear a medal after five years' service.

'At the grotto, everything speaks of water: the rushing Garve River, the drizzling rain from the cloudy sky; the spring of Mosabielle … I want to be purified. I want to be cleansed.

Henri Nouwen

    Lourdes exercises a very important ministry to the sick and handicapped. It is also involved in working out a contemporary theology of suffering that does not seek to glorify or glamorize the condition in any way, but rather emphasizes that those who suffer have their own calling and especially their own dignity and place in Christ's kingdom. This theme was highlighted in a major international conference, 'Called by Name', organized in 2008 by the Handicapped Children's Pilgrim Trust and addressed by Jean Vanier, the founder of the *L'Arche* communities that have brought together able-bodied volunteers and those with profound learning difficulties.

    Although apparently miraculous cures have been effected through contact with the waters of the grotto, this aspect of the pilgrim experience is played down by the authorities who run the shrine. Displays in the modest museum of miracles tucked away on an upper floor of one of the buildings that lines Rosary Square point out that of nearly 7,000 cures registered with the Lourdes medical bureau, only sixty-six have officially been recognized by the church as miracles. The most recent was in 1999 following the complete recovery of a male French nurse from multiple sclerosis twelve years earlier. Over 70 per cent of the officially attested cures have come about through either drinking or bathing in

Left: The daily procession of voitures carrying sick or elderly pilgrims to and from the grotto.

Below: Filling a bottle with Lourdes water from one of the taps beneath the basilica

the waters of the grotto and over 80 per cent have involved women. As at other Marian shrines, female pilgrims easily outnumber men.

The water that now flows copiously from the grotto was discovered by Bernadette after she clawed away at the mud in response to one of the Virgin's commands: 'Go drink at the spring and wash yourself there.' Although no official claims are made for its therapeutic or miraculous properties, the seventeen marble baths in the bath houses beyond the grotto do steady business every morning and afternoon as pilgrims queue up to be immersed in it. Around 400,000 pilgrims a year brave the cold waters, the great majority again being women. Many more fill up containers at a row of stand-pipes beneath the basilica to which water from the grotto is piped. Lourdes lies at the heart of a part of France famous for its spas, and the influence of a culture that emphasizes the health-giving and purifying aspects of spring water is clear in the layout of the grotto and the baths. After a visit in 1990, the Dutch priest and writer on spirituality, Henri Nouwen, commented: 'At the grotto, everything speaks of water: the rushing Garve River, the drizzling rain from the cloudy sky; the spring of Mosabielle … I want to be purified. I want to be cleansed.'

The theme of water's spiritual significance has been imaginatively taken up in a Water Walk laid out along the opposite bank of the River Garve from the grotto in 2002. Its nine stations represent places mentioned in the Bible where water played a key role: Beersheba, where the clans of Abraham and Abimelech made peace after fighting over access to drinking water; the road to Gaza where Philip baptized the Ethiopian eunuch; Meribah, where Moses struck the rock and water gushed forth; En Gedi, the oasis by the side of the Dead Sea; the spring that Ezekiel prophesied would flow through the desert from the new temple; the fountain in Nazareth from which Mary is said to have collected water daily and which is associated with the story of the Annunciation; Jacob's Well where Jesus encountered the Samaritan woman; the pool of Bethesda where he cured a cripple; and the pool of Siloam where he restored the sight of a blind man. Pilgrims are invited to approach each of the water points and wash their faces. Once again, the emphasis is on purification

Priests prepare for
the procession of
the exposition of the
sacrament

and clarification rather than on the miraculous. Those taking part in the Water Walk are encouraged to 'return upstream to recover the sources of our own baptism' and are steered away from any magical interpretation: 'the water is a sign, but the reality is the grace of God'. Bernadette herself, when questioned about the miracles that were occurring around the grotto, insisted that they were not to be attributed to the spring but to faith and prayer.

During the pilgrim season at Lourdes, which lasts from Palm Sunday to the end of October, each day unfolds with a clear ritual and rhythm. From early in the morning an endless procession of wheelchairs and *voitures* wends its way across Rosary Square to the grotto. Masses are celebrated in the many churches and chapels around the sanctuary from 6 a.m. and many pilgrims choose to spend an hour or so, before it gets too hot, walking The Stations of the Cross on the wooded hillside above the main basilica. Jesus' journey to Calvary is dramatically represented by dioramas made up of 115 life-size cast-iron figures. At 9 a.m. on Wednesdays and Sundays an International Mass is celebrated in the huge underground basilica, constructed entirely from reinforced concrete in the shape of an up-turned boat and consecrated in 1958 by Pope John XXIII.

Morning is also the time when many pilgrims make their confessions. There are forty-eight confessionals in the Reconciliation Chapel, manned by thirty chaplains permanently attached to the Sanctuary, who are oblates of the Order of Mary Immaculate, and visiting priests. Father Martin Moran, who is in charge of all services and activities in the English language, believes that Lourdes has become a major international centre for confession, or the sacrament of reconciliation as it is now more commonly known in the Roman Catholic Church: 'People who have a very tenuous connection with the church see this as a last resort. The vast majority haven't been to church for a long time and certainly not to a confession. Something happens here. They experience the knowledge that they are valued and loved by God and have a dignity before God'. Father Paul Horrocks, a South African priest in charge of the English language

'People who have a very tenuous connection with the church see this as a last resort ... Something happens here. They experience the knowledge that they are valued and loved by God and have a dignity before God.'

Father Martin Moran

confessional team, sees Lourdes' mission as being primarily the renewal of faith and hope. As well as the physically handicapped and terminally ill, he is struck by the large number of bereaved people and couples unable to have children who come as pilgrims.

The late afternoon and evening are dominated by two great processions around the sanctuary. The first, the exposition of the Blessed Sacrament and blessing of the sick, begins at 5 p.m. across the river from the grotto and moves through Rosary Square before ending up with a service in the huge underground basilica that accommodates 25,000 people. It is introduced by a thrilling fanfare of trumpets and drums and the singing is led by operatic trained cantors and a choir made up of visiting pilgrims. The consecrated host is carried through the sanctuary, followed by a procession of several thousand pilgrims led by the sick in their *voitures* and on stretchers. In the underground basilica, a moving liturgy is sung and spoken in the six different languages officially recognized and used in the sanctuary (French, English, German, Italian, Spanish and Dutch). The host rests on the central altar before being paraded past the sick pilgrims who, as always, are treated with special reverence and care and given prime positions at the front of the church. Nurses go round throughout

Procession of the Exposition of the Blessed Sacrament

Candles burning at Lourdes

The sheepfold at Bartres

the service with cups of water for those feeling dehydrated or overcome by the heat.

The evening procession, which takes place at 9 p.m., again involves thousands of people processing through Rosary Square following a statue of the Virgin as it is borne round the sanctuary. Everyone carries a lighted candle and sings the distinctive Lourdes *Ave Maria* and *Salve Regina* as well as other hymns and chants. There is a powerful sense of solidarity and devotion as pilgrims from every corner of the world snake across the square, gently marshalled by *hospitaliers,* and line up in front of the façade of the basilica. The thousands of individual candles merge into a great blaze of flickering light, expressing both the warmth and the fragility of faith, and emphasizing the theme of light which is one of the five signs of Lourdes (the others being water, the crowd, the rock and the sick). Many pilgrims go on after the brief service to light a larger candle in the special area set aside for this purpose beyond the grotto. Altogether, 700 tonnes of

A Pilgrim's Impression

My impressions of Lourdes are overwhelmingly of the faith, devotion and friendliness of fellow pilgrims. I think of the group of Japanese pilgrims who shared my couchette compartment on the overnight train from Geneva; the trio of Dominican priests from Singapore whom I met in a café and with whom I discussed Scottish theology; the Irish women from the 1000-strong group from the diocese of Cork who were so proud to have been chosen to lead the evening procession round the sanctuary; the Sri Lankan couple with whom I watched the film about Bernadette; the young Italian family sitting next to me in the underground basilica during the exposition of the sacrament; the group of Polish nuns with whom I walked in the torchlight procession, holding our candles high and singing 'Ave, Ave, Ave Maria' again and again; and the Croatians who were still singing and waving their banner in front of the basilica long after the torchlight procession had ended. Lourdes has a more international feeling than any of the other European pilgrim places that I have visited. It also attracts pilgrims from other faith traditions, notably Hindus but also some Muslims who are moved by the devotion to the Virgin Mary and the overwhelming atmosphere of faith and prayer.

candles are burnt in the sanctuary every year between April and October.

The typical length of time for a pilgrimage to Lourdes is five days. As well as the daily events in the sanctuary, there is much more for the pilgrim to do. A trail round the town *'sur les pas de Bernadette'* takes in important places in Bernadette's life, including the Boly Mill where she was born and the Cachot, a former prison where her family lived in desperate poverty after her father lost his job as a day labourer in the mill. They are remarkably unspoiled and provide a fascinating insight into her life and background. Also well worth undertaking is the 2½-mile (4-km) walk that starts from the hamlet of Bartres where Bernadette lived shortly before the apparitions. It begins from near the sheepfold where she tended sheep, accessed by a rough and stony uphill track. From there a good and well-defined footpath, the *Chemin de Bernadette*, leads down to Lourdes through fields. The first building you come to on the outskirts of the town is the municipal rubbish and recycling centre – which is perhaps appropriate given that many people leave some of their unwanted baggage behind at Lourdes. The path comes down under the railway track and beside the town hospital, formerly a workhouse and school where Bernadette was a pupil and lived for six years with a religious community. A little museum there displays her schoolbooks and other souvenirs. The most recent entry in the visitors' book when I visited read: 'Bernadette, I leave all that is wrong with my life to you in Lourdes.'

Lourdes undoubtedly has its touristy and commercial side. You can chug round the streets in a little tourist train and visit a waxworks museum, a model village and a Nativity display with animated figures. You can also, if you wish, approach the town in the manner of a more traditional pilgrim. Though few do so, the authorities suggest that some might like to make the last part of their journey to Lourdes on foot and offers six routes into the town, including a 25-mile (40-km) hike from Pau offering splendid views of the Pyrenees, an 18-mile (30-km) walk from the Benedictine monastery at Tournay and a 9-mile (15-km) stroll from the Marian shrine at Betharram. It would be good to see these paths more used. The neon sign proclaiming the message '*Tourisme et Religion*' above the shelves of bottled water and plaster statues of the Virgin in the Boulevard de la Grotte well sums up Lourdes' unique atmosphere. It is the home of religious tourism and spiritual junk but it is also a beacon of faith and hope and a wonderful exemplar of the prioritizing of the sick and the suffering who were so central to Jesus' own ministry. It is also manifestly a place of prayer. As such, Lourdes is fulfilling the wishes of the mysterious woman in white who appeared to the young shepherdess at the grotto. Alongside her call for processions, church building and bathing in the water was a starker and simpler injunction: 'Penance, penance, penance – pray for sinners.'

Practicalities

Lourdes can be reached by TGV train from Paris via Bourdeaux in five hours, by road exiting the main Toulouse–Bourdeaux motorway at Tarbes, and by air to Tarbes–Lourdes airport from Paris or to Pau (30 miles or 50 km away) by direct flights from Amsterdam and London. There are numerous hotels at every price range. An excellent website, www.lourdes-france.org, includes live web cameras.

Taizé

18

There are two particularly striking features about the 100,000 or more people who make their way to Taizé every year. The great majority are under the age of twenty-five and there are virtually no tourists or day-trippers among them. Taizé is not an ancient pilgrim shrine but rather a contemporary Christian community that attracts up to 5,000 young people every week to engage in an intense mixture of worship, Bible study, reflection and community life. Instead of cameras slung round their necks, they wear the distinctive Taizé cross based on the letter Tau in the Greek alphabet.

Above: Indian pilgrims packing picnic lunches at Taizé

Right: The towers of Cluny Abbey

Most come in groups. Several buses arrive every Sunday from different departure points in Germany, the country that currently provides the largest number of pilgrims to Taizé. On the Sunday afternoon that I was there, three buses arrived from Italy and two departed to connect with flights for Finland. Others came from further afield, including a group of monks and nuns from a new religious community in Brazil who were making a pilgrimage across France and a squad of volunteers from Catholic churches in India enthusiastically packing picnics.

Some pilgrims come to Taizé on their own, like the young German who was stopping off there as he walked from Coburg in Bavaria to Santiago de Compostela. 'Some bad things happened in my life and I just decided to make the walk' he told me. He added that he relished the silence along the way – for three days after leaving Le Puy he had not met anyone. Another young German had cycled in three days from Freiburg. But for most pilgrims to Taizé it is the destination rather than the journey that is important. It is relatively easy to reach the small Burgundian village that lies just off the A6 motorway from Paris to Lyon and close to Macon station on the TGV railway line from Paris to Geneva. From the station a local bus wends its way through the vineyards and hills of Burgundy and passes the nearby town of Cluny, site of the huge Benedictine Abbey, which throughout the Middle Ages was the largest church in Christendom. The opulence of medieval Cluny, which so offended St Bernard of Clairvaux that he broke away to found the more austere Cistercian order, provides a striking contrast to the simplicity of the modern community at Taizé.

It was to this tiny hamlet perched on a hill that 25-year-old Roger Schütz-Marsauche, the son of a Swiss Lutheran pastor, came in 1940 seeking to work for peace and reconciliation. He offered a welcome to all who needed help or sanctuary, especially Jewish refugees. After the war a small community of brothers grew up around him. Initially all Protestant, they were later joined by Catholic laymen and priests. The community that Brother Roger led until his death in 2005 now numbers around a hundred brothers from twenty-five different countries and many different denominations. About seventy-five are based at Taizé and the rest work in areas of exceptional poverty around

the world including Bangladesh, Senegal and Brazil. The brothers are vowed to poverty, celibacy and simplicity of life and take no donations. Since 1966 the Sisters of St Andrew, an international Roman Catholic community, have lived in the next village and share responsibility for the ministry of welcome.

From an early stage of the community's existence young people started coming to Taizé, drawn by Brother Roger's direct, open teaching. Originally they were billeted 2½ miles (4 km) away so that the brothers would not be distracted from their call to be contemplative and secluded, but Brother Roger later became convinced that the community should welcome the young visitors into its midst. The brothers eat and sleep in their own community house but almost all of them are engaged in a ministry of hospitality, teaching and counselling visitors and supervising the domestic arrangements. There are always a dozen or so standing discreetly around the back of the church at the end of evening worship to talk to those with particular problems or questions, and a team of brothers and volunteers is on duty all day and night to deal with pastoral emergencies.

In 1970 Brother Roger conceived the idea of a worldwide council of youth to parallel and complement the work of the Second Vatican Council. He was concerned at the number of young people who were leaving the church or never joining it. He came to realize, however, that the way to address these questions was not through a formal council but rather through what he described as 'a pilgrimage of trust across the earth', which would inspire young people and encourage them to work in their own communities as peacemakers

The church at Taizé with its onion-shaped domes

and bearers of reconciliation. The pilgrimage is supported by a bi-monthly letter written by one of the brothers from a difficult or depressed part of the world. In the last week of every year, a five-day meeting brings together up to 100,000 young people in one of the major cities of Europe. There have also been meetings in cities further afield, including Madras, Johannesburg, Calcutta, Cochabamba in Bolivia, and Dayton, Ohio.

The principles of this pilgrimage of trust underlie the communal life that so many young people find attractive. At its heart is prayer – Brother Roger said of Taizé that 'the most valuable thing that people experience here is prayer together'. Services take place every day at 8.15 a.m., 12.20 p.m. and 8.30 p.m. in the vast hangar-like church built in 1962 and subsequently extended so that it can take up to 6,000 worshippers. Clad in their white prayer robes, the brothers sit on small stools in their own central enclosure, while everyone else

The Romanesque church in Taizé

huddles together on the floor around them or sits on the steps or benches at the side. Originally the community gathered to worship in the small twelfth-century Romanesque village church and used a set liturgy in French. As more and more young people from many different countries came to join them, the brothers not only had to create a bigger building but also a radically new and simplified form of service.

After some experiment, they found that the most effective form of worship for the huge numbers of young people gathering at Taizé was the use of simple chants that took biblical phrases in several languages and repeated them several times. The first Taizé chants were written by Jacques Berthier, a composer and friend to the community, who died in 1994. Since then many have been written by Joseph Gelineau. The chants, which are sung over and over again by the congregation, often with a solo cantor interposing verses, are interspersed with short spoken prayers and Bible readings, given

in French, English, German and also often in other
languages including Spanish, Italian, Dutch, Polish and
Latin. There are also prolonged periods of silence in
each service.

Each week's devotions culminate in a representation
of the death and resurrection of Jesus. On Friday
evening a large icon of the cross is laid on the floor of
the church and many come forward at the end of the
service to venerate it. On Saturday evening worshippers
light candles, enhancing the strong theme of light conveyed by the mass of
candles that burn throughout every service from large open bricks piled up at
the east end of the church in front of striking yellow and orange drapes.

Following each morning service, the brothers give separate Bible expositions
for adults and young people. Indeed, apart from at worship, those over thirty
are segregated from the young people who form the majority of the visitors to
Taizé. They eat and sleep separately. This arrangement is made largely so that
adults will not dominate discussion, but it does make for a slightly fragmented
atmosphere and seems a pity when the message of Taizé is so much about unity
and reconciliation. Also separate for more obvious reasons are those making a
silent retreat for the week.

The young people's Bible study sessions are further subdivided by age. Fifteen
and sixteen-year-olds explore the theme 'Up to Jerusalem', which looks at the
last week of Jesus' life. Those between seventeen and twenty-nine can choose
between 'I am the bread of life', based around a detailed reading of Chapter 6
of John's Gospel, and 'He opened a way', themed around various passages in
Luke's Gospel. The adult Bible study sessions are more varied, focusing on Jesus'
last words from the cross, among other topics. After each talk people break into
small groups organized according to language to discuss questions posed by
the brothers. For those reflecting on the first session in 'He opened a way', for
example, the questions include:

• Which people living near me show greatest generosity to others?
• What place do others have in my life? How important to me are their
  desires and needs?
• What barriers keep us from going towards others? How can we surmount
  those barriers?
• How can we reply to those who say 'I don't know what to do with my life'?

In the afternoons there is always a music practice for those who want to form a
choir and help keep the chants going. There are also workshops on a variety of
themes, ranging from the environment to further theological and biblical study. The
distinctive gifts of visitors are often harnessed: during my stay a Jewish rabbi staying
for the week with a group from Israel gave a talk on the love of God from a Jewish

*Bless us, Lord Christ, on our pilgrimage,
be with us and all who are dear to us,
and with everyone we meet.
Keep us in the Spirit of the Beatitudes:
joyful, simple, merciful.*

A pilgrim prayer from Taizé

perspective.

The atmosphere at Taizé resembles a cross between a holiday camp and a military base. Visitors stay either in tents or in spartan dormitories known appropriately as barracks and food is served out on trestle tables under canvas in a process reminiscent of the way troops are fed in the field. The basic rations are doled out from huge cooking pots and containers into plastic bowls and cups, and the only piece of cutlery provided is a spoon with which you are somehow expected to spread the butter – and, if you are an adult, the added indulgence of jam – on your morning roll. Many people bring their own tents or come in caravans and mobile homes so that the whole place looks like a vast campsite. As at Iona, visitors are expected to help in chores. You sign up at the beginning of the week for kitchen duties, washing up, lavatory cleaning or other tasks supervised by the resident volunteers. Visitors are also called upon to help in other ways. Twice during meals while I was there the call went out for a car

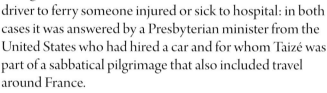

driver to ferry someone injured or sick to hospital: in both cases it was answered by a Presbyterian minister from the United States who had hired a car and for whom Taizé was part of a sabbatical pilgrimage that also included travel around France.

Rules and regulations are kept to a minimum, however, and neither worship nor attendance at the morning Bible study or group meetings are compulsory. The emphasis on openness and trust is greatly appreciated by the young. A German teenager said that what she liked about Taizé was 'the prayers and the atmosphere of trust – it gives you space and also the chance to meet so many young people from all over the world'. An Irish lady told me that she could not wait to bring her 19-year-old son there: 'He is totally turned off by the church at home because of child abuse scandals and the lack of integrity and leadership but here I feel sure that he would experience, as I do, a genuine deep but open spirituality.' The atmosphere is infectiously ecumenical. Nobody bothers if you are Protestant or Catholic and no one parades their denominational identities, except perhaps the occasional visiting Orthodox monk in his distinctive robes. Most visitors share together in the Eucharist, which is presided over by a Catholic priest, although there is a separate Protestant communion service every morning and blessed but unconsecrated wafers are also available at the end of every morning service for those who do not want to receive Communion.

Taizé touches people at turning points in their lives. This is perhaps especially true of the 150 or so volunteers who come for periods ranging from one month to two years to assist the brothers and who do much of the work to keep the place going: cooking, welcoming people, carrying out maintenance and repairs and organizing the work squads of visitors washing up and cleaning. A good number of them are university drop-outs who realized that they had made the wrong choice and are taking time to rethink their future. A high proportion come from Germany, perhaps partly because time at Taizé is one of the forms of social service that the German government allows as an alternative to compulsory military service. The volunteers eat together and have their own separate Bible studies. They are a wonderfully eclectic group: a trio that I encountered serving out tea to new arrivals on Sunday afternoon was made up of a Lithuanian drop-out from university, an Australian training to be an actor and a medical student from Texas. Among the young people coming for a week on their own, as distinct from the majority who come in church or school groups, there are also individuals in a state of indecision or seeking to sort out their lives. Several initially come for a week and then decide to stay on, sometimes for a period of silent retreat, or for longer as a volunteer.

Brother Roger

During an evening service in 2005 Brother Roger was fatally stabbed by a psychologically disturbed visitor. The attendance at his funeral, which included leaders of Roman Catholic, Protestant and Orthodox churches, testified to the strength of his ecumenical witness and the considerable impact that he had made throughout his life. He is buried in a simple grave covered in flowers by the side of the door to the ancient village church, which now serves as an oasis of peace and quiet reflection in contrast to the bustle of the crowds thronging the modern Community buildings up the hill.

> **'Our life is living our humanity in the presence of God, not finding our spirituality floating in the clouds.'**
>
> **Brother Alois, Prior of Taizé**

Many of the adults who come to Taizé are there because of their children. I met several fathers there with their daughters, and two Dutch women – one Catholic and one Protestant – who had never met before, with their daughters who were schoolmates. They found themselves in the same discussion group sharing their stories, their faith and their doubts. Some adults return on their own again and again, like the Dutch local government official who told me that he comes every year to recharge his spiritual batteries and keep his faith and devotional life alive.

The brothers are keen to emphasize that they do not want visitors to return home and seek to set up miniature Taizé communities, but rather to go back into their own churches and communities and live out the gospel message of trust, unconditional love and forgiveness that they have learned about, experienced and shared during their week with the community. At the end of each week, participants in the discussion groups are asked to reflect on what it means to be grounded in their Christian faith, with a capacity to be open to all, and on what commitments towards others they wish to develop or to begin. There is an emphasis on involvement in the world rather than retreat from it into seclusion. Brother Alois, the German Catholic who was chosen by Brother Roger before he died to be his successor as prior, says: 'Our life is living our humanity in the presence of God, not finding our spirituality floating in the clouds.' Much of the preaching of Brother Roger focused on the tension between prayer and contemplation on one side and the struggles of faith and facing one's responsibilities in the world on the other. He also constantly emphasized the theme of pilgrimage, declaring that 'we go from one beginning to another' and observing that 'we are all seekers, searching for the well-springs of the gospel, the peace of heart and the joy that radiates the love of Christ. Peace and joy are always linked. There is no joy without inner peace.'

The theological atmosphere of Taizé is open, inclusive and welcoming to all. Brother Pedro, a Spanish brother, often leads biblical meditations on the doubting apostle Thomas whom he sees as 'a believer of our time, seeking proof and full of uncertainty'. He speaks about finding Jesus in the indecision of doubt as much as in the serenity of faith and insists that 'in our own pilgrimage from doubt to hope and from suffering to joy we are supported by the faith of the church and the faith of others. We are also supported by believers of other religions'. Brother Jean Marc, an Oxford classics graduate, summed up what Taizé is about with the following words:

> We hope that here we create a space where people can find Christ, where the elements of the gospel are all present but we don't push them – people can find their own way for themselves. We seek to model the undivided church as it was in early Christian times, open but rooted in orthodoxy. We don't push any particular denominational or theological line.

Practicalities

Pilgrims to Taizé are encouraged to arrive on Sunday and stay for a week although it is possible to make a shorter visit, preferably from Thursday to Sunday. Registration through the website www.taize.fr is strongly recommended and it is advisable to secure accommodation, although no one is turned away if they turn up without booking. You should bring your own sleeping bag and towel. Depending on age, nationality and length of stay, visitors are asked to contribute a suggested amount for accommodation and meals. If you are travelling via TGV, be warned that the buses to Taizé do not connect with the train arrival times at Macon-Loche station and you may well have a wait of an hour or more.

19 Medugorje

Medugorje boasts the only air-conditioned confessionals in the world. There are twenty-five of them lined up in a highly functional and not very beautiful yellow plastered building, supplemented by another six inside the adjoining church and also by an array of priests in assorted garb, who sit on small stools on the pavement outside behind printed signs indicating the languages in which they can hear confessions.

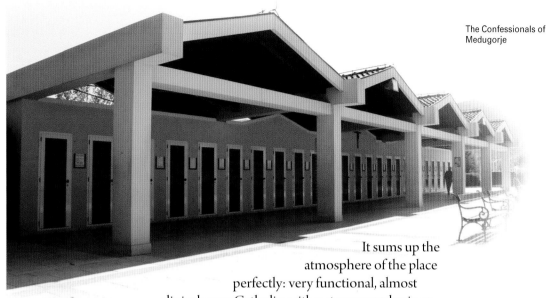

The Confessionals of
Medugorje

It sums up the
atmosphere of the place
perfectly: very functional, almost
clinical; very Catholic, with a strong emphasis on
confession, Mass and devotion to Mary; and above all, very
modern. Medugorje is the most recent major European place of pilgrimage.
Its beginnings can be dated very precisely to 24 June 1981 when six young
people reportedly saw an apparition of the Virgin Mary on a hill outside what
was then a tiny and impoverished village in Yugolsavia. Unlike most pilgrim
shrines, it does not have a medieval atmosphere or a feeling of being rooted in
the past. The apparitions are still going on and three of the original visionaries,
now in early middle-age, regularly receive messages from Our Lady that are
posted on the web and flashed up on an electronic notice board at the entrance
to the church precincts. Everything is very high-tech, as evidenced by the fact
that pilgrims can hear a simultaneous translation of the Croatian services in the
church by tuning into a special FM frequency on their transistor radios.

Not that history is irrelevant to the emergence of this particular place as
a major pilgrim shrine. The troubled past of this part of the Balkans could
perhaps help to explain why the Virgin might appear in Medugorje and why it
now attracts well over a million pilgrims a year. The village lies in what has long
been one of the most disturbed regions of Europe with a long history of intense
suffering and bitter conflict. The nearby River Neretva was the boundary
between the western and eastern parts of the Roman empire. In the south-
eastern corner of what is now the independent state of Bosnia-Herzegovinia,
the population is Croatian and staunchly Catholic. For over 400 years they lived
under Turkish and Islamic rule, which actively suppressed or only grudgingly
tolerated Christianity. The late-nineteenth-century absorption of the region
into the Austro-Hungarian empire ushered in a revival of Christianity but also
introduced intense political and ethnic conflicts, which triggered the First
World War. Following the Second World War, Communist rule meant an even

'Peace, peace, peace and only peace! Peace must reign between God and man and between men.'

more brutal suppression of Christianity. More recently, the civil war between 1992 and 1995 that led to the break-up of Yugoslavia brought more violence and destruction.

This background establishes the context for the apparitions and goes a long way to explaining their hold on the local population and on visitors. The Croatian Catholics of Medugorje and its surrounding region form a small but significant minority of the population of Bosnia-Herzegovinia, which is predominantly Muslim and Orthodox. They display the strength of faith of a persecuted minority.

The Virgin Mary's initial appearance occurred at around 6 p.m. on 24 June 1981 when six local youngsters aged between ten and seventeen, climbing a hill above the village, saw a beautiful young woman with a child in her arms who beckoned to them to come nearer. They were too frightened to approach her, but the following evening four of the group felt drawn back to the place where they had seen the woman, whom they recognized as the Virgin Mary. They were joined by another two teenagers. The woman appeared again to all six and they prayed and spoke with her. From then on these six visionaries, as they became known, had daily apparitions, sometimes when they were together and sometimes alone, in different places around the village. At the end of 1982, two ten-year-old girls started hearing inner locutions from the Virgin Mary.

Panel showing the Annunciation on Apparition Hill

For over a year all six of the visionaries claimed to experience apparitions on a daily basis. Towards the end of 1982, three had their sightings of the Virgin reduced to an annual apparition. In March 1984, after 1,000 days of daily apparitions, the Virgin started appearing on a weekly basis and since 1987 this has moved to a monthly appearance. Three of the original visionaries still experience apparitions and one, Marija Pavlovic, receives a message on the 25th of each month.

The message conveyed in the apparitions and through the locutions has remained remarkably consistent across the twenty-five years or more that they have been said to take place. It has also been very simple and straightforward. The tone was set in the words that Marija reported hearing from the Virgin on her third appearance on 26 June 1981: 'Peace, peace, peace and only peace! Peace must reign between God and man and between men.' The theme of peace and reconciliation has been dominant ever since. So have injunctions to prayer – especially the recitation of the Rosary – regular attendance at the Eucharist, reading of the Bible, fasting two days a week and monthly confession. These five practices are presented as the key weapons with which Christians can confront and defeat Satan. There has also been a strong emphasis on individual conversion, understood in terms of repentance or changing one's mind (the Greek word for repentance, *metanoia,* can be literally translated as 'a change of mind').

Pilgrims began coming to Medugorje soon after the apparitions started to occur, and although there was a falling off during the civil war of the early 1990s there has been a rapid recovery since. In 2006, the twenty-fifth anniversary of the first apparitions, nearly one and a half million people came. Italy provides the largest number of pilgrims – about 30 per cent of the total – with significant contingents coming from France, Austria, Germany, Poland, Hungary, Slovakia, Ireland and the United States. A youth pilgrimage at the end of July attracts 60,000 young people from across Europe. The number of pilgrims is increasingly annually and there are signs of new building all around the town, which already provides 15,000 visitor beds.

Pilgrims usually spend around five days in Medugorje and most follow a programme centred on twice-daily Masses, celebrated by thirty or more priests, recitation of the Rosary and eucharistic adoration in the twin-towered parish church completed in 1966. During their stay pilgrims make at least one journey up the steep, rocky path through thorn bushes to Apparition Hill, where the Virgin first appeared to the visionaries. From the village they walk through

Above: Apparition Hill seen from the track that leads from the village

Below: The rocky way up the hill itself

An Afternoon with Father Jozo

Although the great majority of pilgrims do not stray far from Medugorje during their time there, there is one excursion that is taken by nearly all. This is the 16-mile (25-km) coach ride to the Franciscan monastery in Siroki Brijeg, which was the first Christian community to be established after the end of Turkish rule. Franciscans have provided the priests for this part of Herzegovinia for over 700 years and they remained when the regular clergy fled during the dark days of Islamic domination, growing moustaches to look like their Turkish oppressors. The distinctive spirituality of the Franciscans, with its emphasis on evangelical simplicity, mission and radical conversion and discipleship, is very evident in the atmosphere and ethos of Medugorje. The particular reason for visiting Siroki Brijeg is that it is the home of Father Jozo Zovko, who was parish priest when the apparitions began in 1981.

Initially sceptical of the claims of the children, he himself saw the Virgin during a service in the church and thereafter became a strong supporter of the veracity of the apparitions. He was arrested by the Communist authorities in August 1981 and remained in prison for eighteenth months.

Together with a large group of English-speaking pilgrims I spent an afternoon listening to Father Jozo. Wearing his distinctive brown Franciscan habit, he addressed us in the garden of the monastery where twelve Franciscan priests were brutally killed by Communist partisans in 1945. Asked in turn to renounce their faith, they refused and were shot one by one. They were subsequently thrown into an underground shelter and burned, although some were still alive. A further thirty-one Franciscan brothers were taken away and killed later at various locations. This horrendous massacre provided the starting point for Father Jozo's impassioned sermon, delivered without notes and lasting for well over an hour, which dwelt much on the blood of the martyrs. The nub of his message was the need to live rather than simply know the faith: 'Our faith is not a theory,' he said. 'Theology is about systems but systems don't give birth to saints. A saint is born on his knees, not through study.' Clutching a statue of the Madonna in one hand and a crucifix in the other, he emphasized the five great themes of the apparitions – prayer with the heart, the Eucharist, the Holy Bible, fasting and monthly confession – describing them as 'the little stones for us to use against Goliath'. He gave out plastic rosaries and a card bearing a picture of the face of the Madonna and an invitation to individual conversion, and ended with a series of blessings that led some of those present to fall to the ground.

vineyards and fields along a dusty track lined by booths selling locally grown figs and honey, hand-stitched tablecloths and the ubiquitous rosary beads and statues of the Virgin that are on sale throughout the town. Many pilgrims also make the longer and even steeper climb up Mount Krizevac where local inhabitants, under the direction of the parish priest, erected a 36-foot- (11-m-) high concrete cross in 1933 to mark the 1,900[th] anniversary of the death of Jesus.

There is also a chance every week to hear and meet with one of the people who claim to have seen or heard Mary. I went to hear Marijana Vasilij, one of the two so-called interlocutors, who spoke in what is known as the Yellow Hall, a large hangar-like building behind the church. On the wall behind her was a large cross flanked on one side by a huge picture of Mary with her arms outstretched and on the other by a much smaller picture of the pope. She spoke of how she started hearing Mary in March 1983. Unlike the visionaries, she was not able to see or talk to the Virgin, but described hearing 'a voice quite different from the human voice, more like a voice of consciousness', which only came to her when she was deep in prayer. In response to its injunctions, she set up a prayer group of forty women that met for four years 'with Our Lady as our constant spiritual guide'. Her talk turned into a lecture on prayer, its importance and the proper technique for pursuing it and making it effective.

If Medugorje is in many respects the most Catholic of all the European pilgrim shrines, it is also the most influenced by the Charismatic movement and, in terms of its emphasis on preaching, the most Protestant. In just two days there I heard four long sermons, two preached by local Franciscans and two by visiting Irish priests. All were firmly biblical, superbly crafted and were delivered extempore. An Irish priest giving the homily at the morning English language Mass in the church emphasized the pilgrimage theme and observed: 'Medugorje is not the destination but rather a step towards the destination. It is a place where we gather encouragement to go on. When we leave, we continue our pilgrimage in the Lord, where we are all young and beautiful. As we travel, we travel with Mary, with God, with Jesus and with the Holy Spirit, trying to go back to ourselves, the selves that God made.' Father Edward Murphy, an Irish priest based in Boston who was accompanying a group of North

Above: The multi-lingual sign directing pilgrims to Apparition Hill

Below: Pilgrims pray around the statue of the Virgin Mary on the hill

Plaster Madonnas fill the shelves of the shops in Medugorje

American pilgrims, spoke of his feeling that the special grace of Medugorje as compared with other places of pilgrimage is that it enables people to cleanse themselves within and get rid of baggage from the past. 'Pilgrimage,' he said, 'makes you vulnerable and different. It gives us the freedom to step out of the ordinary and do something heroic and also to empty ourselves completely.'

If the Franciscan influence lies behind this emphasis on the evangelical preaching of the Bible, then it is also evident in the many practical good works that have been directly inspired by the apparitions. Whatever one makes of them, there is no doubt that much good has come from them. Most pilgrims to Medugorje are taken on a visit either to the Cenacolo community on the edge of town, which provides rehabilitation for drug addicts, or to 'Mother's Village', an orphanage set up in 1993 for child victims of the Balkan conflict by Father Slavko Barbaric, Father Jozo's successor as parish priest, and which now caters for vulnerable children and troubled or addicted teenagers. Another initiative directly inspired by the messages of Our Lady is Mary's Meals, a Scottish-based venture that aims to feed the hungry and homeless in Africa, Asia and Latin America.

More than most pilgrim places in Europe, Medugorje is a curious mixture of religious junk, simple faith, charismatic enthusiasm and practical good works. The streets around the church, packed with garish shops loaded with rosaries and plaster Madonnas, look as though they have been transported from some slightly seedy seaside resort. Yet the large plazas immediately in front of and behind the church are oases of quiet with groups of women (who, as usual, far outnumber men among the pilgrims) saying the Rosary or kneeling before the outdoor statue of the Virgin. There is a distinctly charismatic and somewhat dated feel to the worship, with songs from the 1960s such as 'Kumbaya' being sung over and over again in a mantra-like way to soupy guitar chords. These songs also float out across the night air from the booths lining the way to the Hill of Apparition, which remain open until late in the evening. They were, indeed, my first introduction to Medugorje, being played on a CD in the minibus that picked us up from Dubrovnik Airport throughout the two-and-a-half-hour journey to the shrine. There is also a slightly apocalyptic atmosphere. The Virgin has apparently revealed ten secrets to the visionaries and although they pointedly refuse to disclose them, there is speculation that they concern the end times. Certainly some pilgrims, especially those from the United States, seem to be drawn to

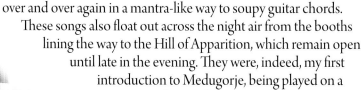

A nun prays in the open air worship area behind the twin towered church

Medugorje by a sense that the end of the world is nigh – when I asked him why pilgrimage is on the rise across Europe one of them told me that people are worried about the imminent appearance of the Four Horsemen of the Apocalypse. Mary's messages do regularly say that this is a time of special graces and that it may not be so easy to convert and be forgiven in the future, but the apocalyptic aspect is generally played down by the visionaries and interlocutors and the local Franciscan priests. When a visiting Irish priest asked Marijana Vasilij whether the messages that she heard mentioned the stark choice that confronts us between heaven and hell, she said that Mary only ever mentioned heaven.

The official position of the Roman Catholic Church on what has been happening in Medugorje over the last twenty-five years or so is one of scepticism. It is not prepared to affirm on the basis of investigations that 'one is dealing with supernatural apparitions and revelations' and it has declared that only when the apparitions cease can a conclusive judgment be made. The local diocesan bishop in Mostar is particularly sceptical of the visionaries' claims. Yet other independent observers are convinced that they are genuine. A recent study by Dr Paul Pandarakalam, a consultant psychiatrist working in the British National Health Service who has spent many years researching the phenomena at Medugorje, concludes that 'the medical observations and synchronisms suggest that the visionaries are responding to an outside power and not internal stimuli. The dual modes of perception also suggest that there is a non-physical agent in front of the visionaries.'

It is difficult to sum up the atmosphere of Medugorje. Of all the pilgrim places that I have visited in the course of researching this book, it is the most overwhelming and intense. In some ways it is also the most undisciplined, with worshippers barging into church in the middle of services (there are back-to-back Masses in different languages from 7.30 a.m. to 2 p.m. every weekday), provoking a rebuke from a priest that ended with the words: 'I'm not even asking you to behave like Christians but just to be decent, civilized human beings.' At the same time there is a very moving atmosphere of genuine devotion. The predominantly young local tour guides who conduct pilgrims around are fired with zeal and enthusiastically launch into the Rosary on every

'Pilgrimage makes us vulnerable and different. It gives us the freedom to step out of the ordinary and do something heroic and also to empty ourselves completely.'

Father Edward Murphy

coach journey. I have never said so many Hail Marys in my life – we were even called on to intone the Rosary when barely awake at 3 a.m. as our coach departed for the airport. There is no doubt that for the hundreds of thousands who return year after year, Medugorje provides real spiritual refreshment and renewal.

Perhaps it also has the potential to contribute to one of the most urgent and important tasks of our age – the peaceful reconciliation of Christians and Muslims. Father Jozo speaks warmly of the devotion to the Virgin that he found among Muslims in Indonesia. One of Mary's messages, delivered in January 1985, said: 'The Muslims and the Orthodox, for the same reason as Catholics, are equal before my Son and me. You are all my children. It does not suffice to belong to the Catholic Church to be saved, but it is necessary to respect the commandments of God in following one's conscience. Those who are not Catholics are no less creatures made in the image of God, and destined to rejoin someday the House of the Father. Salvation is available to everyone without exception.' How wonderful it would be if from this strife-torn region came a movement for mutual respect, reconciliation and peace among the adherents of the Abrahamic faiths.

Practicalities

Most pilgrims to Medugorje fly to either Split or Dubrovnik, both of which are served by budget airlines, and then take a three-hour coach journey. It is best to go with an organized group as this enables visits to Father Jozo, an audience with a visionary or interlocutor and other important elements of the pilgrim experience to be arranged. Of the many websites carrying the messages from the apparitions and giving information about the shrine, www.medugorje.org is probably the best.

St Cuthbert's Way

20

Opened in 1996, St Cuthbert's Way is a long-distance footpath that follows in the steps of one of the great Anglo-Saxon saints beginning at the place where he committed himself to the monastic life and ending on the island where he died. It is 62 miles (100 km) long and can be walked by anyone in a reasonable state of fitness in four or five days. The route crosses from Scotland to England and provides an astonishing variety of scenery, from the broad banks of the River Tweed to the high hills of the Cheviots. Several of the parish churches along the way on both sides of the border have opened their doors and provided imaginative displays and material for pilgrims.

Looking past a marker point for St Cuthbert's Way walk on the Eildon Hills.

Above: Parish church of Lindisfarne

Right: Statue of St Cuthbert by Fenwick Lawson

The original idea for St Cuthbert's Way came from Ron Shaw, project officer with the Till Valley Tourist Initiative in the northernmost part of England's most northerly county, Northumberland. He approached Roger Smith, the walking development officer for the Scottish Borders Council, and together they planned a route based on the life and travels of Cuthbert, one of the key figures in the early Christian history of the British Isles. Access agreements were negotiated with over forty landowners and farmers; stiles, gates and bridges were built or rebuilt; and the whole route was waymarked with a distinctive cross symbol.

St. Cuthbert's Way begins at Melrose Abbey, an early twelfth-century Cistercian foundation. The actual site of the monastery where Cuthbert himself lived and worked is 3 miles (5 km) off the route itself at Old Melrose. It can be

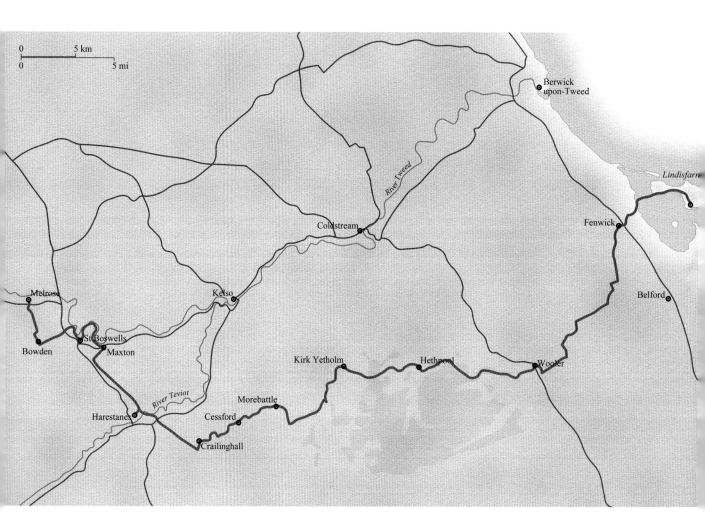

St Cuthbert of Lindisfarne

Cuthbert's exact place of birth is unknown and he first emerges into historical view in AD 651 when, aged around sixteen, he travelled to Melrose with the aim of joining the monastic community there. He studied under the abbot Boisil and was soon ordained a priest. During his time as a monk at Melrose he is described by his biographer, the Venerable Bede, as going out on pastoral journeys for a week or more and searching out in particular 'those steep rugged places in the hills which other preachers dreaded to visit because of their poverty and squalor'. He went for a period to a new monastery in Ripon, North Yorkshire, and then returned to Melrose where he became prior. In AD 664 he was made prior of the monastery at Lindisfarne, the small island off the north Northumbrian coast also known as Holy Island, which had been established thirty years earlier and already played a key role in the evangelization of the north-east of England. From AD 676 Cuthbert spent much of his time in solitary seclusion on the remote Inner Farne Island further out in the North Sea. With much reluctance, he was persuaded to accept the bishopric of Lindisfarne in AD 685, but after two years in the post he retired on health grounds and returned to his remote island retreat where he died in AD 687. Although he had asked to be buried on Farne Island, his body was taken to Lindisfarne, wrapped in elaborate vestments and placed in an elaborate wooden sarcophagus. When it was opened eleven years later, his body was found to be perfectly preserved, confirming his saintly status, which had already been attested by miracles around his tomb.

In AD 875 following Viking raids, Cuthbert's body was removed from Lindisfarne by monks. For the next eight years it travelled around Northumbria, eventually coming to rest at Chester-le-Street near Durham in AD 883. It remained there until AD 995 when it was moved to a specially built church in Durham. In 1093 the monastic community at Durham began building a magnificent cathedral to house Cuthbert's relics and in 1103 they were placed in a chapel behind the high altar. They remain there to this day, a continuing object of pilgrimage and devotion. Those walking the St Cuthbert's Way should, ideally, stop off at Durham Cathedral on their return from Lindisfarne to pay their final respects to the saint and savour the atmosphere of one of Europe's greatest Christian buildings, which also contains the tomb of Cuthbert's biographer, Bede, the first historian of the church in the British Isles.

reached by making a detour over the chain bridge across the River Tweed between Newton St Boswells and St Boswells and then taking a track past a statue of the Scottish hero, William Wallace, to a viewpoint near Bemersyde that was a favourite of the novelist, Walter Scott, who lived nearby. From this viewpoint the site of Cuthbert's monastery can be seen on a hill enclosed by a bend in the river. Nothing is left of this early monastic settlement, which was raided and burned down in AD 839, although a chapel dedicated to Cuthbert was built there by the Cistercian monks of the new Melrose Abbey in the thirteenth century.

The first day of walking St Cuthbert's Way provides a good introduction to the variety of scenery to be encountered on the walk as a whole. It begins with a stiff climb over the

The refuge for those caught by the incoming tide while crossing to Lindisfarne

Eildon Hills where, according to one legend, King Arthur lies sleeping and ready to return to life when needed. At the foot of the hills lies the first and in many ways the most atmospheric of the churches along the way, Bowden Kirk, with its unusual laird's loft running along the north side. There is much spiritual fare provided here for pilgrims, including a Welcome Book in which visitors are invited to note their observations and impressions. One such message reads: 'Thank you for the open door to quietness allowing me prayerfully to reflect on the life of my dear mum who passed away this morning.' The way then follows the bank of the Tweed, passing the ruins of Dryburgh Abbey, where Walter Scott and Field Marshal Haig lie buried, and the quiet country kirk at Maxton before joining the route of Dere Street, a wonderfully straight Roman road built on the orders of Agricola to link York and Edinburgh. On this stretch, Roman helmets replace the cross of St Cuthbert as the main waymarkers. Most of those walking St Cuthbert's Way make Harestanes country park their finishing point on the first day and seek overnight accommodation in nearby Ancrum or Jedburgh. There is one rather luxurious bed and breakfast establishment just off the long straight Dere Street section of the way. I have happy if slightly guilty memories of luxuriating in a hot

Lindisfarne Castle

tub in its garden while my fellow pilgrim, an Episcopal priest, said his evening office in our shared bedroom inside. I am sorry to say that he was rewarded for his asceticism by bad blisters later on in the walk.

The second section of St Cuthbert's Way goes from Harestanes to Yetholm and involves a climb of 1,300 feet (400 m) over Grubbit Law and Wideopen Hill. Yetholm is famed for its long connection with gypsies who elected their king and queen there and is a good place to reflect on the connections between pilgrims and travelling people.

The third day's walk crosses the border into England, involves another steep climb, this time up into the Cheviots, and affords a fine view over Yeavering Bell, the site of an important prehistoric hill fort and also later of an Anglo-Saxon settlement known as Gelfrin – both names mean 'the hill of the goats' and wild goats still roam in this area. It was at Gelfrin that the Anglo-Saxon bishop, Paulinus, is said to have baptized over 3,000 Northumbrians in the River Glen over a one-month period in AD 627 at the invitation of King Edwin.

The final section of the walk, for those doing it in four days, starts at Wooler, the small town that nestles on the English side of the Cheviots, and passes Doddington Moor where Cuthbert is said to have tended sheep as a boy. A dramatic sandstone overhang known as St Cuthbert's Cave, situated in the middle of a wooded stretch, is thought to have been one of the places where the

The parish church and priory ruins on Lindisfarne seen from the tiny St Cuthbert's Isle

Upturned boats used as storehouses by fishermen on Holy Island

saint's body was taken after its removal from Lindisfarne in AD 875. A ridge just a few hundred yards from here affords pilgrims on St Cuthbert's Way their first view of Holy Island, although there is still a good deal of walking to be done, including a crossing of the busy A1 road and the main east coast railway line. The final walk across to Lindisfarne itself is dependent on the tide – the island is cut off by the sea for two five-hour periods every twenty-four hours and it is important to consult the tide tables before venturing across as the sea can come in very quickly. There are, in fact, two ways to approach Lindisfarne when the tide is out: either by the main causeway used by cars, or by the Pilgrim's Route marked out by stakes across the sand – a shorter crossing but best tackled either barefoot or with boots on as it is extremely squelchy and wet under foot.

'Lindisfarne is still very much a place of pilgrimage and retreat and an increasing number of people visit it for this purpose'.

Lindisfarne is still very much a place of pilgrimage and retreat and an increasing number of people visit it for this purpose, quite apart from those walking St Cuthbert's Way. There are several buildings on the island that are well suited for quiet prayer and contemplation, including: the ruins of the priory that was established around 1120 on the site of Cuthbert's monastery; the thirteenth-century parish church; the Roman Catholic Church dedicated to St Aidan, the first great abbot of Lindisfarne; and the United Reformed Church, which has been turned into a centre for conferences and retreats as well as worship. Marygate House is a residential retreat in the centre of the village with a fine library. Many pilgrims find inspiration from sitting on the shore and looking out towards the nearby St Cuthbert's Isle, where Cuthbert first sought retreat before withdrawing to the more remote Farne Islands. I well remember sitting there on my first visit to Lindisfarne watching the 'Cuddy ducks', as the eiders are locally known in commemoration of Cuthbert, and talking with David Adam, who was then the local vicar and whose Celtic-style prayers, often inspired by the ebb and flow of the tides around the island, have been such an inspiration to many.

Lindisfarne is the base of the Community of Aidan and Hilda, a dispersed community with members across the world who follow a disciplined rule of life and prayer based on that found in Celtic monasticism. Rooted in the charismatic renewal movement, the Community was launched in 1994 at an Anglican Renewal Conference. It runs a residential retreat house on the island known as the 'Open Gate' with a chapel where prayers are said every weekday at 12 noon and 9 p.m. Those making an individual retreat can also stay in Lindisfarne Retreat, the home of the Community's founder and guardian, Ray Simpson, which also houses a Celtic Study library.

Pilgrimage is central to the ethos and mission of the Community of Aidan and Hilda, which describes itself as 'a world-wide pilgrim people reconnecting with the Spirit and the Scriptures, the saints and the streets, the seasons and the soil' and communicates its vision as being 'to cradle a Christian spirituality for today, to raise up a renewed pilgrim people, to resource the

Statue of St Aidan, Cuthbert's predecessor as leader of the monastic community on Lindisfarne

The ruins of Lindisfarne Priory

emerging and existing church and to heal fragmented people and places'. Those interested in finding out more about the Community and its way of life are invited to become explorers and test their vocation with the help of a soul friend. If after a year of living the way of life, which is founded on the principles of simplicity, purity and obedience, they wish to commit to it, they make their first vows, known as 'taking the first voyage in the Coracle', and become voyagers.

Along with life-long learning, a rhythm of prayer, work and recreation, simplicity of lifestyle, care for creation, commitment to unity and mission, and an openness to God's spirit, the concept of spiritual journey is a central element of the Community's way of life. It is primarily expressed in two ways: through regular retreats and through a commitment to pilgrimage. In the words of the booklet introducing the Community to potential explorers and voyagers:

> 'Pilgrims are persons in motion – passing through territories not their own – seeking something we might call contemplation, or perhaps the word clarity will do as well, a goal to which only the spirit's compass points the way.'
>
> **Richard Niebuhr**

The purpose of pilgrimage is to tread in the shoes of Christ or his saints in order to make contact with the many rich experiences which are to do with being a pilgrim. Such pilgrimages draw us into deeper devotion to our Lord Jesus and will inspire us to mission. Members might seek out communities of prayer. The Community recommends pilgrimage to sites of the Celtic Christian tradition, such as Iona and Lindisfarne, as well as to new 'places of resurrection'.[1]

The emphasis on spiritual journey in the Community's way of life and its implications are well brought out in a recent book by Ray Simpson entitled *A Pilgrim Way*, which draws both on the biblical tradition of pilgrimage and the specifically Celtic approach epitomized by the sermons of Columbanus and the rules of Columba and other Irish monks. In another booklet, he provides suggestions for a retreat on Holy Island with a 'menu' of activities that includes building a cairn with each stone representing a hurt, anger or mistake to be left behind, finding a rhythm with the tides, and observing the birds – 'notice the wild geese flying in formation. They tell us something about unity. When they fly together in this instinctive way they travel three times as fast as when they fly alone. What does this say to us?'[2]

Ray Simpson also has some helpful thoughts on how a pilgrimage to Lindisfarne can prepare us to head for home:

Go to the harbour and look at the boats. Celtic 'pilgrims for the love of God' sailed wherever God's wind blew them, and wandered wherever God's spirit led them. Celtic-inspired Christians see all life as a journey. Where is God wanting to take you at this time? How do you need to prepare? What ties need to be broken in order that you become free to go? Remember, we can be free to move with the spirit even when we feel as if we are in a desert.

The boats here are used in varying weathers to catch lobsters, crab and other fish; but there are times when the fisherfolk know that the boat should be left at their moorings. There is a time in our lives to set sail and a time to down anchor.

Review your life. Try and discern the ways God has led you. In what ways are you being called to up-anchor or to down-anchor? For some people, the final journey into eternity will be the focus for their meditation. This is often portrayed in the image of the boat coming calmly into harbour in the setting sun.[3]

Practicalities

Melrose can be reached from Edinburgh by bus. It is also possible to leave your car there at the start of walking St Cuthbert's Way and return from Lindisfarne by bus via Berwick-on-Tweed. Accommodation along the way can be booked in advance through the Scottish Borders Tourist Information Centre. Several companies organize walking holidays along St Cuthbert's Way: the most local is Scotwalk (www.scotswalk.co.uk) and the baggage company Carry-lite (www.carrylite.com) will transport your luggage. The Community of Aidan and Hilda organizes regular retreats and has an excellent website: www.aidanandhilda.org.

Endnotes

Introduction

1. M.L. & S. Nolan, *Christian Pilgrimage in Modern Western Europe* (University of North Carolina Press, 1989), pp.1–2, 8.
2. *Santiago de Compostela* (Catholic Truth Society, London, 2001), p. 82.
3. *Pilgrimage and Beyond* (Pax Travel, London, 2007).
4. *The Great Pilgrimage in the Jubilee*, Pontifical Council for the Pastoral Care of Migrants and Itinerant People, Rome, 1998, p. 1.
5. *The Pilgrim Way* (Pilegrimskontoret, Oslo, 1997), p. 18.
6. *Pilegrimsvandring* (Nidaros, 1994), p. 7.
7. 206 Tours, Smithtown, New York, 2007.
8. *Chester Cathedral News*, June 2007, p. 4.
9. V. & E. Turner, *Image and Pilgrimage in Christian Culture* (Columbia University Press, New York, 1978), p. 6.
10. N. Frey, *Pilgrim Stories on and off the road to Santiago* (University of California Press, Berkeley, 1998), p. 71.
11. *The Great Pilgrimage in the Jubilee*
12. Georgia Greenia, 'Pilgrimage as Therapy', *W&M News* (22 September 2005) <www.wm.edu/news/id=5210>

Chapter 1 The Biblical Roots of Pilgrimage

1. R. Giles, *Creating Uncommon Worship* (Canterbury Press, Norwich), p. 22–23.

Chapter 2 Pilgrimage in the Early Church

1. Eusebius: *Life of Constantine* (Clarendon Press, Oxford, 1999), p. 137.
2. Cyril of Jerusalem, *Catechetical Lectures* 14.23; 13.22.
3. J. N. D. Kelly, *Jerome* (Duckworth, London, 1975), p. 120.
4. E. Yarnold, *Cyril of Jerusalem* (Routledge, London, 2000), p. 69.
5. Gregory of Nyssa, *Epistle 2*.
6. Jerome, *Letter 58*.

Chapter 3 Celtic Pilgrimage

1. T. Clancy & G. Markus (eds), *Iona: The Earliest Poetry of a Celtic Monastery* (Edinburgh University Press, 1995), p. 147.
2. Bede, *Ecclesiastical History of the English People*, Book III, Chapter 19.
3. *Celtic Spirituality* (Classics of Western Spirituality, Paulist Press, 1999), p. 353, 355, 356.
4. *Ibid.*, p. 189.

Chapter 4 The Golden Age of Pilgrimage

1. Quoted in G. Hartwell Jones, *Celtic Britain and the Pilgrim movement* (Hon. Society of Cymmrodorion, London, 1912), p. 77.
2. Quoted in J. G. Davies, *Pilgrimage Yesterday and Today* (SCM Press, 1988), p. 74.
3. Debra Birch, 'Jacques de Vitry and the Ideology of Pilgrimage' in J. Stopford (ed.), *Pilgrimage Explored*, p. 84.
4. J. Sumption, *Pilgrimage*, p. 125.
5. W. Hilton, *The Scale of Perfection*, II, 21.
6. J. G. Davies, *Pilgrimage Yesterday and Today* p. 93.

Chapter 5 After the Reformation

1. Ieuan ap Rhydderch quoted in H. Lewis, T. Roberts & I. Williams, *Cywyddau Iolo Goch ac Eraill* (University of Wales Press, 1972), p. 245.
2. T. Wright, *Letters Relating to the Suppression of the Monasteries* (Camden Society, 1843), pp. 184, 207.
3. Mary Lee Nolan and Sidney Nolan, *Christian Pilgrimage in Modern Western Europe*, (UNC Press, 1989) pp. 111–13.
4. J. G. Davies, *Pilgrimage Yesterday and Today*, pp. 146, 148.
5. *Ibid.* p. 146.

Chapter 6 Pilgrimage Today

1. Barbara Butler and Jo White, *To Be A Pilgrim* (Kevin Mayhew, 2002), p. 327.
2. *Ibid.*, p. 131.
3. Pilgrimage to Nidaros. A practical pilgrimage theology (Liturgical Centre, Trondheim, 2003), pp. 163-202.
4. *Ibid.*, p. 185.

Chapter 7 How to Be a Pilgrim

1. 'Bringing the Pilgrimage Home', *Coracle* (October/November 2007), p. 20.
2. R. Giles, *Creating Uncommon Worship*, p. 22.

Chapter 9 Santiago

1. A. Crockett, *Account of pilgrimage from Le Puy to Santiago* (unpublished, 1995), p. 47.
2. D. Lodge, *Therapy* (Secker & Warburg, 1995), pp. 292–93.
3. Nancy Frey, *Pilgrim Stories on and off the Road to Santiago* (University of California Press, Berkeley, 1998), p. 4.
4. *Ibid.*, pp.187–88.

Chapter 11 Iona

1. N. Shanks, *Iona: God's Energy*, p. 84.
2. *Ibid.*, p. 96.
3. P. Millar, *An Iona Prayer Book* (Canterbury Press, Norwich, 1998), p. 6. Reproduced with permission.

Chapter 13 Wales

1. 'Small Pilgrim Places', *Country Way* (Arthur Rank Centre, Stoneleigh), summer 2006, p. 24.
2. A.M. Allchin, *Bardsey: A Place of Pilgrimage* (locally published, 2002), p. 3
3. R.S. Thomas, *Collected Poems, 1945–1990* (Phoenix, London, 1993), p. 364.

Chapter 15 Assisi

1. D. Kirkpatrick (ed.), *Joy In All Things: A Franciscan Companion* (Canterbury Press, 2002), p. 205.

Chapter 17 Lourdes

1. W.M. Gesler, *Healing Places* (Rowman & Littlefield, Lanham, 2003), p. 67.

Chapter 20 St Cuthbert's Way

1. *Introducing the Community of Aidan and Hilda* (Holy Island, 2007), p. 10.
2. Ray Simpson, *Give Yourself a Retreat on Holy Island* (St Aidan Press, Holy Island, 1998), p. 16.
3. *Ibid.*, p. 30.

Further reading

General studies of pilgrimage

Ruth Barnes & Crispin Branfoot, *Pilgrimage: The Sacred Journey* (Ashmolean Museum, Oxford, 2006).
Craig Bartholomew & Fred Hughes, *Explorations in a Christian Theology of Pilgrimage* (Ashgate, Aldershot, Hampshire, 2004).
J. G. Davies, *Pilgrimage yesterday and today: Why? Where? How?* (SCM Press, London, 1988).
John Eade & Michael Sallnow (eds.), *Contesting the Sacred: The Anthroplogy of Christian Pilgrimage* (Routledge, 1991).
Victor Turner, *Image and Pilgrimage in Christian Culture: Anthropological Perspectives* (Basil Blackwell, Oxford, 1978).

Anthologies and classics of pilgrim literature

Bridal Wreath, Mistress of Husaby and *The Cross*, a trilogy of Kristin Lavransdatter novels by the Norwegian author Sigrid Unset are set at the height of the Nidaros pilgrimage in the early fourteenth century. There are several English translations, including by Charles Archer (Bantam, 1978 & Abacus, 1995).
John Bunyan, *Pilgrim's Progress* (numerous editions).
P. Henderson (editor), *A Pilgrim Anthology* (Confraternity of St James, London, 1994).
Martin Robertson, *Sacred Places, pilgrim paths: An Anthology of Pilgrimage* (Fount, London, 1997).
Edward Sellner, *Pilgrimage* (Sorin Books, Notre Dame, Indiana, 2004).
Andrea Skevington, *The Pilgrim Spirit* (Lion Hudson, 2007).
The Way of a Pilgrim, the Russian classic available in several translations, including by H. Bacovcin (Image Books, New York, 1978) and R. M. French (Triangle, London, 1995).

Celtic Pilgrimage

Ian Bradley, *Columba, Pilgrim and Penitent* (Wild Goose Publications, Glasgow, 1997).
T. O'Fiaich, 'Irish Monks on the Continent' in J. Mackey (ed) *Celtic Christianity* (T. & T. Clark, Edinburgh, 1989).
Andrew Jones, *Every Pilgrim's Guide to Celtic Britain and Ireland* (Canterbury Press, Norwich, 2002).

Katharine Lack, *The Eagle and the Dove: The Spirituality of Columbanus* (Triangle, 2000).
John Marsden, *The Sea Roads of the Saints* (Floris Books, Edinburgh, 1995).
Philip Sheldrake, *Living Between Worlds* (Darton Longman & Todd, London,1995).
G. S. M. Walker, *Sancti Columbani Opera* (Dublin Institute for Advanced Studies, 1957).

Pilgrimage in the Middle Ages

Debra Birch, *Pilgrimage to Rome in the Middle Ages* (Boydell Press, Woodbridge, Suffolk, 1998).
Canterbury Tales. The best text is *The Riverside Chaucer* (Oxford University Press, 1988). A good introduction is Helen Phillips, *An Introduction to the Canterbury Tales* (Macmillan, 2000).
Anthony Goodman, *Margery Kempe and Her World* (Longman, 2002).
Colin Morris & Peter Roberts (eds.), *Pilgrimage: The English Experience from Becket to Bunyan* (Cambridge University Press, 2002).
Jonathan Sumption, *Pilgrimage: An Image of Medieval Religion* (Faber, 1975).
Diana Webb, *Pilgrims and Pilgrimage in the Medieval West* (I.B.Tauris, 2001).
Barry Windeatt, *The Book of Margery Kempe* (Longman, 2000).

Pilgrimage today

Barbara Butler and Jo White, *To Be A Pilgrim* (Kevin Mayhew, 2002).
Magnus Fladmark (editor), *In Search of Heritage As Pilgrim or Tourist?* (Donhead, Shaftesbury, Dorset, 1998).
Mary Lee & Sidney Nolan, *Christian Pilgrimage in Modern Western Europe* (University of North Carolina Press, 1989).
Eleanor Nesbitt, *Interfaith Pilgrims* (Quaker Books, London, 2003).
Cintra Pemberton, *Soulfaring* (Morehouse, Harrisburg, PA, 1999).
Edward Sellner, *Pilgrimage* (Sorin Books, Notre Dame, Indiana, 2004).
Ray Simpson, *A Pilgrim Way: New Celtic Monasticism for Everyday People* (Kevin Mayhew, Stowmarket, 2005).

Specific pilgrim places

Rome

Matilda Webb, *The Churches and Catacombs of Early Christian Rome* (Sussex Academic Press, Brighton, 2001).

Santiago

Nancy Frey, *Pilgrim Stories on and off the road to Santiago* (University of California Press, Berkeley, 1998).

James Hogarth (translator), *The Pilgrim's Guide* (Confraternity of St James, 1996).

Cees Nooteboom, *Roads to Santiago* (Harvill Press, London, 1997).

Francois Taillandier, *L'Épopée de Compostelle* (L'Instant Durable, Clermont-Ferrand, 2006).

J. Williams & A. Stones (eds.) *The Codex Calixtinus and the Shrine of St James* (Gunter Narr Verlag, Tübingen, 1992).

St Andrews

Peter Yeoman, *Pilgrimage in Medieval Scotland* (Batsford/Historic Scotland, 1999).

Iona

Ewan Campbell, *Saints and Sea Kings* (Historic Scotland, Edinburgh, 1999).

Jessica Christian & Charles Stiller, *Iona Portrayed* (New Iona Press, Inverness, 2000).

Ron Ferguson, *Chasing the Wild Goose* (Wild Goose Publications, Glasgow, 1998).

Peter Millar, *Pilgrim Guide: Iona* (Canterbury Press, Norwich, 1997).

Norman Shanks, *Iona – God's Energy* (Hodder & Stoughton, London, 1999).

Ireland

M. Haren & Y. de Pontfarcy, *The Medieval Pilgrimage to St Patrick's Purgatory* (Clogher Historical Societ, Enniskillen, 1988).

J-M Picard, *St Patrick's Purgatory* (Four Courts Press, Dublin, 1985).

Wales

A. M. Allchin, *Pennant Melangell: Place of Pilgrimage* (Pennant Melangell, 1994).

A. M. Allchin, *Bardsey: A Place of Pilgrimage* (locally published, 2002).

T. Charles-Edwards, *Saint Winefride and Her Well* (Holywell, 1997).

Brendan O'Malley, *A Welsh Pilgrim's Manual* (Gomer, Llandysul, 1989).

Nidaros

B. Hardeberg & O. Bjordal, *Pilgrimage to Nidaros: A practical pilgrimage theology* (Liturgical Centre, Trondheim, 2003).

A. Raju, *Pilgrim Roads to Nidaros* (Cicerone, Milnthorpe, Cumbria, 2001).

S. Thue, *On The Pilgrim Way to Trondheim* (Tapir, Trondheim, 1998).

There are a number of excellent books and guides on the Nidaros pilgrimage in Norwegian by Eivind Luthen. There are plans to translate them into English. An excellent guide in English to the pilgrim route to Nidaros from Borgsjö in Sweden was published in 2007.

Assisi

Giuseppe De Roma, *Assisi: Encounters That Make History* (published in numerous languages, 2002).
Judith Dean, *Every Pilgrim's Guide to Assisi* (Canterbury Press, Norwich, 2002).
Paolo Maiarelli, *Assisi – Franciscan Itinerary* (Edizioni Porziuncola, Assisi, 2006).
Angela Seracchioli, *Di Qui Passo Francesco* (Terre di Mezzo, Milano, 2006).

Częstochowa

J. D. Gracz, *Golgota Jasnogórska* (Jasna Góra, 2004).
Robert Maniura, *Pilgrimage to Images in the Fifteenth Century* (Boydell Press, Woodbridge, 2004).

Lourdes

W.M. Gesler, *Healing Places* (Rowman & Littlefield, Lanham, 2003).
Ruth Harris, *Lourdes: Body and Spirit in the Secular Age* (Penguin Compass, 1999).
Suzanne Kaufman, *Consuming Visions: Mass Culture and the Lourdes Shrine* (Cornell University Press, 2005).
Patrick Marnham, *Lourdes – A Modern Pilgrimage* (Heinemann, 1980).
S. Martin, *Every Pilgrim's Guide to Lourdes* (Canterbury Press, Norwich, 2005).
Official Guide to the Lourdes Sanctuary (published in six languages)

Taizé

Brother Roger, *The Sources of Taizé* (GIA, Chicago, 2000).
Kathleen Spink, *A Universal Heart: The Life of Brother Roger of Taizé* (SPCK, London 2006 and translated into several languages).

Medugorje

David Baldwin, *Medjugorje* (Catholic Truth Society, London, 2002).
Joe & Eleanor McFadden, *Messages of the Queen of Peace* (Dublin, 2007).
Viktor Nuic, *Medugorje – Pilgrim's Monograph* (published in numerous languages, Zagreb, 2006).
Paul Pandarakalam, *Like A Heavenly Breeze* (Pandarak Paul Bros Publication, 1997).

St Cuthbert's Way

Mary Low, *St Cuthbert's Way: A Pilgrim's Companion* (Wild Goose
Publications, Glasgow, 2000).
Dominic Marner, *St Cuthbert: His Life and Cult in Medieval Durham*
(British Library, London, 2000).
Roger Smith & Ron Shaw, *St Cuthbert's Way: Official Trail Guide*
(Stationery Office, Edinburgh, 1997).

Index

Picture Acknowledgments

Alamy – pp. 11 Graeme Peacock, 38 Caro, 53, 73 Interfoto Pressebildagentur, 59 Jon Arnold Images Ltd, 62 Arco Images GmbH, 68 Danita Delimont, 83 Oso Media, 86–87 Peter Bowater, 102 G.P. Bowater, 111b Phil Seale, 120 AA World Travel Library, 128 Peter Horree, 131 Stephen Emerson, 134–135 David Lyons, 137 Steve Lewis ARPS, 139 David Wrench, 141l Topix, 171 Leslie Garland Picture Library, 203 Scottish Viewpoint

Ian Bradley – pp. 2–3, 4–5, 5, 7, 16, 34, 37, 74, 78, 80, 89al, 89ar, 90, 91, 92, 93, 94, 95, 96a, 96m, 96b, 97, 99a, 99bg, 101, 103l, 103r, 104, 106bl, 106ar, 107al, 107b, 108, 109, 111ar, 112, 113bl, 113ar, 118, 121, 123, 125, 126a, 126b, 127, 130, 137 (inset), 140, 141r, 142, 145a1, 145a2, 145m, 145b, 146, 147al, 147br, 149, 152, 153, 155, 156a, 156b, 157a, 157b, 158a, 158b, 159l, 159r, 160a, 160b, 161bg, 161ar, 161b, 162a, 162b, 163, 165, 166 (inset), 167a, 168b, 168, 169l, 169r, 170l, 170m, 170r, 173a, 173b, 174, 175bl, 175ar, 176, 177, 178–9, 180, 181a, 181b, 182a, 182b, 183, 185a, 185b, 186l 186r, 187a, 187b, 188, 190a, 190b, 191, 192, 194, 195, 196, 197a, 197b, 198, 199a, 199b, 200a, 200b, 201, 202, 204, 205, 206-207, 206al, 206br, 207a, 208, 209a, 209b, 214

British Library – p. 47 © British Library Board. All Rights Reserved. Royal 14 C. VII. ff.4v–5

Corbis – pp. 3, 9, 67, 88–89, Atlantide Phototravel, 12 Reuters, 15 Pascal Manoukian/Sygma, 23 Pierre Vauthey/Sygma, 24 Nik Wheeler, 25 Andrea Jemolo, 26 Brooklyn Museum, 27 Arte & Immagini srl, 31 Christie's Images, 33 Hanan Isachar, 45 Fine Art Photographic Library, 52 David Lees, 55 Ricardo Spila/Grand Tour, 64 Homer Sykes, 69 Philippa Lewis, Edifice, 71 Darren Staples/Reuters, 75 Markus Botzek/zefa, 77 Ammar Awad/Reuters, 105 Bernard Bisson/Sygma, 132 Barry Lewis, 133 Peter Guttman, 143 Alison Hall, Cordaiy Photo Library Ltd, 150 Christophe Boisvieux, 166 Antoine Gyori/Sygma, 172 Paul Thompson, 179 Pascal Deloche/Godong

Historic Scotland – p. 116 © Crown Copyright reproduced courtesy of Historic Scotland

Scala – p. 49 © Photo SCALA, Florence

Richard Watts – pp. 14, 40, 56, 100, 114, 149, 164, 204

Lion Hudson
Commissioning editors: Morag Reeve, Stephanie Heald
Project editors: Catherine Sinfield, Miranda Powell
Proof reader: Liz Evans (freelance)
Designer: Jonathan Roberts
Picture researchers: Jonathan Roberts, Kate Leach, Jenny Ward
Production manager: Kylie Ord